Lena Maier-Hein

Computer-assisted needle insertion

Lena Maier-Hein

Computer-assisted needle insertion

Motion compensation and guidance

Südwestdeutscher Verlag für Hochschulschriften

Impressum/Imprint (nur für Deutschland/ only for Germany)
Bibliografische Information der Deutschen Nationalbibliothek: Die Deutsche Nationalbibliothek verzeichnet diese Publikation in der Deutschen Nationalbibliografie; detaillierte bibliografische Daten sind im Internet über http://dnb.d-nb.de abrufbar.

Alle in diesem Buch genannten Marken und Produktnamen unterliegen warenzeichen-, marken- oder patentrechtlichem Schutz bzw. sind Warenzeichen oder eingetragene Warenzeichen der jeweiligen Inhaber. Die Wiedergabe von Marken, Produktnamen, Gebrauchsnamen, Handelsnamen, Warenbezeichnungen u.s.w. in diesem Werk berechtigt auch ohne besondere Kennzeichnung nicht zu der Annahme, dass solche Namen im Sinne der Warenzeichen- und Markenschutzgesetzgebung als frei zu betrachten wären und daher von jedermann benutzt werden dürften.

Verlag: Südwestdeutscher Verlag für Hochschulschriften Aktiengesellschaft & Co. KG
Dudweiler Landstr. 99, 66123 Saarbrücken, Deutschland
Telefon +49 681 37 20 271-1, Telefax +49 681 37 20 271-0
Email: info@svh-verlag.de
Zugl.: Karlsruhe, Universität Karlsruhe (TH), PhD thesis, 2009

Herstellung in Deutschland:
Schaltungsdienst Lange o.H.G., Berlin
Books on Demand GmbH, Norderstedt
Reha GmbH, Saarbrücken
Amazon Distribution GmbH, Leipzig
ISBN: 978-3-8381-0848-3

Imprint (only for USA, GB)
Bibliographic information published by the Deutsche Nationalbibliothek: The Deutsche Nationalbibliothek lists this publication in the Deutsche Nationalbibliografie; detailed bibliographic data are available in the Internet at http://dnb.d-nb.de.

Any brand names and product names mentioned in this book are subject to trademark, brand or patent protection and are trademarks or registered trademarks of their respective holders. The use of brand names, product names, common names, trade names, product descriptions etc. even without a particular marking in this works is in no way to be construed to mean that such names may be regarded as unrestricted in respect of trademark and brand protection legislation and could thus be used by anyone.

Publisher: Südwestdeutscher Verlag für Hochschulschriften Aktiengesellschaft & Co. KG
Dudweiler Landstr. 99, 66123 Saarbrücken, Germany
Phone +49 681 37 20 271-1, Fax +49 681 37 20 271-0
Email: info@svh-verlag.de

Printed in the U.S.A.
Printed in the U.K. by (see last page)
ISBN: 978-3-8381-0848-3

Copyright © 2010 by the author and Südwestdeutscher Verlag für Hochschulschriften Aktiengesellschaft & Co. KG and licensors
All rights reserved. Saarbrücken 2010

ABSTRACT

Clinical practice is increasingly replacing traditional open surgical procedures with minimally invasive techniques for cancer diagnosis and therapy. These procedures typically require placement of a surgical instrument into the organ of interest with a high degree of accuracy. In general, the success of a treatment or of a diagnosis is highly dependent on the accuracy of instrument insertion and thus depends crucially on the skills and experience of the physician. While intra-operative navigation has been proven to be highly effective in interventions on bony or sufficiently rigid structures, such as the spine and the brain, computer aided soft tissue procedures are still limited to non-invasive diagnostics and surgical planning. This can primarily be attributed to the lack of robust methods for compensation of intra-interventional organ motion caused by respiration, heartbeat, patient movement and manipulation by surgical instruments.

In this thesis, new concepts for computer-assisted soft tissue interventions were developed, implemented and evaluated. The main contributions include (1) development and evaluation of a real-time capable motion compensation method for percutaneous abdominal interventions based on fiducial needles, (2) development and evaluation of a guidance method to allow for fast and precise insertion of a needle-shaped instrument along a predetermined trajectory and (3) development of a respiratory liver motion simulator for evaluating the proposed methods in a realistic setting. As the liver is one of the most common sites for metastatic disease and, at the same time, one of the organs most affected by respiratory motion, a prototype system for navigated liver punctures was developed according to the proposed concepts. Based on an analysis of the sources of error associated with the approach, the system was evaluated in two stages. Firstly, the individual system modules were evaluated in various *in-silico*, *in-vitro*, and *in-vivo* experiments. Secondly, the system was evaluated in the clinical workflow in close cooperation with medical partners. According to an *in-vivo* accuracy assessment study, the novel approach is highly accurate compared to state of the art work, yielding an overall needle insertion error below 4 mm. Furthermore, the proposed method outperforms the conventional CT-guided needle insertion method with respect to accuracy and radiation exposure to the patient. The developed methods are broadly applicable to various organs and procedures and are thus an important contribution to the field of computer-assisted medical interventions.

PUBLICATIONS

Some ideas, figures and tables from this thesis have appeared previously in the following publications:

INTERNATIONAL JOURNALS

1. L. Maier-Hein, A. Tekbas, A. Seitel, F. Pianka, S. A. Müller, S. Satzl, S. Schawo, B. Radeleff, R. Tetzlaff, A. M. Franz, B. P. Müller-Stich, I. Wolf, H.-U. Kauczor, B. M. Schmied, and H.-P. Meinzer. In-vivo accuracy assessment of a needle-based navigation system for CT-guided radiofrequency ablation of the liver. *Med Phys*, 35(12):5385-5396, 2008.

2. L. Maier-Hein, A. Tekbas, A. M. Franz , R. Tetzlaff, S. A. Müller, F. Pianka, I. Wolf, H.-U. Kauczor, B. M. Schmied, and H.-P. Meinzer. On combining internal and external fiducials for liver motion compensation. *Comp Aid Surg*, 13(6):369-376, 2008.

3. L. Maier-Hein, F. Pianka, S. A. Müller, U. Rietdorf, A. Seitel, A. M. Franz, I. Wolf, B. M. Schmied, and H.-P. Meinzer. Respiratory liver motion simulator for validating image-guided systems ex-vivo. *Int J CARS*, 2(5):287-291, 2008.

4. L. Maier-Hein, S. A. Müller, F. Pianka, S. Wörz, B. P. Müller-Stich, A. Seitel, K. Rohr, H.-P. Meinzer, B. M. Schmied, and I. Wolf. Respiratory motion compensation for CT-guided interventions in the liver. *Comp Aid Surg*, 13(3):125-138, 2008.

5. S. A. Müller, L. Maier-Hein, A. Mehrabi, F. Pianka, U. Rietdorf, I. Wolf, L. Grenacher, G. Richter, C. N. Gutt, J. Schmidt, H.-P. Meinzer, and B. M. Schmied. Creation and establishment of a respiratory liver motion simulator for liver interventions. *Med Phys*, 34(12):4605-4608, 2007.

PEER-REVIEWED INTERNATIONAL CONFERENCES

1. L. Maier-Hein, C. J. Walsh, A. Seitel, N. C. Hanumara, J.-A. O. Shepard, F. Pianka, S. A. Müller, B. M. Schmied, A. H. Slocum, R. Gupta, and H.-P. Meinzer. Human vs. robot operator error in a needle-based navigation system for percutaneous liver interventions. In *SPIE Medical Imaging 2009: Visualization, Image-Guided Procedures, and Modeling*, 7261:72610Y (12 pages), 2009.

2. A. Seitel, C. J. Walsh, N. C. Hanumara, J.-A. O. Shepard, A. H. Slocum, H.-P. Meinzer, R. Gupta, and L. Maier-Hein. Development and evaluation of a new image-based user interface for robot-assisted needle placements with the Robopsy system. In *SPIE Medical Imaging 2009: Visualization, Image-guided Procedures and Modeling*, 7261:72610X (9 pages), 2009

3. M. Seitel, L. Maier-Hein, U. Rietdorf, S. Nikoloff, A. Seitel, A. M. Franz, H. Kenngott, M. Karck, R. DeSimone, I. Wolf, and H.-P. Meinzer. Towards a mixed reality environment for preoperative planning of cardiac surgery. In *Health Technol Inform*, 142:307–309, 2009.

4. H.-P. Meinzer, L. Maier-Hein, I. Wegner, M. Baumhauer, and I. Wolf. Computer-assisted soft tissue interventions. In *IEEE International Symposium on Biomedical Imaging: From Nano to Macro*, pages 1391–1394, 2008.

5. L. Maier-Hein, A. M. Franz, J. Neuhaus, H.-P. Meinzer, and I. Wolf. Comparative assessment of optical tracking systems for soft tissue navigation with fiducial needles. In *SPIE Medical Imaging 2008: Visualization, Image-Guided Procedures, and Modeling*, 6918:6981Z (9 pages), 2008.

6. A. Tekbas, L. Maier-Hein, S. A. Müller, A. Seitel, B. Radeleff, S. Satzl, R. Tetzlaff, A. M. Franz, F. Pianka, I. Wolf, H.-U. Kauczor, H.-P. Meinzer, and B. M. Schmied. In-vivo comparision of the conventional CT-guided liver biopsy method with a novel computer-assisted approach. *Int J CARS 3 (Suppl 1)*, pages 142–143, 2008.

7. L. Maier-Hein, F. Pianka, A. Seitel, S. A. Müller, A. Tekbas, M. Seitel, I. Wolf, B. M. Schmied, and H.-P. Meinzer. Precision targeting of liver lesions with a needle-based soft tissue navigation system. In *Medical Image Computing and Computer-Assisted Intervention (MICCAI) 2007 (2)*, 4792, pages 42–49, 2007.

8. A. Seitel, L. Maier-Hein, S. Schawo, B. A. Radeleff, S. A. Müller, F. Pianka, B. M. Schmied, I. Wolf, and H.-P. Meinzer. In-vitro evaluation of different visualization approaches for computer assisted targeting in soft tissue. *Int J CARS 2 (Suppl 1)*, pages 188–190, 2007.

9. L. Maier-Hein, S. A. Müller, F. Pianka, A. Seitel, B. P. Müller-Stich, C. N. Gutt, U. Rietdorf, G. Richter, H.-P. Meinzer, B. M. Schmied, and I. Wolf. In-vitro evaluation of a novel needle-based soft tissue navigation system with a respiratory liver motion simulator. In *SPIE Medical Imaging 2007: Visualization and Image-Guided Procedures*, 6509: 650916 (12 pages), 2007.

10. L. Maier-Hein, D. Maleike, J. Neuhaus, A. M. Franz, I. Wolf, and H.-P. Meinzer. Soft tissue navigation using needle-shaped markers: Evaluation of navigation

aid tracking accuracy and CT registration. In *SPIE Medical Imaging 2007: Visualization and Image-Guided Procedures*, 6509: 650926 (12 pages), 2007.

PEER-REVIEWED NATIONAL CONFERENCES

1. L. Maier-Hein, A. Tekbas, A. M. Franz , R. Tetzlaff, S. A. Müller, F. Pianka, I. Wolf, H.-U. Kauczor, B. M. Schmied, and H.-P. Meinzer. Reduktion der Invasivität bei nadelbasierter Bewegungskompensation fur navigierte Eingriffe im Abdomen. In *Bildverarbeitung für die Medizin 2009*, pages 82–86, Springer, 2009.

2. J. Neuhaus, I. Wegner, J. Kast, M. Baumhauer, A. Seitel, I. Gergel, M. Nolden, D. Maleike, I. Wolf, H.-P. Meinzer, and L. Maier-Hein. MITK-IGT: Eine Navigationskomponente für das Medical Imaging Interaction Toolkit. In *Bildverarbeitung für die Medizin 2009*, pages 454–458, Springer, 2009.

3. J. Kast, J. Neuhaus, F. Nickel, H. Kenngott, M. Engel, E. Short, M. Reiter, H.-P. Meinzer, and L. Maier-Hein. Der Telemanipulator daVinci als mechanisches Trackingsystem - Bestimmung von Präzision und Genauigkeit. In *Bildverarbeitung für die Medizin 2009*, pages 341–345, Springer, 2009.

4. A. M. Franz and L. Maier-Hein and I. Wolf and H.-P. Meinzer. Robustheitsuntersuchung des optischen Trackingsystems MicronTracker 2. In *Tagungsband der 53. Jahrestagung der Deutschen Gesellschaft für Medinische Informatik, Biometrie und Epidemiologie*, pages 149–151, 2008.

5. L. Maier-Hein, A. Tekbas, A. Seitel, F. Pianka, S. A. Müller, S. Schawo, B. Radeleff, R. Tetzlaff, A. M. Franz, A.-M. Rau, I. Wolf, H.-U. Kauczor, B. M. Schmied, and H.-P. Meinzer. In-vivo targeting of liver lesions with a navigation system based on fiducial needles. In *Bildverarbeitung für die Medizin 2008*, pages 227–231, Springer, 2008.

6. L. Maier-Hein, F. Pianka, S. A. Müller, A. Seitel, U. Rietdorf, I. Wolf, B. M. Schmied, and H.-P. Meinzer. Atembewegungssimulator für die in-vitro Evaluation von Weichgewebe-Navigationssystemen in der Leber. In *Bildverarbeitung für die Medizin 2007*, pages 379–283, Springer, 2007.

PATENTS

1. L. Maier-Hein, B. P. Müller-Stich, H. Kenngott, and H.-P. Meinzer. System and method for computer assisted surgery. *US 61/166,370*, Apr 2009.

2. H. Kenngott, B. P. Müller-Stich, C. N. Gutt, L. Maier-Hein, and H.-P. Meinzer. Cutting tool for soft tissue surgery. *US 61/166,327*, Apr 2009.

3. L. Maier-Hein, A. Seitel, I. Wolf, and H.-P. Meinzer. A system for computer assisted targeting in soft tissue. *US 61/075,467*, Jun 2008.

ACKNOWLEDGMENTS

The work described in this thesis was performed at the Division of Medical and Biological Informatics at the German Cancer Research Center (DKFZ).

First, I would like to thank the head of the division, Pitt Meinzer, for his support, the ideal working conditions in his department, the great atmosphere in his group, and the opportunity to conduct this thesis in an exciting research area. Many thanks also go to Rüdiger Dillmann for accepting the supervision at the University of Karlsruhe.

I also gratefully acknowledge the German Research Foundation (DFG) for funding this work and the *Research Training Group 1126: Intelligent Surgery* for the opportunity of working in a fruitful cooperation with medical partners. Thanks to Frank, Aysun, Sascha, Beat Müller and Bruno Schmied for contributing to the success of this project.

I would like to thank all my colleagues and friends at the department for the great times we had at the office, at conferences and during other activities (Neckarwiese, Schwarzwald, Beachbasketball...). All of you contributed to this work in some way! In particular, I would like to thank Ivo, Alex and Alfred for all their contributions to this project in the last couple of years and for proofreading my thesis (Alex). I am also deeply indebted to Nevan who checked the grammar and language.

Special thanks go to my boyfriend Klaus for his valuable comments and suggestions regarding this document and his "psychological support" in the past few weeks! Thank you so much!

Last but not least, I would like to thank my parents for supporting me over all these years: DANKE!

CONTENTS

1 INTRODUCTION 1
  1.1 Motivation 1
  1.2 Objectives 2
  1.3 Approach 3
  1.4 Outline 6
2 MEDICAL BACKGROUND 9
  2.1 Anatomy of the liver 9
  2.2 Characterization of hepatic motion 10
  2.3 Percutaneous liver interventions 13
    2.3.1 Liver biopsy 13
    2.3.2 Radiofrequency ablation of liver tumors 14
3 STATE OF THE ART 19
  3.1 History of computer-assisted interventions 19
  3.2 Computer-assisted needle insertion into soft tissue 21
    3.2.1 Imaging 23
    3.2.2 Tracking 26
    3.2.3 Initial registration 30
    3.2.4 Real-time motion compensation 33
    3.2.5 Guidance 36
4 APPROACH 43
  4.1 Fundamental design decisions 43
  4.2 Workflow 46
  4.3 Implementation 49
  4.4 Sources of error 52
    4.4.1 Tracking error 52
    4.4.2 Target registration error 56
    4.4.3 User error 57
    4.4.4 Discussion 58
5 RESPIRATORY LIVER MOTION SIMULATOR 61
  5.1 Design 61
  5.2 Motion analysis 65
  5.3 Results 68
  5.4 Discussion 69
6 TRACKING: TOOL DESIGN, ACCURACY, AND ROBUSTNESS 73
  6.1 Navigation tools 75
    6.1.1 Polaris tools 75
    6.1.2 MicronTracker 2 tools 77

ix

- 6.2 Tracking accuracy and precision 79
  - 6.2.1 Accuracy phantom 79
  - 6.2.2 Experiments 79
  - 6.2.3 Results 84
  - 6.2.4 Discussion 89
- 6.3 Tracking robustness 90
  - 6.3.1 Experiments 90
  - 6.3.2 Results 91
  - 6.3.3 Discussion 92

7 INITIAL REGISTRATION 95
- 7.1 Initial registration method 95
- 7.2 Fiducial needle localization 97
  - 7.2.1 Methods 97
  - 7.2.2 Registration phantom 100
  - 7.2.3 Experiments 100
  - 7.2.4 Results 101
  - 7.2.5 Discussion 102
- 7.3 Prediction of registration accuracy 103
  - 7.3.1 Experiments 104
  - 7.3.2 Results 109
  - 7.3.3 Discussion 110

8 MOTION COMPENSATION 115
- 8.1 Basic approach 115
  - 8.1.1 Mathematical background 116
  - 8.1.2 Motion compensation method 117
- 8.2 Comparison of deformation models 119
  - 8.2.1 Experiments 119
  - 8.2.2 Results 122
  - 8.2.3 Discussion 123
- 8.3 Fiducial placement 128
  - 8.3.1 Experiments 128
  - 8.3.2 Results 129
  - 8.3.3 Discussion 129
- 8.4 Integration of skin markers 131
  - 8.4.1 Experiments 131
  - 8.4.2 Results 134
  - 8.4.3 Discussion 134
- 8.5 Accuracy vs. invasiveness 136
  - 8.5.1 Experiments 136
  - 8.5.2 Results 137
  - 8.5.3 Discussion 138

8.6 Automatic gating   140
    8.6.1 Experiments   141
    8.6.2 Results   141
    8.6.3 Discussion   142

9 GUIDANCE   145
    9.1 Visualization methods   145
        9.1.1 3D Overview   146
        9.1.2 Projection View   146
        9.1.3 Tool Tip Camera View   149
        9.1.4 Fixed Camera View   150
    9.2 Experiments   150
    9.3 Results   153
        9.3.1 Quantitative evaluation   153
        9.3.2 Qualitative evaluation   155
    9.4 Discussion   157
    9.5 Derived guidance method   159

10 SYSTEM EVALUATION IN THE CLINICAL WORKFLOW   165
    10.1 Study I: In-vitro accuracy assessment   165
        10.1.1 Study design   166
        10.1.2 Results   169
        10.1.3 Discussion   170
    10.2 Study II: In-vivo accuracy assessment   172
        10.2.1 Study design   172
        10.2.2 Results   176
        10.2.3 Discussion   178
    10.3 Study III: Navigated vs. conventional liver biopsy   184
        10.3.1 Study design   184
        10.3.2 Results   189
        10.3.3 Discussion   191

11 DISCUSSION   197

12 SUMMARY   205
    12.1 Summary of contributions   205
    12.2 Conclusions   209

BIBLIOGRAPHY   211

ACRONYMS

2D	2-dimensional
3DoF	3-Degrees-of-Freedom
3D	3-dimensional
4D	4-dimensional
5DoF	5-Degrees-of-Freedom
6DoF	6-Degrees-of-Freedom
AR	Augmented Reality
CT	Computed Tomography
FLE	Fiducial Localization Error
FOM	Field of Measurement
FRE	Fiducial Registration Error
fMRI	functional MRI
GUI	Graphical User Interface
HU	Hounsfield Unit
MR	Magnetic Resonance
MRI	Magnetic Resonance Imaging
MPR	Multi-planar Reformatting
PACS	Picture Archiving and Communication System
PET	Positron Emission Tomography
RFA	Radiofrequency Ablation
RMS	Root Mean Square
SPECT	Single Photon Emission Computed Tomography

TRE	Target Registration Error
TIPS	Transjugular Intrahepatic Portosystemic Shunt
US	Ultrasound

1

INTRODUCTION

The secret of getting ahead is getting started.
— Mark Twain

1.1 MOTIVATION

Cancer is one of the leading causes of death world-wide. It accounted for 7.9 million deaths (or approximately 13% of all deaths) in 2007, and the number is expected to increase further to approximately 11.5 million in 2030 [159]. Irrespective of the primary tumour, the liver is one of the most common sites for metastatic disease [120]. As many patients are not eligible for surgery, image-guided percutaneous[1] approaches to diagnosis and treatment of liver cancer are increasingly applied in clinical routine. These procedures typcially require insertion of an elongate instrument into the liver with a relatively high degree of accuracy. Thermal ablation therapies, for example, are receiving increasing attention as minimally invasive strategies for the treatment of focal malignant disease [120], but exact placement of the instrument is essential for the success of the therapy [28, 124]. In the future, accuracy requirements will even further expand as targets for therapy become smaller due to improved image quality [28].

Percutaneous liver procedures rely heavily on image guidance to achieve the required precision. In general, the needles are placed under real-time image guidance (ultrasound (US), fluoroscopy) or under magnetic resonance (MR) or computed tomography (CT) guidance [102]. Real-time imaging modalities can continuously visualize the instrument in relation to the patient's anatomy and at the same time capture tissue motion caused by patient movement, respiration and cardiac motion. However, these modalities are not always available or sufficient for guiding the procedure (e.g., because the tumor is not visible in the image), or radiation dose concerns may prohibit their use. When sonographic placement is not possible, CT is often the method of choice. In this case, the operator has to "mentally" register the patient with the planning CT scan acquired pre-interventionally in

---

[1] Percutaneous: Through the skin

order to transfer the planned trajectory to the patient. This requires a lot of practice, especially when in-plane needle insertion is not possible. To lower the risk of needle misplacement, the needle position is checked repeatedly in control CT scans, which leads to high radiation exposure to the patient and long procedure times. In addition, each correction increases the risk of tumor seeding and post-procedure complication [73, 140, 145]. The introduction of CT fluoroscopy brought improvement through real-time feedback [45], but the physician's hand-eye coordination still remains a limiting factor, and both the patient and the physician are exposed to additional doses of radiation [111, 139].

Image-guided systems aim at complementing the physician's ability to understand the patient specific anatomy by integrating medical images and other sources of information, such as tracked instruments [166]. To date, however, such systems are only available for bony or sufficiently rigid structures such as the spine and the brain. These systems rely on the assumption that pre-operatively acquired images used to guide the intervention accurately represent the morphology of the tissue during the procedure [166]. In soft tissue interventions, however, the target organ can be subject to considerable organ shift and deformation caused by respiration [28], heartbeat [76], patient movement and manipulation by surgical instruments [149]. In consequence, the established navigation systems designed for rigid structures cannot be applied in these procedures, and soft tissue navigation remains a subject of ongoing research [166].

1.2 OBJECTIVES

The main objective of this work was to develop and evaluate a concept for computer-assisted percutaneous needle insertion into soft tissue featuring the following characteristics:

- High accuracy: A motion compensation concept capable of capturing and compensating for intra-interventional organ shift and deformation.

- Efficient guidance: An intuitive visualization scheme which allows for fast and precise needle insertion along a predetermined trajectory and does not require extensive training.

- Clinical applicability: A clinically feasible workflow in terms of time requirements and costs.

- Benefits for the patient: Improved clinical outcome in terms of radiation dose, complication rates and applicability to difficult cases.

As the liver is one of the most common sites for metastatic disease and at the same time one of the organs most affected by respiratory motion, the concept was to be implemented and evaluated by means of example for percutaneous liver punctures. It was, however, intended to be readily applicable to other abdominal organs and procedures.

1.3 APPROACH

Based on the above requirements, a soft tissue navigation approach was developed, which estimates the position of an abdominal target (e.g., a tumor) continuously from a set of tracked fiducial[2] needles. The workflow is illustrated in Fig. 1. Prior to the intervention, the needles are inserted in the vicinity of the target. Next, a planning CT scan is acquired on which a trajectory from the skin to the target is planned. Finally, the fiducials are located, both in image space and in tracking space, and a transformation between the tracking coordinate system and the CT coordinate system is established based on these fiducial locations (*initial registration*). During the intervention, the fiducial needles are continuously located by a tracking system, and a real-time deformation model is used to estimate the position of the target point based on the poses of the fiducials. To allow for fast and accurate needle insertion, a navigation monitor guides the physician towards the moving target.

The primary contributions of this work can be summarized as follows:

RESPIRATORY LIVER MOTION SIMULATOR: To reduce the number of animal experiments for evaluating the proposed methods, a respiratory liver motion simulator was developed, which allows for *in-vitro*[3] experiments in a respiring patient model [90, 91]. In an *in-vitro* study, the movement of explanted porcine and human livers mounted to the simulator was compared to the natural human liver movement (chapter 5).

TRACKING: As both the applied instruments as well as the fiducial needles should be trackable with high accuracy and at the same time not handicap the operator, different commercially available optical tracking systems were evaluated with regard to their suitability for needle-based soft tissue navigation [86]. For this purpose, different tool designs were developed and compared both experimentally and theoretically via error propagation methods. Furthermore, the sensitivity of the tracking systems to the pose of a tool within the measurement volume, illumination conditions, and motion was assessed (chapter 6).

---

2 The meaning of the term *fiducial* depends crucially on the context. In this thesis, it may refer to feature points locatable by a tracking system (cf. section 3.2.2), to reference markers attached to the patient for motion compensation, or to control points used for point-based registration.
3 *In-vitro*: Refers to the technique of performing an experiment in a controlled environment outside of a living organism

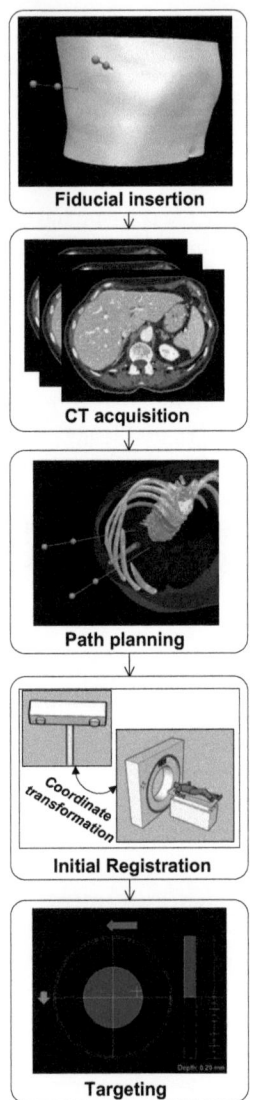

Figure 1: Workflow for navigated needle placement. Prior to the intervention, a set of fiducial needles is inserted in the vicinity of the target. Next, a planning CT scan is acquired, and a trajectory to the target is planned. Finally, the image coordinate system is registered with the tracking coordinate system, based on the fiducial poses. During the intervention, the fiducial needles are continuously located by an optical tracking system, and a real-time transformation is used to estimate the position of the target point accordingly. A suitable visualization scheme guides the physician towards the moving target.

REGISTRATION: To allow for visualization of surgical instruments in relation to the patient's anatomy, the image coordinate system must be registered with the tracking coordinate system based on the fiducial poses. This process requires accurate localization of the fiducial needles in both coordinate systems. To automatically locate fiducial needles in CT images with high accuracy, a novel localization algorithm was developed which applies a stochastic optimizer to fit geometrical models of the navigations aids into the image [87]. The main motivation for applying fiducial needles as opposed to skin markers is the ability to track reference points inside the target organ itself for capturing organ movement. Yet, even if the morphology of the tissue at the time of registration is approximately identical to the morphology of the tissue during image acquisition ("rigid body assumption"), it can be advantageous to use needles because the degree of influence of the fiducial localization error (FLE) on the target registration error (TRE) depends on the proximity of the fiducials to the target. To address this issue, an *in-silico*[4] study based on Monte-Carlo simulations was performed for evaluating the benefits of fiducial needles compared to skin markers when registering the tracking coordinate systems with the image coordinate system under the rigid body assumption (chapter 6).

MOTION COMPENSATION: Due to the high accuracy requirements, the navigation approach requires a mechanism to compensate for intra-interventional organ shift and deformation in real-time. In this work, a motion compensation method based on fiducial needles was developed, which allows for continuous estimation of the position of an abdominal target during continuous breathing [88, 89]. In this context, different deformation models to update the anatomy in real-time [88, 89], different fiducial placement strategies [89], and methods to reduce the invasiveness of the approach [94, 95] were investigated. Furthermore, an automatic gating method based on the tracked fiducials was derived [94] (chapter 8).

GUIDANCE: An important factor to the overall performance of a navigation system is the guidance module, which presents the positional information extracted from imaging and tracking data to the operator to facilitate needle insertion along a predetermined trajectory. To provide optimal guidance, different visualization schemes for targeting of an anatomical structure with a needle-shaped instrument were developed and compared [134, 135]. Based on the results of an *in-vitro* evaluation of the proposed methods, a three-stage visualization scheme for clinical use was derived [93, 96] (chapter 9).

EVALUATION: To evaluate the clinical applicability of the proposed approach, a prototype system for percutaneous needle insertion into the liver was developed. The overall targeting accuracy of the system, which is the accuracy of hitting a

---

4 *In-silico*: Via computer simulation

predefined target with the tip of a needle-shaped instrument, results from a variety of different sources of error as illustrated in Fig. 2. To obtain a meaningful error analysis, the developed methods were evaluated in two stages:

1. Evaluation and optimization of system modules: To assess and minimize the contribution of different sources of error, the accuracy of the individual system components were assessed separately from each other, namely the instrument tracking error [86] (chapter 6), the FLE in tracking space [86] (chapter 6), the FLE in image space [87] (chapter 7), the TRE [88, 89] (chapter 8), and the user error [135, 92, 96] (chapter 9).

2. Evaluation of the system in the clinical workflow: Three studies were conducted to evaluate the clinical applicability of the approach (chapter 10):

    a) *In-vitro* accuracy assessment: Evaluation of the accuracy of the system in the respiratory liver motion simulator [92].

    b) *In-vivo*[5] accuracy assessment: Evaluation of the accuracy of the system in swine [96, 97].

    c) *In-vivo* comparison to the conventional method: Comparison of the conventional CT-guided biopsy method with the computer assisted approach with respect to accuracy, time and radiation exposure [147].

1.4 OUTLINE

This thesis is organized as follows: Chapter 2 provides the reader with the medical background relevant to this work.

Chapter 3 reviews the history of navigation in medical interventions and provides an overview on computer-assistance in percutaneous abdominal interventions. Chapter 4 presents the proposed navigation approach on the basis of related work and describes the individual sources of error contributing to the overall needle insertion error associated with the concept.

Chapter 5 describes the motion simulator that was developed to evaluate the proposed methods in a realistic setup. Thereon, chapters 6 through 9 describe and evaluate the individual modules of the system: Chapter 6 presents the navigation tools developed for this thesis, evaluates two commercially available tracking systems with regard to their suitability for the proposed application, and assesses the FLE in tracking space. Chapter 7 introduces the developed method for locating the fiducial needles in the planning CT, assesses the FLE in image space, and evaluates the initial registration accuracy for different combinations of internal and external fiducials. Chapter 8 describes the motion compensation approach in detail and assesses the TRE for different real-time deformation models, placements strategies,

---

5 *In-vivo*: Inside an organism

and combinations of applied fiducials. Finally, the presentation of the system modules ends with chapter 9, which introduces and compares several visualization schemes for computer-assisted needle insertion along a predetermined trajectory, presents the guidance method derived for clinical use, and assesses the user error associated with the chosen method.

Subsequently, chapter 10 presents the three *in-vitro* and *in-vivo* studies that were performed to evaluate the performance of the developed prototype navigation system in the clinical workflow. Based on the results of these studies, chapter 11 discusses the developed navigation concepts in the context of the state of the art in clinical practice and in related work. Finally, chapter 12 summarizes the contributions and results of this work.

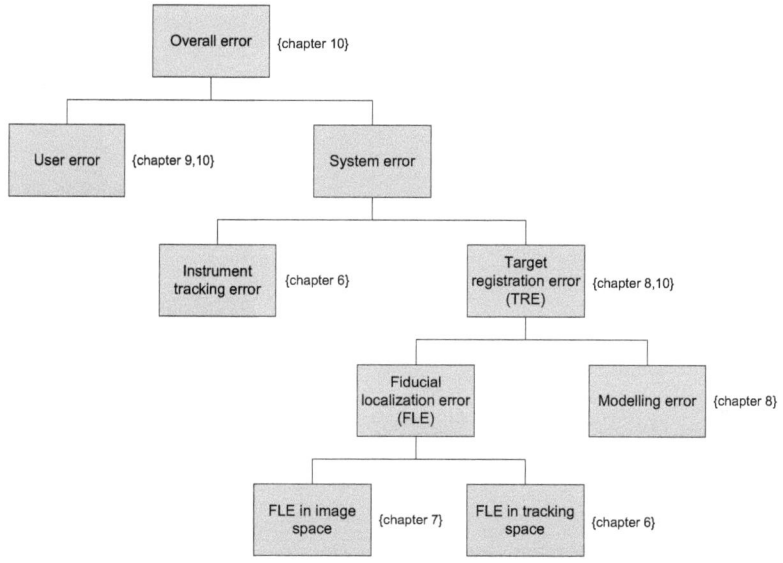

Figure 2: Hierarchical representation of the sources of error associated with the presented approach. The overall targeting error is represented by the root node. The children of a node e represent the sources of error causing e, that is, if all children $c_i(e)$ of e are associated with no error ($c_i(e) = 0; i = 1, \cdots, n$), then the error of that node is zero ($e = 0$). For example, if the fiducials are located accurately ($FLE = 0$) and the applied deformation model accurately reflects reality (*Modelling error*= 0), then the position of the target can be estimated accurately ($TRE = 0$).

2

MEDICAL BACKGROUND

> *When you discover your mission,*
> *you will feel its demand.*
> *It will fill you with enthusiasm*
> *and a burning desire to get to work on it.*
>
> — W. Clement Stone

Clinical practice is increasingly replacing traditional open surgical procedures with minimally invasive techniques [166]. This development results in a transition from direct visual feedback to image-based feedback. The physician can no longer directly see and feel the anatomical structures but needs to mentally establish the spatial relationship between the imagery and the patient. As many diagnostic and therapeutic procedures require high accuracy in placing an instrument inside the target structure (e.g., biopsy, radiofrequency ablation (RFA)), they require a high degree of operator skill. This holds especially for soft tissue organs, which are effected by breathing motion, patient movement and manipulation of surgical instruments.

This chapter is intended to describe the challenges associated with percutaneous interventions in clinical practice and to provide the reader with the general medical background relevant to the remaining part of this thesis. It briefly describes the anatomy of the liver (section 2.1), summaries the published studies on characterization of hepatic motion (section 2.2) and illustrates the challenges associated with percutaneous needle insertion by means of two example procedures (section 2.3): Liver biopsy and liver RFA.

2.1 ANATOMY OF THE LIVER

The human abdomen is the part of the body between the pelvis and the thorax. It consists among others of the lower esophagus, the stomach, the intestine, the liver, the kidneys, the pancreas and the spleen. The liver is the largest gland in the human body and is situated in the right upper quarter of the abdominal cavity under the right lower ribs (Fig. 3). Traditional gross anatomy divides the liver into four *lobes* [14], two of which (right liver lobe and left liver lobe) are shown in Fig. 4. The liver plays a major role in metabolism and has a number of vital functions including glycogen storage, decomposition of red blood cells, plasma protein synthesis and detoxification [131].

The liver receives arterial blood supply via the hepatic artery, but unlike other organs, it has a second venous blood supply; the blood that leaves the organs of the intestinal tract flows through the portal vein into the liver (cf. Fig. 4). As the blood flow allows for cancer cells originating from other organs to be carried into the liver, the liver is one of the most common sites for metastatic disease [120].

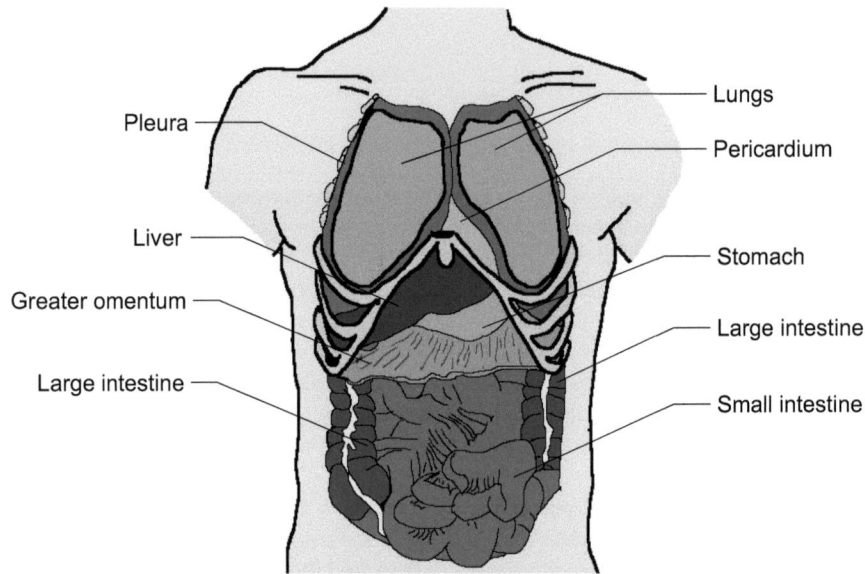

Figure 3: Location of the liver in the human abdomen (guideline: Faller *et al.* [38]).

2.2 CHARACTERIZATION OF HEPATIC MOTION

Liver motion is a significant obstacle to precise percutaneous needle placement [28]. Due to high anatomic variabilities as well as to numerous sources of movement and deformation, quantitative analysis of hepatic motion is challenging. Clifford *et al.* [28] reviewed the published efforts to characterize liver motion secondary to respiration, with the specific goal of defining the limitations and potential applications of image-guided systems in percutaneous liver interventions. The nine reviewed reports showed liver movement to be complex, with cranio-caudal, lateral, and anterior-posterior motion, in addition to movement due to deformation of the tissue. All studies agree that cranio-caudal motion is the most significant, with translation ranging from 10 to 26 mm in quiet respiration. In contrast, measurements of movement in both the anterior-posterior and lateral directions varied markedly with the assessment technique used, but the authors concluded that translation is significant in all three directions, especially when tracking targets within liver tissue. Furthermore, the studies demonstrate that there is wide variation between individuals in the degree and direction of liver movement.

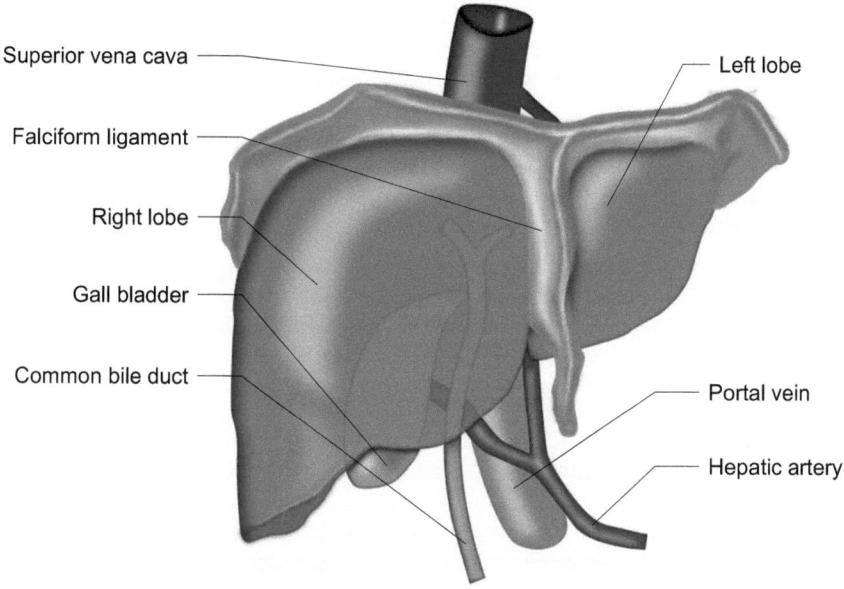

Figure 4: Anatomy of the liver.

According to the analysis by Rohlfing *et al* [126], the liver also shows significant motion due to deformation. When point-by-point measurements of locations within the liver were tracked throughout the respiratory cycle, they differed from the predictions made by rigid motion models by between 2 and 19 mm with an average of 6 mm. As the liver is nonregular in shape and nonuniform in composition, the degree of deformation varies markedly within the organ.

Kolen et al. [76] measured the cardiovascular component of natural liver motion (i.e, the motion resulting from heartbeat). The authors found cardiovascular motion in the liver to be complex, both temporally and spatially, but cyclic in every liver segment. Approximately 70% of the liver motion could be described by only one vector, and the mean liver displacement was generally below 1 mm.

Several groups investigated respiratory gating protocols, which assume that the liver reoccupies the same position at identical moments in the respiratory cycle. Suramo et al. [144] investigated the ability to suspend respiration repeatedly leaving the liver in exactly the same position with the aid of given instructions. The authors found the range of movement of the liver to be 5.5 cm during maximum respiration, 2.5 cm during normal respiration and 0.9 cm during suspended respiration. In a related study, Olbrich et al. [116] analyzed respiratory motion patterns of the liver caused by a respirator in swine. The authors concluded that repositioning after one breathing cycle was within a range of 1mm.

The liver as one of the most mobile organs does not have a fixed relationship to the skin surface or surrounding organs during the respiratory cycle. Shimizu et al. [137] analyzed the position of hepatic tumors relative to the overlying skin surface for possible radiotherapy treatment volume reduction by respiratory gating. The authors reported that the position of the tumor contours was not constant relative to the skin surface at peak exhalation or inhalation. In a related study, Wong et al. [165] used electromagnetically tracked skin fiducials and one fiducial needle to simultaneously monitor internal liver motion and external skin motion. The authors found a strong correlation between external anterior-posterior motion and internal inferior-superior motion.

In summary, liver motion can be characterized as follows:

- Liver movement due to respiration is complex, with cranio-caudal, lateral, and anterior-posterior motion, in addition to movement due to deformation of the tissue [28].

- There is wide variation between individuals in the degree and direction of liver movement [28].

- Cranio-caudal motion is the most significant, with translation ranging from 10 to 26 mm [28].

- The cardiovascular component of natural liver motion is relatively small (below 1 mm) [76].

- Skin motion correlates with internal liver motion [165].

- Respiratory gating should be used with care [137, 144].

2.3 PERCUTANEOUS LIVER INTERVENTIONS

Image-guided percutaneous approaches to diagnosis and treatment of liver disorders are already widely used in clinical routine. Diagnostic procedures include percutaneous biopsy (cf. *Liver biopsy*) of intrahepatic masses presumed to be tumors and internal/external biliary drainage[1] for benign and malignant biliary duct obstruction. Therapeutic procedures include tumor ablation (cf. *Radiofrequency ablation*), tumor embolization[2], and delivery of gene therapy vectors[3] [28]. These procedures typically require precise insertion of an elongate instrument into the target organ. In this section, we present the challenges associated with needle insertion into soft tissue by means of two examples: Liver biopsy and liver RFA.

2.3.1 Liver biopsy

A biopsy is a medical test involving the removal of cells or tissues for examination. The tissue sample is generally analyzed under a microscope by a pathologist and/or chemically. Liver biopsies may be taken percutaneously, transvenously (i.e., through the blood vessels) or directly during surgery [50]. The procedure has been routinely performed since early in the 20th century [101] and is generally done to aid diagnosis of liver disease, to assess the severity of known disease, and to monitor the progress of treatment [50]. While it is generally a safe procedure, there is a small risk of complications. The reported mortality from percutaneous liver biopsy varies considerably, but is of the order of magnitude of 0.1 to 0.01% [50]. The main cause of mortality is intraperitoneal haemorrhage. Furthermore, there is a risk of puncturing other organs such as the lung, the diaphragm, or the intestines [50].

Liver biopsies are generally performed under US, CT or CT-fluoroscopy guidance [75, 130]. When sonographic placement is not possible (e.g., because the tumor is not visible in US images), CT is generally the method of choice. In its original form, the procedure requires a pre-interventional CT scan which is used to plan a trajectory to the target. The operator then has to "mentally" register the patient with the images to transfer the planned trajectory to the patient. Due to the lack of real-time imaging information this requires a lot of practice, especially when in-plane needle insertion is not possible. To lower the risk of needle misplacement,

---

1 Drainage: Withdrawal of fluids from a wound or other cavity [103]. Biliary drainage is a procedure in which a catheter is placed percutaneously into the liver to drain the bile.
2 Embolization: Therapeutic introduction of various substances into the circulation to occlude vessels, either to arrest or prevent hemorrhaging, to devitalize a structure, tumor, or organ by occluding its blood supply, or to reduce blood flow to an arteriovenous malformation [103].
3 Gene therapy: Process of inserting a gene artificially into the genome of an organism to correct a genetic defect or to add a new biologic property or function with therapeutic potential [103].

the needle position is checked repeatedly in control CT scans leading to high radiation exposure to the patient and long procedure times (cf. Fig. 5).

In addition, each correction increases the risk of tumor seeding and post-procedure complication [73, 140, 145]. The introduction of CT fluoroscopy brought improvement through real-time feedback [45], but the physician's hand-eye coordination still remains a limiting factor and both the patient and the physician are exposed to additional doses of radiation [111, 139].

2.3.2 Radiofrequency ablation of liver tumors

The term tumor ablation is defined as the "direct application of chemical or thermal therapies to a specific focal tumor (or tumors) in an attempt to achieve eradication or substantial tumor destruction" [49] where the term "direct" aims to distinguish these therapies from others that are either applied orally or via an intravascular or peripheral venous route. The methods of tumor ablation most commonly used in current practice can be divided into the categories *chemical ablation* and *thermal ablation* [49]. In chemical ablation, chemical agents such as ethanol and acetic acid are applied to induce tissue necrosis[4] and cause tumor ablation. In thermal ablation procedures, energy is applied to destroy a tumor either with heat (e.g., radiofrequency, laser) or cold (cryoablation).

Principles of thermal ablation therapy

Ablation techniques can be classified according to the energy source used to achieve tumor destruction [49] as follows:

RADIOFREQUENCY ABLATION (RFA): Application of electromagnetic energy with frequencies less than 30 MHz (typically 375 to 500 kHz range [48]). An alternating electric current is applied, which induces frictional heat due to ion agitation [26] near a needle-shaped applicator inserted into the target organ. In monopolar systems, an electrical circuit develops between the applicator and a set of neutral pads fixed on the patient's skin. In bipolar systems, the electric circuit is closed between two RF electrodes placed in or at the periphery of the tumor and no grounding pads are required. In multipolar RF systems, more than two electrodes are placed in the target tissue and RF energy can be applied by a consecutive activation of every possible pair of electrodes [26].

MICROWAVE ABLATION: Application of electromagnetic energy with frequencies from 30 MHz to 30 GHz [49]. In contrast to RFA, in which the inserted electrode functions as the active source, the inserted probes function as

---

[4] Necrosis: Pathologic death of one or more cells, or of a portion of tissue or organ, resulting from irreversible damage [103].

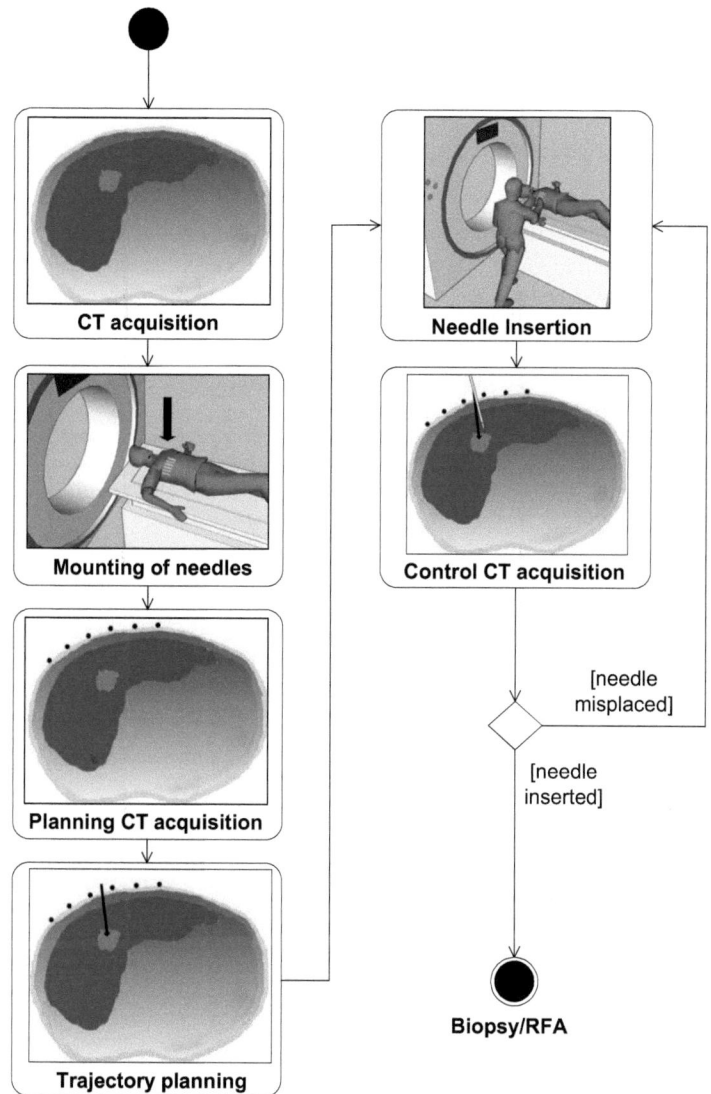

Figure 5: Workflow for CT-guided liver puncture. First, a planning CT is acquired to locate the tumor. Next, a set of needles is placed above the tumor region, and a second CT is acquired based on which a trajectory to the target is planned. Finally, the needle is gradually advanced and/or redirected while its position is repeatedly reassessed with new static images until the desired needle position is obtained.

antennae for externally applied energy [3]. The applied energy causes rotation of polar molecules, which is opposed by frictional forces and induces heating of the tissue.

LASER ABLATION: Ablation with light energy applied via fibres inserted directly into the tissue [29]. The fibers transmit intense light which is converted into heat [3].

ULTRASOUND ABLATION: Application of ultrasound energy for tumor ablation either transcutaneous or direct for percutaneous application with a needle-like applicator and for intracavitary devices.

CRYOABLATION: Application of lowtemperature freezing for destroying tissue. The freezing of tissue with rapid thawing leads to the disruption of cellular membranes and induces cell death [129].

The interested reader may refer to the overview article by Ahmed and Goldberg [3] for an introduction to the different techniques including their advantages and shortcomings.

Indications and limitations of RFA in liver metastasis

Thermal ablation strategies are receiving increasing attention as minimally invasive strategies for the treatment of focal malignant disease [120] with RFA being the most promising ablation technique for the treatment of liver metastases [124]. The advantages of RFA over surgical resection are that it can be used to treat tumors that are not surgically resectable due to anatomic constraints or inadequate liver reserve, that it is associated with reduced morbidity and mortality, and that it is technically easier to perform [2]. Furthermore, it appears safer (compared with cryotherapy), easier (compared with laser ablation), and more effective (compared with chemical ablation) than other minimally invasive therapies [120]. At present, it is applied for metastatic liver disease only in patients who are not candidates for surgical resection [120].

Pereira *et al.* [120] and Crocetti *et al.* [29] provide a broad review on long-term clinical results of RFA in liver tumors. In general, the success of RFA treatment depends crucially on the ability to ablate all viable tumor tissue and an adequate tumor-free margin of about 5-10 mm [29]. In consequence, the size of the metastases to be treated remains the major prognostic factor [120]. As the size and shape of the coagulated volume is variable and not always sufficient to cover the entire tumor [2], it is often necessary to reposition the applicator during the procedure to obtain overlapping spheres of treatment [124]. Ideal candidates for RFA have tumors with a maximum diameter less than 3.5 cm [120]. Beyond this size a high number of needle repositionings is necessary leading to a loss of reproducibility of the coagulation volume, long procedure times and higher complication and recurrence rates [120].

Like all thermal ablation techniques, RFA is negatively influenced by blood flow which potentially removes heat during the procedure [49]. In consequence, the coagulation volume is altered away from blood vessels and depends crucially on the individual patient's anatomy. Although several strategies have been developed to overcome this problem (c.f. [102]), the cooling effect often leads to incomplete tumor ablation.

Image guidance for RFA of the liver

Imaging is used for planning, targeting, monitoring, controlling, and assessing treatment response of ablation therapy [26]. In this section, we focus on the modalities used to guide the RF instrument to the tumor.

Percutaneous RF ablation can be either performed under general anesthesia or under local anesthesia in combination with analgosedation [26]. Depending on the type of anesthesia, needle insertion is typically performed by holding respiration in expiratory phase via the ventilator or during active breath-hold.

The positioning of the RF applicator into the tumor and the monitoring of the ablation process can be performed using US, CT, CT-fluoroscopy, MRI, or laparoscopy (with or without US) [26, 80, 124].

US imaging offers the distinct advantage of real-time imaging capability without using ionizing radiation [28], but is inadequate when overlapping ablations are necessary because heat-produced air bubbles spread peripherally during ablation resulting in bad image quality and thus hindering the exact repositioning of the electrodes [124]. Other weaknesses of US include high interoperator variability and inability to monitor the ablation course [28].

Compared to US, CT provides excellent visualization of target-tissue detail, but successful instrument placement is a repetitive needle-repositioning exercise [28]: The applicator is gradually advanced and/or redirected while its position is reassessed with a new static image until the desired needle position is obtained (cf. Fig. 5). The primary disadvantages of this approach are the high time requirements caused by repeated image acquisition [136] and the inaccuracies introduced by respiratory or patient motion. Furthermore, needle placement for interventions requires a high degree of operator skill [28]. CT fluoroscopy (cf. section 3.2.1) may be used to combine the anatomic resolution of CT with the real-time imaging capabilities of fluoroscopy but is associated with high radiation doses not only to the patient but also to the physician [111, 139]. Furthermore, monitoring the ablation course with CT is still a subject of ongoing research.

The current literature regarding percutaneous RF ablation mainly describes the use of CT and US guidance, but MR guidance is also gaining increasing attention [26]. The major advantages of MR are excellent soft tissue contrast (not limited to a time window after administration of contrast media), sensitivity to thermal effects allowing control of the endpoint of RFA after complete coagulation of the tumor, and direct multiplanar image acquisition [26]. On the other hand, MR is associated with high costs and requires construction of MR compatible devices. Clasen *et al.* [26] reviews clinical studies of MR guided RFA.

Regardless of the imaging modality employed, percutaneous interventions in the liver using the described advance-and-check technique for instrument placement share complication risks that increase with the number of needle passes undertaken [28]. Complications include hemobilia, intraperitoneal hemorrhage and seeding of the needle tract with tumor. Rhim *et al.* [124] further claim that inaccurate targeting is the major reason for tumor undertreatment.

3

STATE OF THE ART

> *[Science is] a great game. It is inspiring and refreshing.*
> *The playing field is the universe itself.*
> — *Isidor Isaac Rabi (Nobel prize 1944)*

Due to rapid developments in the research areas of medical imaging, image processing and robotics, medical interventions are increasingly supported by image-guided systems. To date, however, such systems are only available for bony or near bony structures such as the spine and the brain, and the use of computer assistance in soft tissue is still limited to diagnostics and surgical planning. This chapter reviews the history of navigation in medical interventions (section 3.1), and gives an overview of the approaches to motion compensation and guidance in percutaneous abdominal interventions (section 3.2).

3.1 HISTORY OF COMPUTER-ASSISTED INTERVENTIONS

Computer-assisted navigation has its roots in stereotactic neurosurgical procedures [122], which were developed early in the 20th century by Horsley and Clarke [59]. As reported by Gildenberg *et al.* [46], they were first applied in human neurosurgery by Spiegel and Wycis in 1947 who used the concept of a three-dimensional Cartesian coordinate system for the human brain to enable intraoperative orientation [142]: Prior to medical image acquisition, a *stereotactic frame*, a mechanical tool, was attached to the skull and thus allowed for the establishment of a spatial relationship between medical image space and stereotactic frame space. As the location of subcortical structures relative to the stereotactic frame could be approximated as constant, the position of the target could be described in terms of the frame-based coordinate system, and the mechanical device could be used to guide an instrument to deep brain structures. As frame-based stereotaxy soon achieved a reputation as a reliable way for accurately localizing structures [4, 47, 53] it was established as a standard method for supporting various interventions in open and minimally invasive neurosurgery [12].

For many years, image-guided surgery was confined to stereotactic procedures and was performed without the use of a computer (apart from that employed by the scanner to reconstruct the image) [122]. With the end of the 1980s, advantages in computer technology and robotics began to change the field of medical interventions again [12]: On the basis of industrial robots, robotic arm systems were constructed, which facilitated accurate positioning of surgical instruments [79]. In addition, electromagnetic [67] and optical [69, 161] tracking systems became commercially available in the early Nineties. These systems allow for continuous localization of surgical instruments based on small sensors attached to the devices, which can be tracked with high accuracy. Due to these systems, the localization of surgical instruments relative to the patient's anatomy no longer required a mechanical connection of the instrument to the patient. These technical advances soon expanded the range of applications for navigation systems to other disciplines [12]; Computer-assisted navigation emerged in ear, nose and throat surgery, for sinus and skull-base surgery [35], as well as in orthopedics for navigated placement of pedicle screws into the spine [104, 115]. Systems for navigated hip [9] and knee [33] replacement followed. In maxillofacial surgery, navigation systems are now used for osteo-synthesis implantation [37]. In dental implant surgery, computer-assisted design and manufacturing of implants as well as surgical navigation have been established in clinical routine [65, 105].

A typical image-guided procedure comprises (at least) the following three phases:

1. *Pre-operative planning:* The goal of the first phase is to create a patient and procedure specific plan based on pre-interventional images and other available sources of information (e.g., functional information).

2. *Registration:* At the beginning of the intervention, the coordinate system in which the plan was specified is aligned to the reference coordinate system in the operating room that is used to guide the intervention.

3. *Intra-operative plan execution:* The image-guided system then provides visual assistance to the physician, by displaying the spatial relationship between tracked instruments and anatomical structures. Intra-operative images may be acquired to update the anatomical picture.

Regardless of the target organ, the key component of a navigation system is the ability to register pre-operative images accurately to the patient. In commercially available systems, the registration is typically performed via a set of fiducials attached near anatomical regions of interest, for example to the skin or the bone of the patient [162]. These fiducials are located in the planning image and in the tracking coordinate system (by the tracking system itself) and from this, the transformation for mapping objects from image space to tracking device space is calculated. In general, the navigation systems have been designed for rigid structures and rely on the assumption that the pre-operatively acquired images used to guide the surgery accurately represent the morphology of the tissue during the procedure [166]. In soft tissue interventions, however, the target organ can be subject to considerable organ shift and deformation caused by respiration, heart beat, patient movement and manipulation by surgical instrument (cf. section 2.2). In consequence, the established navigation systems designed for rigid structures cannot be applied in soft tissue interventions, and image-guided systems for deformable anatomical structures are still a subject of ongoing research [166].

The next section presents current approaches to *soft* tissue navigation focussing on navigated needle insertion in percutaneous abdominal interventions. The interested reader may refer to the review articles of Raabe *et al.* [123], Grunert *et al.* [52], and Maciunas [85] for a more elaborate review of the history of navigation in neurosurgery. Sugano [143], and Ewers *et al.* [37] provide more information about the fields of orthopedic surgery and maxillofacial surgery respectively. Baumhauer *et al.* [12] reviews navigation concepts in endoscopic soft tissue surgery. Elaborative articles about navigation in medical interventions in general have been given by Peters [122], DiMaio *et al.* [34], as well as by Yaniv *et al.* [166].

3.2 COMPUTER-ASSISTED NEEDLE INSERTION INTO SOFT TISSUE

Table 1 provides a selection of the navigation systems presented for computer-assisted needle insertion in abdominal interventions. The approaches differ mainly in (1) the applied imaging modality, (2) the tracking method, (3) the initial registration approach, (4) the method for compensating for organ motion in real-time and (5) the method for guiding the operator to the planned target. It should be pointed out, that motion compensation is essentially an intra-interventional registration procedure and can apply the same methods used for initially registering the tracking coordinate system with the image coordinate system. However, this chapter distinguishes between the initial registration approach and the method for continuously compensating for organ motion because the initial registration does not need to be conducted in real-time. In consequence, several groups apply different methods for these two steps.

In the following paragraphs, the above mentioned aspects are discussed individually in the context of percutaneouos abdominal interventions. As the methods developed in the scope of this thesis were particularly designed for percutaneous liver biopsy and liver RFA, this chapter focusses on computer-assistance for needle insertion in the abdomen. The interested reader may refer to the review article of Baumhauer *et al.* [12] for an overview of soft tissue navigation in *endoscopic* minimally invasive surgery.

Authors	Tracking	Registration	Motion compensation
Banovac et al. [6, 7]	electromagnetic	skin fiducials and one fiducial needle	gating
Fichtinger et al. [40]	CT image overlay system	phantom for manually calibrating image overlay system with CT scanner	gating
Khamene et al. [71]	electromagnetic, optical, and image-based	plate equipped with magnetic and optical markers	deformation model describing correlation between internal and external motion
Khan et al. [72]	optical and electromagnetic	skin fiducials	gating
Krücker et al. [78]	electromagnetic	skin fiducials, previous instrument positions	gating
Nagel et al. [110, 109]	optical or electromagnetic	reference frame equipped with CT markers and optical/electromagnetic markers	gating, vacuum mattress stabilization
Nicolau et al. [113]	optical (color-based)	skin fiducials	gating
Wacker et al. [30, 151]	optical	reference frame equipped with CT/MR markers and optical markers	gating, patient immobilization
Wallace et al. [152]	electromagnetic	skin sensor	gating

Table 1: Selection of navigation approaches to computer-assisted needle placement in the liver.

Modality	Intra-operative Availability	Accessability	Dimensionality
X-ray	available	high	2D projection
X-ray fluoroscopy	available	high	2D projection
CT	available	high	3D
CT fluoroscopy	available	moderate	2D
3D C-arm CT	available	low	3D
US	available	high	2D/3D
MRI	available	high	3D
fMRI	not available	moderate	3D
PET	not available	moderate	3D
SPECT	not available	moderate	3D
Optical imaging	available	high	2D projection

Table 2: Classification of imaging devices according to their availability for intra-operative use, their accessability to physicians around the world, and the dimensionality of the data they acquire (modified from Yaniv et al. [166]). Modalities: Computed Tomography (CT), Ultrasound (US), Magnetic Resonance Imaging (MRI), functional MRI (fMRI), Positron Emission Tomography (PET), Single Photon Emission Computed Tomography (SPECT) and optical imaging.

3.2.1 Imaging

In rigid organ navigation, the entire procedure can be conducted based on only one planning image because the anatomy can be regarded constant. In contrast, soft tissue navigation requires a mechanism to compensate for intra-interventional organ shift and deformation. In some applications, real-time images are acquired for this purpose (cf. *Registration* below). Table 2 provides a classification of imaging modalities according to their availability for intra-operative use, their accessability to physicians around the world and the dimensionality of the data they acquire. In the following paragraphs, we discuss these imaging modalities in the context of percutaneous abdominal interventions.

Projection radiography

Projection radiography refers to the technique of exposing an image receptor (e.g., a photographic film) to X-rays to produce a two-dimensional projection image of an object. It is especially useful in the detection of pathology of the skeletal system, but can also be applied for detecting some disease processes in soft tissue [122]. Very cheap, X-rays have two major limitations: First, they reduce the three-dimensional information contained in an object to two, which results in the loss of information about the dimension parallel to the beam. Second, X-rays are a form of ionizing radiation and as such carcinogen.

The term *X-ray fluoroscopy* refers to an imaging technique based on X-rays that provides real-time moving images of the internal structures of a patient. This technique was introduced into medical use shortly after the discovery of X-rays and is widely used in orthopedics and interventional radiology [166]. Images can, for example, be obtained using an image intensifier mounted on one side of a C-shaped frame (*C-arm*) with the radiation source on the other side. Real-time images are displayed on a screen, allowing the physicians to monitor the position of surgical instruments and the patient's anatomy. The main drawback of this modality is that it exposes both the physician and the patient to radiation. Furthermore, the images are characterized by a small field of view and exhibit geometric and intensity distortions [166].

Projection radiography is applied by the image-guided radiosurgery system CyberKnife (Accuray Inc., Sunnyvale, CA), which combines real-time tracking of skin fiducials with occasional detection of *implanted* internal fiducials based on X-ray imaging for motion compensation during radiosurgery [117] (cf. section 3.2.4).

Computed tomography

Computed tomography (CT) is a medical imaging method which creates a three-dimensional image of the inside of an object from a large series of two-dimensional X-ray images taken around a single axis of rotation. In contrast to projection radiography, it provides high-contrast, high resulution and a true 3D volume and has become a gold standard in the diagnosis of a large number of different disease entities [122]. Its main drawback is the radiation dose delivered to the patient [166].

For many years, CT was only used for diagnosis and therapy planning, but it is now increasingly used as an intra-operative imaging modality. In *CT fluoroscopy*, tomographic images can be acquired in real-time with a high update rate [122]. The fact that most machines only provide the physician with a single image slice view led to the recent introduction of C-arm CT imaging that uses iso-centric motorized C-arms to acquire small 3D tomographic data sets [51]. Although the quality of these images is still lower than that of standard CT, further improvements can be expected with advances in technology [166].

Due to the numerous advantages of CT modalities and large installed base of systems, the majority of navigation systems apply CT for computer-based planning and therapy support (e.g. [30, 40, 72, 82, 110]).

Ultrasound

Ultrasound is a real-time modality that uses high frequency sound waves that are reflected by tissue to varying degrees to produce a 2D or 3D image of the patient. It is widely used for soft tissue and blood flow imaging but is not suitable for imaging the internal structure of bones or bodies of gas, such as the lung [166].

Ultrasound is cheap, safe and easy to use, non-invasive and produces no radiation exposure to the patient. Images are acquired at arbitrary orientations via free-hand scanning, and not as a stack of parallel slices. Compact and flexible, ultrasound scanners can be taken to critically ill patients in intensive care units, avoiding the danger caused by moving the patient to the radiology department.

On the other hand, image quality available from ultrasound is inferior to that of CT and even of low-field intra-operative MRI. Images are characterized by variable contrast, image speckle and shadowing artifacts [166]. In consequence, they are hard to interpret. Furthermore, the data is acquired as a set of uncorrelated 2D images at arbitrary orientations, requiring the physician to mentally reconstruct the underlying anatomical structures, which requires a high degree of operator skill. In addition, the ultrasound transducer must be in direct contact with the tissue during imaging and thus presents an intrusion into the operating field.

There are two basic ways for acquiring a 3D US data set [166]:

1. Acquiring a set of 2D images using standard probes and 1D detector transducers coupled with their positional information. This can be achieved using mechanical positioning of the transducer, or free-hand, by tracking the device.

2. Using 2D detector transducers that directly acquire a 3D volume. These images still suffer from poor image resolution and a low frame rate.

3D ultrasound has played a particularly important role in the guidance of prostate biopsy and brachytherapy [125, 154] and is generally gaining increasing attention in image-guided systems due to its real-time compatibility [8, 16, 56].

MRI

A Magnetic Resonance Imaging instrument (MRI scanner) uses powerful magnets to polarise and excite hydrogen nuclei in water molecules, producing a detectable signal which is spatially encoded resulting in tomographic images of the body. Unlike CT, MRI does not involve the use of ionizing radiation and is therefore not associated with the same health hazards. Compared to CT, it provides excellent soft tissue contrast but exhibits both geometric and intensity distortions [166].

A small percentage of centres have MRI scanners located in the operating room. These are typically low field open magnets (0.2-0.5 Tesla), allowing intra-operative image acquisition in close to real-time. One of the most attractive features of intra-operative MR systems is their capability to monitor the progress of certain therapies in real-time by measuring changes in MR characteristics that are undergone by the tissues during freezing or heating (cf. [122]). On the other hand, the limitations placed on an open magnet in the OR result in low resolution, poor image quality and high noise. Furthermore, the surgeon has only limited access to the patient, and the presence of the magnetic field creates a potentially unsafe environment requiring instruments to be modified for compatibility.

Recently, MRI has been increasingly used as imaging modality for navigated interventions (cf. [16, 71, 151]). For a comprehensive review of the current state of the art and future perspectives on interventional MRI the interested reader is referred to [66].

Other imaging modalities

The use of functional imaging such as functional MRI (fMRI), Positron Emission Tomography (PET), and Single Photon Emission Computed Tomography (SPECT) as well as optical imaging obtained from endoscopes and microscopes has played a minor role in related work and is discussed by Yaniv *et al.* [166].

3.2.2 Tracking

The term *tracking* refers to the process of determining and following the position and orientation of an object with respect to some reference coordinate system over time. A core component of an image-guided navigation system is the ability to track instruments in real-time during the procedure and to display them as part of a realistic model of the operative volume.

Tracking technologies

The commercially available systems are generally based on one of the following concepts:

MECHANICAL TRACKING: Mechanical tracking approaches generally employ a probe that is physically linked to a mechanical basis attached firmly to the patient. The position of tracked instruments is determined via angle encoders.

OPTICAL TRACKING: In optical tracking systems, two or more cameras, with known poses to each other, are applied to locate feature points, or *fiducials*, attached to the objects to be tracked. Each camera locates the individual fiducials on the object in a 2D image, and the information from all cameras is merged to obtain a 3D image via triangulation (Fig. 6).

ACOUSTIC TRACKING: Sound point sources are attached to the objects to be tracked, and the time of flight between the source and a number of detectors is used to estimate the location of the source.

MAGNETIC TRACKING: A magnetic field transmitter generates an electromagnetic field, and sensor coils are embedded into the objects to be tracked. By measuring the voltage induced in these coils, the position within the coordinate system defined by the field transmitter can be determined.

OPTICAL EGO-MOTION (SELF-MOTION) TRACKING: Video images are processed to compute camera motion (cf. e.g. [13]).

FIBER-OPTIC BASED TRACKING: Fiber optic curvature sensors produce an output voltage proportional to curvature or displacement of an object [118]. This information is used to generate a 3D image of the position, orientation and shape of a flexible object.

Reviews of some of these technologies and their characteristics can be found in [44, 121, 166]. For a comprehensive review of tracking technologies, not specific to medical applications, the reader may refer to [157].

According to Yaniv et al. [166], an ideal tracking system should be small, accurate, robust, wireless and inexpensive with high refresh rates and a room sized working volume. It should be able to estimate all six degrees of freedom, concurrently track up to 100 objects, and not require line-of-sight to the tracked objects. None of the commercially available tracking system fulfills all of these requirements, hence, the tracking technology to be applied for a given application must be chosen carefully. According to Yaniv et al. [166], the tracking technologies enumerated above can be divided into two classes: Those, that can only track a single object at a time (mechanical, ego-motion, fiber-optics), and those that can track multiple objects concurrently, namely, acoustic, optical, and magnetic tracking systems. In this report, we focus on the second class because soft tissue interventions generally require tracking of more than one object at a time.

The tracking technique most frequently employed in image-guided systems is the optical approach (cf. e.g. [30, 110, 113]), because the devices generally achieve high and robust tracking accuracy and precision [161]. The fiducials localizable by an optical tracking systems include infrared light emitting diodes (IREDs) (e.g., FlashPoint 5000 (Boulder Innovation Group, Boulder, USA)), reflective markers that are illuminated with infrared light (e.g., Polaris® (Northern Digital Inc., Ontario, Canada)), and markers that exhibit high contrast in the visible spectrum (e.g., MicronTracker 2 (Claron Technology, Inc.; Toronto, Ontario, Canada)). All optical systems provide submillimetric FLEs, refresh rates that are sufficient for medical procedures, and robust performance with regard to the environment [166]. Their main drawback is the line-of-sight requirement which limits their use to rigid instruments.

Acoustic systems are unobtrusive, wireless and compute an object's pose with sufficient accuracy in a sufficiently sized work volume for medical applications [166]. Despite this, they are rarely used in image-guided systems because they generally

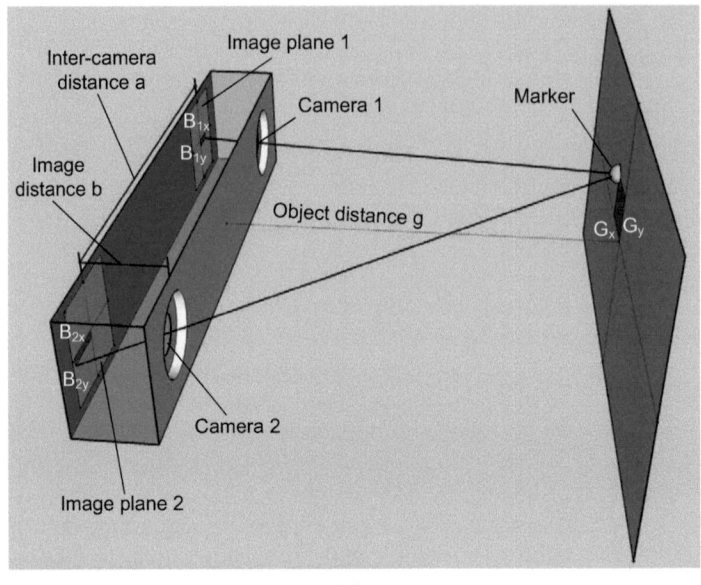

Figure 6: Simplified illustration of the principle of triangulation (a) and derivation of the 3D marker position from two camera images (b).

require that a single emitter fires at a time, and that there be a time delay between them in order for their location to be estimated. In consequence, reliable pose estimation is mostly limited to static objects. Furthermore, ultrasonic systems also impose the line-of-sight constraint between emitters and detectors.

Magnetic systems such as the Aurora® system (Northern Digital Inc., Ontario, Canada) or the microBIRD™ (Ascension Technology Corp., Burlington, VT, USA), on the other hand, do not suffer from the line-of-sight constraint and can track flexible instruments inside the body. Refresh rates are sufficient for most medical procedures [166]. The main drawback of electromagnetic systems, on the other hand, is the fact that their performance is often limited by the presence of metal in the vicinity of the magnetic field transmitter or the sensors [122]. Manufacturers have strived to make their systems more robust with respect to their environment with some recent success (cf. [166]), and users have addressed the issue by developing a variety of correction schemes for electromagnetic field distortions using mechanical devices, robots, and optical tracking systems to establish ground truth (cf. e.g. [74]). Recently, some efforts have been made to develop hybrid systems combining the advantages of optical and magnetic devices (cf. e.g. [15, 72]). When there is no line-of-sight between a tool and the optical tracking system, the magnetic system takes over. Due to the recent development of smaller sensors with a diameter of the order of magnitude of 1 mm, which can be embedded at the tips of medical instruments, electromagnetic tracking systems are increasingly applied in soft tissue navigation systems (e.g. [78, 109, 169]).

Tracking errors

Many different sources of errors contribute to the final error of a tracking system as discussed at length by Bauer *et al.* [11]. A useful representation of errors in measurement systems is the so-called root mean square (RMS) error [11]. Let $\{\vec{x}_j\}$ be a set of measurement with corresponding ground truth values $\{\vec{x}_j^{ref}\}$ ($j = 1, \ldots, N$). Then the RMS error ϵ_{RMS} is computed as:

$$\epsilon_{RMS} = \sqrt{\frac{1}{N} \sum_{j=1}^{N} \left\| \vec{x}_j - \vec{x}_j^{ref} \right\|^2} \qquad (3.1)$$

where $\|.\|$ is usually chosen as the Euclidean norm. The accuracy of a tracking system is generally given as the RMS error of tracking a fiducial/sensor within the measurement volume of the system.

In general, the user is not interested in the accuracy of tracking a single fiducial, but in the accuracy of tracking a target connected rigidly to a set of fiducials, such as the tip of a needle-shaped instrument. This error is referred to as TRE. Section 3.2.3 ($\rightarrow$ *Point matching*) describes how to predict the TRE from the FLE and the tool geometry. Bauer *et al.* [10, 11] further presented a method for estimating the expected accuracy in optical systems for a given camera configuration and a specific target at a specified pose inside the tracking volume.

Tool design

As the expected TRE depends crucially on the fiducial configuration, tool design is important when developing an image-guided system. West et al. [158] analyzed the tracking error for various fiducial configurations and gave design advices for optically tracked pointing devices and endoscopes. In general, the following rules of thumb should be considered when designing a tool [11]:

1. Use many fiducials: It can be shown that the expected squared TRE is inversely proportional to the number n of fiducials [42]. Using many fiducials is thus helpful for reducing the expected TRE. It should be noted, however, that increasing n also leads to higher weight of the tracked tool and - in the case of volumetric markers - increases the occurrence of occlusions between the fiducials.

2. Put the centroid close to the point of interest: The expected TRE is minimal at the centroid of the markers [42] and increases linearly with the distance from the centroid [11].

3. Use a larger diameter for the marker distribution: It can be shown that increasing the diameter of the marker distribution increases tracking accuracy [11, 42].

3.2.3 Initial registration

In the context of image-guided therapy, the term registration refers to the process of determining a transformation that maps positions in one coordinate system to corresponding positions in another coordinate system. At the beginning of an image-guided intervention, the coordinate system in which the surgical plan was specified must be aligned to a coordinate system in the OR, e.g., the tracking coordinate system. The most wide-spread approaches applied for this purpose are presented in the following paragraphs. As this thesis applies a point-based registration approach, this method receives the most attention.

Point matching

Point-based registration involves identification of homologous structures in both the image and on the patient and estimation of a geometrical transformation that maps corresponding points onto each other. The commercially available systems generally assume a rigid transformation $\Phi(\vec{p}) = R\vec{p} + \vec{t}$ with a rotation matrix R and a translation vector $\vec{t}$. Let $P = \{\vec{p}_j\}$ be a point set to be registered with another point set $Q = \{\vec{q}_j\}$, where each point $\vec{p}_j$ corresponds to the point $\vec{q}_j$ with the same index ($j = 1, \ldots, N$). Then Φ is defined as the rigid-body transformation that minimizes the cost function:

$$\epsilon_{RMS}(\Phi) = \sqrt{\frac{1}{N} \sum_{j=1}^{N} \|\vec{q}_j - \Phi(\vec{p}_j)\|_2^2} \qquad (3.2)$$

where $\|.\|_2$ denotes the Euclidean norm. A unique solution exists if and only if the point sets P and Q contain at least three noncollinear points. Several closed form solutions for the problem have been derived (e.g. Horn et al. [58]).

In neurosurgery, possible landmarks used for point based registration include the outer canthi of the eyes, the tragus of the ears and the nasion [122]. One approach employs a tracked pointer to identify landmarks on the patient, and the same structures are then identified via a cursor within the pre-operative planning image of the patient. While widely used, the point based registration approach has several limitations. First, it can be difficult to precisely identify the locations of the landmark points on the patient. Second, the registration accuracy depends crucially on the number and distribution of the chosen landmarks [42]. The accuracy of point matching procedures can be improved by using artificial landmarks (as opposed to anatomical landmarks), namely skin adhesive or implantable fiducials [99]. These markers can either be tracked themselves or be precisely located by a tracked pointer in patient space. Furthermore, the landmarks can potentially be extracted automatically from the planning image.

In soft tissue navigation, the use of anatomical landmarks is generally not feasible, and skin fiducials are often applied for the registration process (cf. e.g. [6, 72, 78, 141]). To avoid attaching markers to the patient, Das et al. [30] as well as Nagel et al. [110] apply a calibration phantom providing both image markers and tracking markers with known distances to each other. Furthermore, Nagel et al. [110] use a vacuum matress to minimize patient movement during the registration process as well as during the intervention. Recently, Krücker et al. [78] expanded the point based registration approach by using previous instrument positions extracted from repeated control CT scans for improving registration precision obtained from skin markers.

In general, there are three useful measures of error for analyzing the accuracy of point-based registration methods [99]:

- Fiducial localization error (FLE): Error in locating the points (*fiducials*) used for registration.

- Fiducial registration error (FRE): RMS distance between corresponding fiducials after registration (eq. 3.2).

- Target registration error (TRE): Distance between corresponding points other than the fiducials after registration.

In many applications, the FRE is used as a figure of merit for registration accuracy [146]. However, Fitzpatrick et al. [42] showed that this may be misleading because unlike the TRE, the FRE does not depend on the fiducial configuration. It can, however, be used as an estimate of the FLE [100].

Fitzpatrick et al. [42] were the first to derive a closed-form solution to estimate the expected squared value of the TRE in rigid-body point-based registration. Assuming an identical and isotropic Gaussian distribution of the FLE, the authors showed that the TRE depends crucially on (1) the FLE, (2) the number of fiducials, and (3) the fiducial configuration. Subsequently, several different approaches have been developed to estimate either the mean squared value of the TRE [84, 160] or the distribution of the TRE [41, 10, 106, 107, 138] under different noise conditions. Moghari et al. [108] recently compared the different methods for estimating the TRE and verified that in the presence of isotropic and identical zero-mean Gaussian noise for the FLE, all algorithms estimate the same distribution of the TRE. However, under heterogenous zero-mean Gaussian distribution, the different methods yield considerably different results. In general, the theoretical models of the TRE can only be as good as the noise models they use, and prediction of the TRE in point-based registration remains an active field of research.

Monte-Carlo simulation is another method for simulating the behavior of complex systems which is often used for error propagation [11]. To compute the Monte-Carlo simulation of a function $f(\vec{x})$, where $\vec{x}$ is a vector with several possibly independent random variables with arbitrary distributions, samples $\vec{x}_i$ are drawn randomly from the distributions and the function value $f(\vec{x}_i)$ is computed accordingly. By repeating the procedure sufficiently often, the distribution of the TRE can be computed from the distribution of the FLE with this method. While Monte-Carlo simulation is a very useful tool for offline accuracy analysis due to its flexibility, it has only limited use when the computing time is restricted, as in online error estimation.

Surface matching

In surface matching, a surface extracted from the planning image is mapped to the same surface in patient space. The latter can for example be acquired as a point cloud with a tracked pointer. Some commercially available neurosurgical systems use the patient's face for this purpose. Herline et al. [55] applied surface matching in the liver in an open procedure. An optically-tracked pointer was used to capture the surface of the liver and the obtained point cloud was fitted to the segmented liver surface obtained from a pre-operative CT scan. Cash et al. [22] used laser range scanning for intra-operative surface registration. According to a recent literature research, however, surface matching has not yet been applied in percutaneous abdominal interventions.

Imaging device calibration

An intra-interventional imaging modality such as ultrasound or C-arm is calibrated and tracked to establish a relationship to the tracking system. The images, patient, and tracking system are thus intrinsically registered. This approach is very fast, but image quality is low, and there is no transfer from pre-interventional planning data to the patient [166]. In addition, calibration of imaging devices with high accuracy is challenging.

Several groups [8, 56, 70, 119] applied a calibrated tracked US probe for registering image space with patient space. Feuerstein *et al.* [39] introduced a laparoscopic navigation system, which combines an isocentric C-arm with an optical tracking system for port placement planning and vessel visualization during resection interventions of liver or kidney. By tracking both the calibrated C-arm and the laparoscope, the intra-operatively acquired CT volume can be augmented on the laparoscope video.

3.2.4 Real-time motion compensation

In rigid organ navigation, a single registration procedure at the beginning of the medical intervention is performed because the target structures are assumed to hold a constant position throughout the intervention. This also holds for navigation systems for neurosurgery, although several studies showed that the morphology of the brain can change dramatically after the opening of the skull (*brain shift*). Peters *et al.* [122] reviewed the efforts to compensate for this effect. In soft tissue procedures, shift and deformation of the organs is even more dramatic. Although tracking of and correction for organ movement is of high concern, the lack of robust solutions has limited the use of image-guided approaches in this area to date [122]. The following paragraphs introduce the motion compensation approaches that have been proposed so far.

Gating

Gating techniques [32] are based on the assumption that the target organ re-occupies the same position at identical points in the respiratory cycle. This approach permits the approximation of a motionless target organ, provided that the intervention is conducted exclusively in a predefined state within the breathing cycle. End-exhalation is the state most often chosen, because it represents the longest natural pause in the respiratory cycle [5]. To prevent the patients from moving, they can be immobilized via a vaccuum mattress as proposed by Nagel *et al.* [110] and Kenngott *et al.* [68]. Gating techniques allow applying the initial registration (cf. section 3.2.3) throughout the intervention. While very simple, the approach has two major drawbacks: First, it requires identification of corresponding states in successive respiratory cycles. Second, several studies indicate that abdominal organs do not reliably reassume the same positions at equivalent states within the breathing cycle (cf. section 2.2).

Fiducial based motion compensation

A set of trackable fiducials[1] is placed onto the skin (*external fiducials*), and/or inside the target organ (*internal fiducials*), and the position of the target is continuously estimated with either a rigid transformation compensating for patient movement or with a non-rigid deformation model which can additionally capture organ deformation.

Most groups apply only external fiducials because they are not invasive and perform gated experiments [72, 78, 113]. Levy *et al.* [81, 82] apply one electromagnetically tracked internal fiducial to determine the timing of the pause in respiratory-related organ motion and thus indirectly the optimal target position. In a recent study, Krücker *et al.* [77] performed experiments in a porcine model to investigate registration and motion correction methods in the presence of respiratory motion. The authors applied either a set of skin fiducials or a set of fiducial needles for this purpose and concluded that respiratory motion can be compensated throughout the respiratory cycle when using internal fiducials.

Surface based motion compensation

The organ surface is captured intra-interventionally (e.g., via a laser scanner [22, 23, 24]), and a deformation model can be applied to estimate the target position accordingly. According to a recent literature search, this approach has only been applied to open procedures.

Image-based motion compensation

A tracked real-time imaging modality, such as ultrasound or X-ray, is applied to update the image guidance system with the current anatomy. Hong *et al.* [57] published first efforts to segment both the tumor and the instrument in real-time from 2D US images. Wei *et al.* [155] proposed a method for segmenting and tracking brachytherapy needles inserted along oblique trajectories from 3D transrectal US in near real-time.

---

[1] As already mentioned above, the meaning of the term *fiducial* depends crucially on the context. In this thesis, it may refer to a to a feature point locatable by a tracking system (cf. section 3.2.2), to reference markers attached to the patient for motion compensation, or to control-point in point-based registration.

To avoid real-time segmentation, a tracked instrument can be visualized in the intra-interventionally acquired images if the imaging device was calibrated prior to the intervention (cf. [8, 39, 56]). Intra-interventional instrument guidance additionally requires extraction of the target position in real-time. This can be achieved by continuously registering pre-operatively acquired images to the incoming intra-operative images. Wein *et al.* [156] simulated US images from CT images for fully-automatic alignment of a freehand US sweep with CT data. The approach is promising but needs further investigation to be applied for real-time motion compensation. In conclusion, fast, robust and accurate image-based motion compensation is still the subject of ongoing research.

Motion compensation with a trained model

A model characterizing organ movement is computed in a pre-interventional learning phase and applied to update the patient's anatomy in real-time during the intervention. Some groups investigated estimating internal organ motion from the movement of the skin. Schweikard *et al.* [133] combined real-time tracking of skin fiducials with occasional detection of *implanted* internal fiducials based on X-ray imaging for motion compensation during radiosurgery. During an initialization phase, a correlation model relating internal and external movement is learnt. This model is continuously updated during treatment to compensate for other, non-respiratory motion. The concept has been in clinical use for several years now [117], but has the major disadvantage of relying on implanted fiducials and of delivering high doses of radiation to the patient.

Khamene *et al.* [71] utilized 4D MRI and tracked magnetic skin fiducials to correlate internal organ motion with skin movement in a pre-interventional learning phase. The approach showed promising results in an experimental study.

Blackall *et al.* [16] presented a method for incorporation of a respiratory motion model into a non-rigid registration algorithm for registering 3D pre-interventional images to intra-interventionally acquired 2D US images. In a pre-interventional learning phase, a set of MR images is acquired to establish a model characterizing respiration induced organ motion. During the intervention, this model constraints the search space of a non-rigid registration algorithm. The approach showed promising accuracy but a single slice registration took 15 min, which is not fast enough for real-time guidance.

Biomechanical approaches

Biomechanical models allow priors about the realistic behaviour of tissue to be introduced as additional constraints [21]. In general, a computational model that can simulate deformations is used to warp pre-interventional images to reflect the intra-interventional situation. Carter *et al.* [21] provide a broad review of biomechanical modelling for compensating for soft tissue deformation during

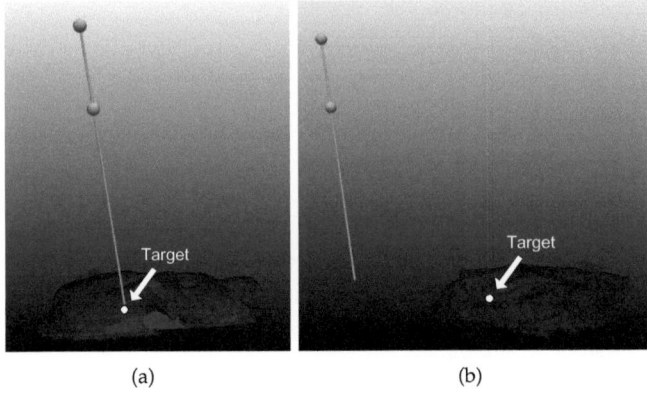

Figure 7: Classical 3D overview showing the same scene from two different perspectives. The target appears to be hit in image (a), but the instrument has not even been inserted into the liver, as shown in image (b).

image-guided surgery. While physics-based concepts such as finite element models have been applied in surgery simulation with success to simulate organ deformation [21], the methods have not yet successfully been applied to percutaneous soft tissue interventions. This can be attributed to the fact that (1) they require that the material properties, constitutive equations and boundary conditions are known and (2) they are computationally very expensive. To overcome these problems, Hostettler et al. [60, 61] proposed a method for predicting internal organ motion induced by breathing from the abdominal skin position based on a single planning CT. The approach is based on the assumption that the volume of the viscera and the tissue thickness between skin and organs remains constant. In consequence, the position of the diaphragm can be induced from the position of the abdominal skin, which is optically tracked in real-time. Although promising, this approach is still under development and needs further investigation.

3.2.5 Guidance

The goal of data visualization in image guided procedures is to concisely convey the relevant information for the successful completion of the intervention [166]. Existing methods for displaying 3D information are presented and discussed extensively in the review articles by Yaniv et al. [166] and Baumhauer et al. [12]. In this section, we focus on the proposed concepts for targeting an anatomical structure with a needle-shaped instrument. As illustrated in Fig. 7, a simple 3D visualization of the scene is not sufficient to guide the operator to the target.

Classical display techniques

Multi-planar reformatting (MPR), or multiplanar reconstruction is a term used in medical imaging to refer to the reconstruction of images in the coronal and sagittal planes in conjunction with the original axial dataset. Many image-guided systems provide an MPR view in addition to a 3D virtual environment generated from the reconstructed 3D imaging data. Some systems further present the planned trajectory by a tube-shaped object as shown by means of example in Fig. 8 and Fig. 9.

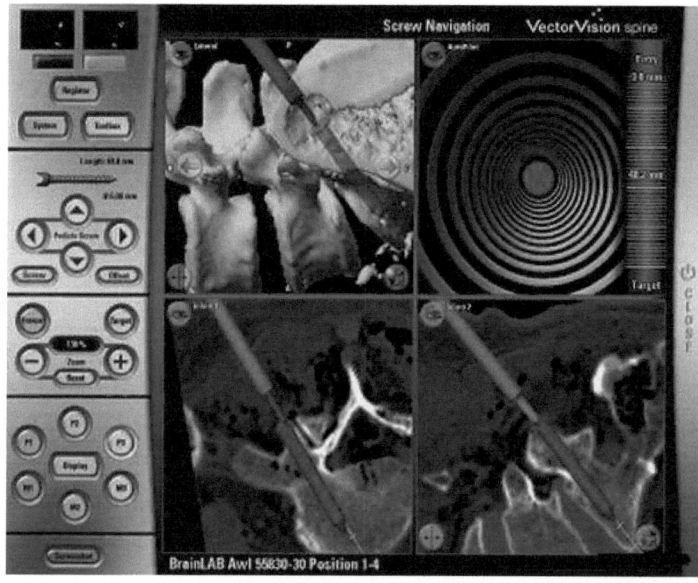

Figure 8: Visualization scheme provided by the "AutoPilot" (BrainLAB®, Feldkirchen, Germany). In addition to the MPR, a helical channel is shown representing the trajectory to the target (source: BrainLAB®).

Levy et al. [81] provide a fourth view, in addition to the MPR view, showing color-coded crosshairs representing target, needle tip, and needle hub, which must be overlapped for successful puncture (Fig. 10).

Nicolau et al. [112] presented a visualization approach showing the scene from a virtual camera placed in the tip of the instrument with the view direction along the needle axis (Fig. 11).

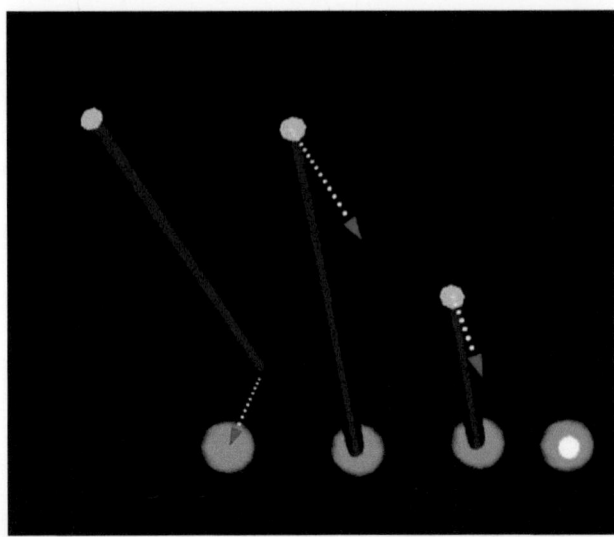

Figure 9: Visualization scheme provided by the "BrainNavigator" [20] developed by LOCALITE GmbH (Sankt Augustin, Germany). The generated guidance image shows the navigation scence from the perspective of a virtual camera placed onto the axis defined by the planned trajectory. (Reprinted with permission from Bublat et al. [20].)

Video-based augmented reality visualization

Video-based augmented reality (AR) systems provide guidance by overlaying the video imagery with information about the anatomical structures and tools that are underneath the visible surface. Information can be displayed either on a screen (cf. Fig. 11) or directly into the optical device used to view the anatomy. Das et al. [30] use a video-see-through head-mounted display for AR guidance in abdominal interventions. Both the optical tracking camera and the scene camera are attached to a helmet (Fig. 12(a)), such that the line-of-sight between the tracking camera and the optical markers is not obscured by the operators body. The device provides two visualization screens showing augmented live video streams (Fig. 12(b)). A virtual cylinder serves as a linear extension of the needle from its tip to facilitate aiming the instrument at the target.

Tomographic image overlay

Tomographic image overlay systems provide guidance using an image display approach that incorporates semi-transparent mirrors (Fig. 13(a)). Fichtiger et al. [40] apply the concept for computer-guided needle insertion (Fig. 13(b)). A monitor and

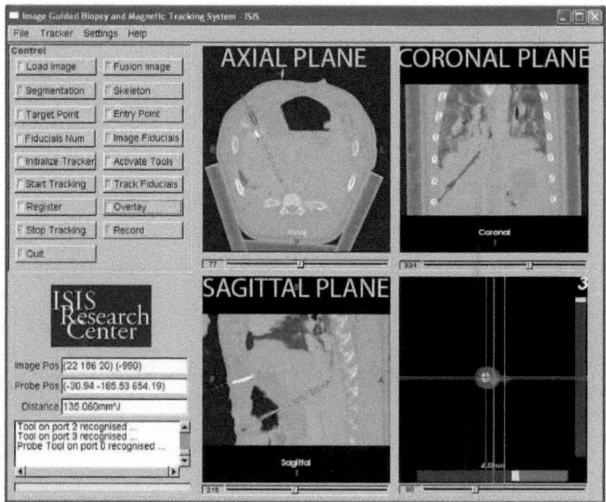

Figure 10: Visualization scheme provided by Levy *et al.* [81]. The puncture needle position is superimposed on the planned trajectory in the axial, coronal and saggital slices. In a fourth window, color-coded crosshairs represent target, needle tip and needle hub, which must be overlapped for successful puncture. (Reprinted with permission from Levy *et al.* [81].)

a semi-transparent mirror are positioned such that the reflected image from the monitor appears to float inside the patient. System operation involves a calibration step which assures that the reflection in the mirror is physically accurate. Calibration is valid as long as the spatial relationship between the mirror, monitor, and imaging device is constant. System accuracy depends on the geometric accuracy of the images and the accuracy of the calibration procedure. One advantage of this concept is that it enables the physician to focus his attention to the interventional site. On the other hand, the mirror restricts access to the patient. According to a recent literature search, tomographic image overlay systems have not yet been combined with motion compensation methods (only with gating).

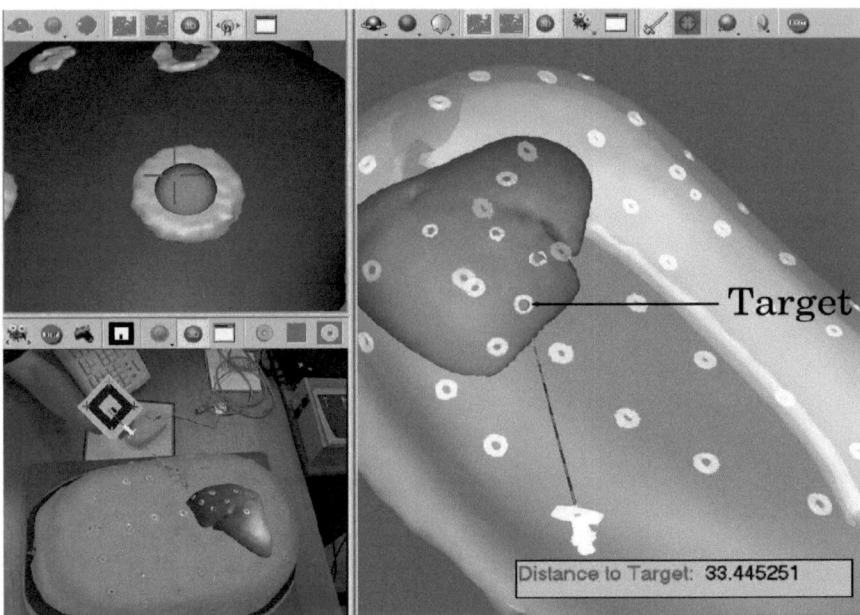

Figure 11: Visualization scheme provided by Nicolau et al. [112]. It shows an augmented video image (bottom, left), a virtual reconstruction of the scene (right), and an image showing the scene from the view of a virtual camera placed in the tip of the instrument with the view direction along the needle axis. (Reprinted with permission from Nicolau et al. [112].)

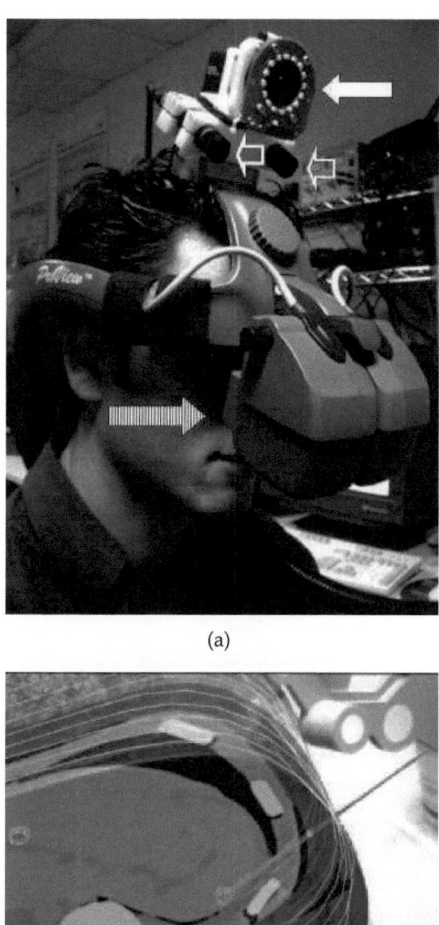

Figure 12: Visualization scheme provided by Das et al. [30]. Two visualization screens (striped arrow) allow exploration of the augmented scene from a variety of viewpoints. The camera triplet has a stereo pair of scene cameras (open arrows) to capture the scene and a dedicated tracking camera (solid arrow) with dedicated light-emitting diodes to generate a constant infrared flash (a). Augmented scene, as viewed by the operator, demonstrates a thin colored cylinder that represents the virtual needle. A second cylinder represents the extrapolated needle trajectory extending from the needle tip. The white grid superimposed on the outer perimeter of the interventional phantom provides additional depth cues (b). (Reprinted with permission from Das et al. [30].)

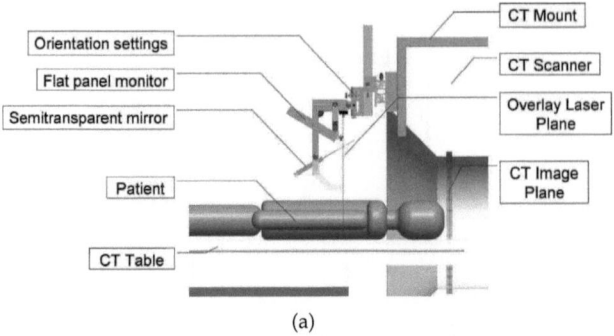

(a)

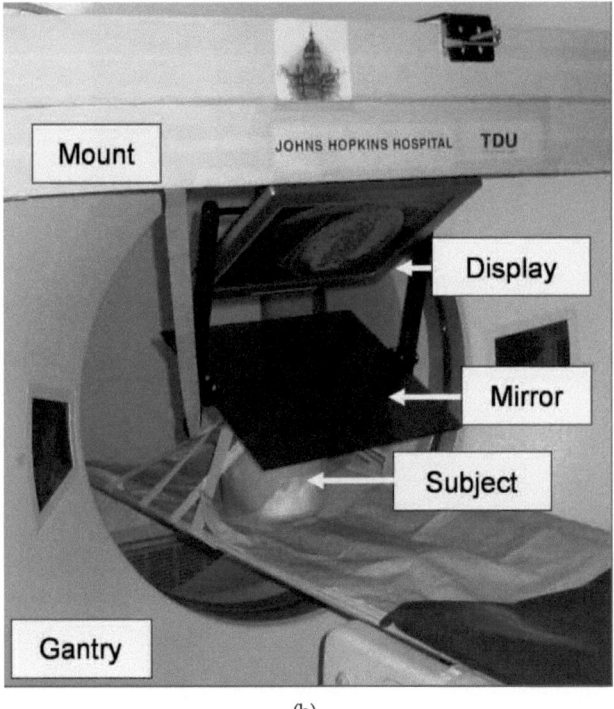

(b)

Figure 13: Concept of the 2D tomographic image overlay: A flat display and a semi-transparent mirror are co-aligned with the CT scanner to produce an image to guide interventions (a). Image overlay system that creates the floating image in the scan plane of the CT gantry (b). (Reprinted with permission from Fichtinger et al. [40].)

4

APPROACH

> *A good idea will keep you awake during the morning,*
> *but a great idea will keep you awake during the night.*
>
> — Marilyn vos Savant

The main objective of this work was to design, implement and evaluate a clinically applicable concept for computer-assisted percutaneous needle insertion into soft tissue that is capable of capturing and compensating for intra-interventional organ motion. This chapter presents the fundamental design decisions that were made to meet these requirements (section 4.1), the clinical workflow implied by the design (section 4.2) and an overview of the implementation of the developed prototype system (section 4.3). Furthermore, it provides a hierarchical model of the sources of errors associated with the novel concept (section 4.4).

4.1 FUNDAMENTAL DESIGN DECISIONS

Based on the state of the art in computer-assisted abdominal interventions discussed in chapter 3, the following design decisions were made:

IMAGING: CT was chosen as imaging modality because it is widely available, provides high image quality and is employed by our clinical partners in image-guided abdominal interventions (cf. section 3.2.1). Due to its high resolution and high contrast images, it is well suited for fiducial-based registration of the tracking coordinate system with the image coordinate system. In contrast to MRI, it does not make complex demands on the material properties of the employed instruments, and is associated with low costs. Compared to US, it does not require extensive operator training for image acquisition, does not present an intrusion into the operating field and can acquire large 3D volumes. One of the main disadvantages of CT guidance - the use of ionizing radiation - can be reduced by providing computer assistance for the needle insertion process: If the system is accurate, the needle position does not need to be checked repeatedly in control CT scans, and the radiation exposure to the patient can be reduced. Furthermore, the use of a

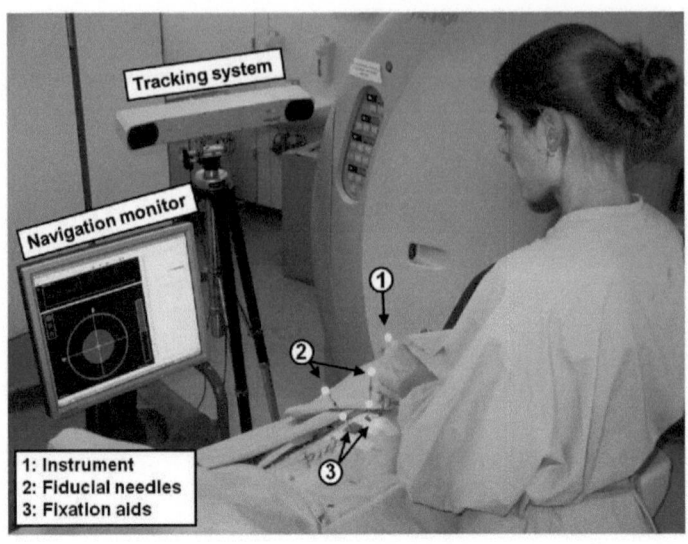

Figure 14: Navigation system in the intervention room. (Reprinted with permission from [96])).

tracking system in combination with a motion compensation method allows for providing real-time positional information throughout the intervention, although the CT images themselves can only be acquired at discrete points in time.

TRACKING SYSTEM: An optical tracking device is employed for instrument tracking because optical systems have the distinct advantage of allowing for concurrent tracking of several dynamic targets with high accuracy *and*, at the same time, providing robust performance with regard to the environment (cf. section 3.2.2). As the presented navigation approach relies on pre-interventionally acquired static images and does not incorporate real-time imaging data, robust tracking accuracy is of high concern. In contrast to electromagnetic systems, optical systems impose the line-of-sight requirement between the tracking systems and the tracked objects. However, *if* the targets are detected, tracking accuracy is high, and the maximum error (95% confidence interval) is small compared to other systems.

INITIAL REGISTRATION: As the navigation concept should be highly accurate, needle-shaped fiducials (*fiducial needles*, or *navigation aids*) inserted in the vicinity of the target are utilized for registering the tracking coordinate system with the image coordinate system. Unlike other registration approaches (cf. section 3.2.3) this methods allows for using points inside the target organ itself to be used for the registration procedure and does not require additional hardware such as an ultrasound device. According Fitzpatrick *et al.* [41], the TRE decreases with an increasing proximity of the fiducials to the target. The fact that the use of fiducial needles *initially* increases the invasiveness of the intervention can be compensated by eliminating the need for repeated instrument insertions.

MOTION COMPENSATION: Like the initial registration procedure, the motion compensation method is based on the fiducial needles. Depending on the location of the target relative to the fiducials and the type of respiration (mechanical ventilation or spontaneous breathing), an appropriate deformation model (e.g., rigid, affine, spline-based) is selected which continuously estimates the current position of the target from the initial and current poses of the fiducial needles. As this project was part of the *Research Training Group 1126: Intelligent Surgery*, the objective was to develop a concept which could be implemented and clinically evaluated within a time-frame of three years. In consequence, biomechanical models and image based approaches to motion compensation were excluded from consideration because they were not expected to be sufficiently fast and robust for clinical trials (cf. section 3.2.4). Due to the generally irregular respiratory pattern of freely breathing patients, a concept based on a trained model was also rejected. Instead, a needle-based navigation approach was chosen because, unlike all other methods, it allows for robust real-time tracking of points inside the target organ that move similar to the target itself and was thus expected to yield high accuracy.

GUIDANCE: To keep the required equipment minimal and thus to allow for a cost-efficient, clinically applicable workflow, all guidance information is displayed on a single external monitor, and no special hardware such as a head-mounted display or a tomographic image overlay system is applied (Fig. 14). The developed visualization scheme is adapted to the actions taken by the physician during the targeting procedure, namely finding the entry point (*tip positioning*), directing the instrument to point toward the target point (*needle alignment*) and inserting the needle towards the target (*needle insertion*). In each step, the relevant information is extracted and presented such that the user understands intuitively how to move the instrument.

EVALUATION: To evaluate the novel approach, a prototype system for percutaneous needle insertion into the liver was developed and evaluated in two stages. First, the individual modules of the system were developed and evaluated individually (*stage 1*). This allowed for quantification of the different errors contributing to the overall needle insertion error. Once, the individual system modules had been optimized individually, the prototype system was evaluated in the clinical workflow (*stage 2*). To reduce the number of animal experiments in this context, a respiratory liver motion simulator was developed to serve as patient model for *ex-vivo*[1] experiments in porcine and human livers. Based on an *ex-vivo* study, the system was then further refined and finally, evaluated *in-vivo*. For this purpose, the needle insertion accuracy was assessed and compared to the targeting accuracy obtained from other systems published in related work. In addition, the novel approach was compared to the conventional CT-guided needle insertion method with respect to radiation exposure to the patient, accuracy and time.

4.2 WORKFLOW

The detailed workflow associated with the presented navigation concept is shown in Fig. 15. The procedure is based on a 3D diagnostic image (typically CT or MRI) acquired before the intervention (not necessarily on the day of the procedure) and comprises the following steps:

1. *Pre-interventional planning:* Depending on the type of the procedure (e.g., RFA, biopsy) and the physical condition of the patient, the physician decides on the type of anesthesia and thus on the type of respiration (mechanical ventilation or spontaneous breathing). Furthermore, the number of fiducial needles is chosen based on the size and the location of the tumor extracted from the pre-interventional image as well as on the type of anesthesia. This decision requires considering the tradeoff between accuracy and invasiveness: In ventilated patients, for example, only one or two fiducial needles are likely to yield sufficiently high accuracy in many cases because a specific state within the breathing cycle (and the corresponding target position) can be assumed to be reproducible more easily than in freely breathing patients. In contrast, a small tumor in a freely breathing patient may require higher accuracy and thus more fiducials.

2. *Intra-interventional preparation:* Once the patient has been prepared for the intervention (i.e., brought to the CT room, anesthetized, etc.), the following steps are necessary for computer-assisted needle insertion:

    a) *Fiducial insertion:* The fiducial needles are inserted in the vicinity of the target either without real-time guidance based on the planning image (if there is no significant risk of injuring risk structures) or with a US device. If more than two navigation aids are used, the target should be located in the volume spanned by the needles. If two needles are used, they should be placed along the cranio-caudal axis and enclose the target. If only one fiducial needle is used it should be inserted as close as possible to the

---

[1] *ex-vivo*: Outside of the living body. Refers to experimentation or measurements done in or on living tissue in an artificial environment outside the organism.

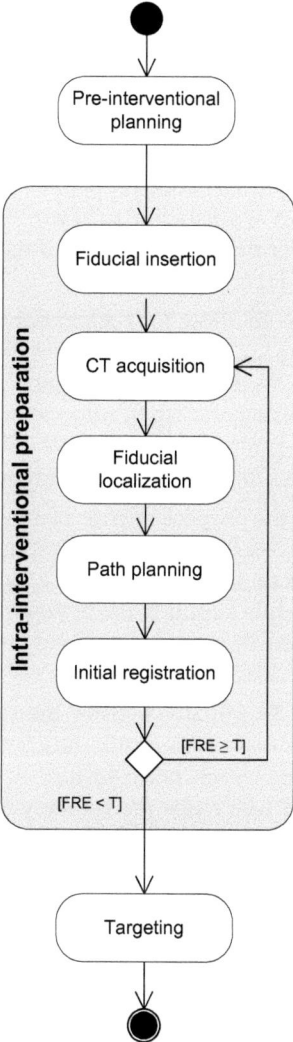

Figure 15: Detailed workflow for computer-assisted needle insertion. The parameter T defines the maximally allowed FRE and can be computed from the fiducial arrangement, the target position and the maximally allowed value of the TRE [42].

target. To prevent the needles from slipping out they should be anchored within the tissue or be affixed to the skin of the patient.

b) *CT acquisition:* Once the fiducials have been inserted, a high resolution planning image is acquired and transferred to the navigation PC. As the resolution of the planning image has a direct effect on the registration accuracy, the slice thickness should be of the order of magnitude of 1 mm. To allow for fast data transfer from the CT scanner to the navigation system, the developed software can be run as a plugin within the CHILI® Report workstation software (CHILI GmbH, Heidelberg, Germany) as part of the CHILI® Picture Archiving and Communication System[2] (PACS) [36] (cf. section 4.3).

c) *Fiducial localization:* To allow for registration of the tracking coordinate system with the image coordinate system, the navigation aids must be located accurately in the planning image. For this purpose, models of the fiducials are automatically fit into the image. If the operator is not satisfied with the result, he can modify the poses of the navigation aids manually (e.g., via drag and drop) or semi-automatically.

d) *Path planning:* For the purpose of path planning, the tumor is segmented semi-automatically on the basis of the graph-cut algorithm [18], and the target is by default set to the center or gravity of the segmented lesion. A path planning module supports the operator in choosing a trajectory to the target. This module provides different views for judging the quality of the chosen trajectory.

e) *Initial registration:* To initially register the tracking coordinate system with the CT coordinate system, the fiducials are tracked over several breathing cycles. For each point in time t, a rigid transformation Φ_t is determined that best maps the registered fiducials onto the tracked fiducials. The transformation $\Phi_{\hat{t}}$ yielding the best match (represented by the associated FRE) is then chosen as the transformation defining the initial registration. If the fiducials do not match well, the planning CT scan can be re-acquired. It is worth noting that, unlike the TRE, the FRE is approximately independent of the fiducial configuration and thus a poor indicator for the TRE. It can, however, be used to estimate the FLE, which in turn allows for predicting the TRE based on the target position and the arrangement of the fiducials [41].

3. *Targeting:* In the preferred setup, the tracking system and the navigation monitor are placed on one side of the patient, and the operator stands on the other side as shown in Fig. 14. The fiducial needles are continuously located

---

[2] PACS: Computers or networks dedicated to the storage, retrieval, distribution and presentation of medical images

by a tracking system, and a real-time deformation model is used to estimate the position of the target point based on the initial and current poses of the fiducials. The chosen deformation model depends on the number and location of the fiducial needles as well as on the type of intervention (ventilated and thus gated or freely breathing). To allow for fast needle insertion along the planned trajectory, a navigation monitor guides the physician towards the moving target.

This workflow requires additional preparation time compared to the conventional liver puncture workflow (cf. Fig. 5). However, due to the guidance mechanism, there is no need for repeated redirecting and advancing of the instrument, and the actual targeting can be performed extremely fast as compared to the conventional method.

4.3 IMPLEMENTATION

The navigation software was implemented in the programming language C++ and drew upon the following toolkits:

INSIGHT SEGMENTATION AND REGISTRATION TOOLKIT (ITK): Open-source cross-platform application development framework implemented in C++ which employs leading-edge segmentation and registration algorithms in two, three, and more dimensions [63].

THE VISUALIZATION TOOLKIT (VTK): Open-source cross-platform graphics toolkit implemented in C++ [132] which can be regarded as the de facto standard for 3D visualization in medical imaging applications [164].

MEDICAL IMAGING INTERACTION TOOLKIT (MITK): Open-source cross-platform library based on ITK and VTK which provides methods of developing interactive medical imaging applications [164]. MITK extends ITK and VTK with an application layer that adds user interaction, data management, and other features needed to build end user image processing applications.

Although MITK is a toolkit rather than an application, it also provides an application environment into which new modules can be integrated. The application-level support classes are graphical user interface (GUI)-toolkit dependent and are currently implemented for Qt - a cross-platform application framework widely used for the development of GUI programs. Among others, the application-level support includes a concept for the structured combination of application-specific modules, so-called *functionalities*. A functionality combines a user interface with algorithmic function for a specific task. MITK based applications can be run as plugins within the CHILI® Report workstation software as part of the CHILI® PACS, allowing all application modules to access the contents of a PACS database [36].

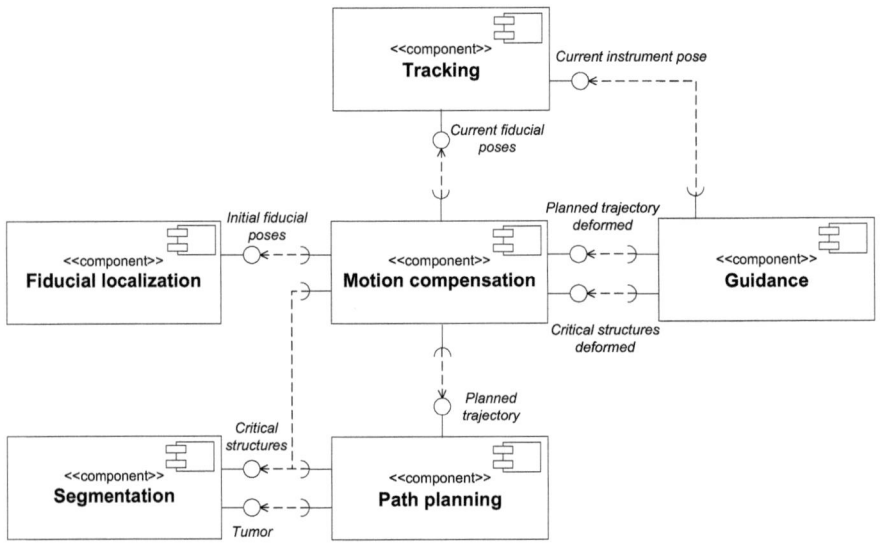

Figure 16: Simplified representation of the software components developed for the navigation software. Apart from the *Tracking* component and the *Segmentation* component, which were re-used from other projects, the components were developed especially for the proposed navigation system and are now realized as individual *functionalities* in the MITK framework. The data flow between the components (boxes) is visualized via interfaces (spheres). In practice, all data produced by the individual funtionalities is stored in a globally accessible *data tree*. For means of clarity, the planning CT, which is accessed by almost all components via the data tree, is not shown in the diagram.

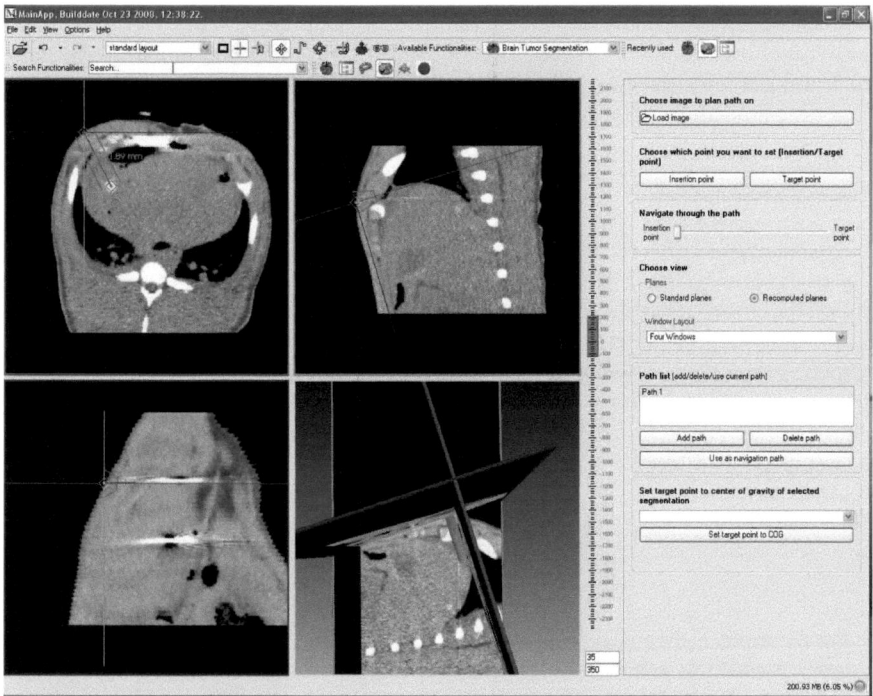

Figure 17: Screenshot of the *Path planning* functionality, which provides means for planning a trajectory from the skin of the patient to an anatomical target.

MITK allows hierarchically organizing the data at run-time in a tree-like structure, called the *data tree*, which is globally accessible. This allows for communication between functionalities without making them dependent on each other: Each functionality accesses the data objects contained in the tree, changes them and/or creates new data objects. Other functionalities can continue to work on the changed and/or newly created data tree entries. For this purpose, the individual objects in the data tree, called *data tree nodes*, can be assigned so-called *properties* of arbitrary type. For example, a segmentation functionality may assign the boolean property critical_structure with the value true to all segmentations that represent a critical structure in the current context. A path planning functionality may then iterate over the data tree to identify all anatomical structures to be taken into consideration and optimize a trajectory to the target accordingly.

The concept of a common data structure is suitable for navigation software because it allows for modelling the complex workflow as a pipeline of functionalities that may have, in part, been developed independently of each other. A tumor segmentation functionality, for example, can potentially be used in a variety of medical applications. The navigation software developed for this project comprises individual functionalities for object localization, path planning, motion compensation and guidance as shown in Fig. 16. Figure 17 shows a screenshot of one of the functionalities developed for this project.

4.4 SOURCES OF ERROR

Each module of the developed prototype system effects the overall targeting accuracy during an intervention. To allow for a systematic evaluation of the proposed approach, this section presents a hierarchical reprentation of the most important sources of error contributing to the overall error. The targeting error, which is the error of hitting a predefined target with the tip of a needle-shaped instrument, is represented by the root node of the diagram shown in Fig. 18. The children $c(e) = \{c_1(e), \cdots, c_n(e)\}$ of a node e represent the sources causing error e, that is, if all children $c_i(e)$ of e are associated with no error, then the error of that node is zero:

$$c_i(e) = 0 \; \forall i \in \{1, \cdots, n\} \Rightarrow e = 0 \qquad (4.1)$$

For example, if the instrument could be tracked with no error (*Instrument tracking error*= 0), and the position of the target could be estimated perfectly ($TRE = 0$), then there would be no system error (*System error*= 0). For means of clarity, the entire error tree was split into subtrees representing the instrument tracking error (Fig. 19), the TRE (Fig. 20), and the user error (Fig. 21). The leaves of the tree are associated with *influencing factors* that affect the error. For example, the user error depends highly on the provided guidance method (Fig. 21). In some cases, the degree of influence of a source of error (child) on its parent can be determined by additional factors not shown in the diagram. For example, the degree of influence of the FLE on the TRE depends crucially on the configuration of the fiducials as well as on the position of the target.

The following sections describe the most important sources of error in detail.

4.4.1 *Tracking error*

As described in section 3.2.2, optical tracking systems apply two or more cameras with known poses to each other to locate *feature points* attached to the objects to be tracked. In the following, these feature points will be referred to as *markers*, and the tool tracking error refers to the error of determinining the pose (i.e., the position and orientation) of a tracking target connected rigidly to a set of markers (e.g., the tip of a tracked tool) in the tracking coordinate system. In this context, the term *tool* may refer to a fiducial needle used for motion compensation or to the

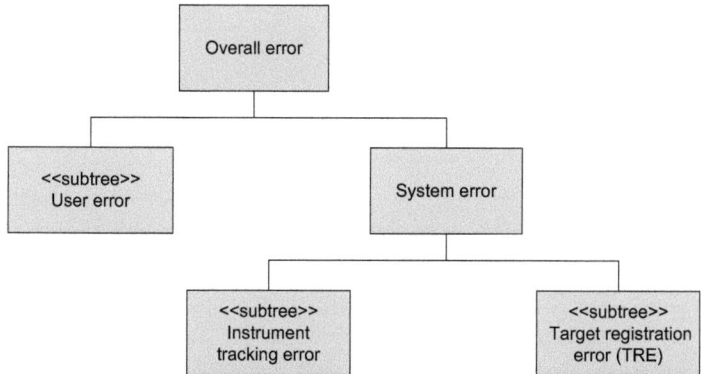

Figure 18: Hierarchical representation of the sources of error associated with the presented approach. The overall targeting error is represented by the root node. The children of a node e represent the sources of error causing e, that is, if all children $c_i(e)$ of e are associated with no error ($c_i(e) = 0; i = 1, \cdots, n$), then the error of that node is zero ($e = 0$). For means of clarity, the tree was split into subtrees representing the tracking error (Fig. 19), the TRE (Fig. 20), and the user error (Fig. 21).

instrument used for targeting a given anatomical structure. It is worth noting that the *Tracking* subtree appears twice in the error hierarchy because it applies to both the instrument and the fiducials.

The tool tracking error results from (1) the 3D marker localization error, and (2) an erroneous tool geometry (Fig. 19) as described in the following paragraphs.

3D marker localization error

In optical systems, each camera locates the individual markers on the object in a 2D image, and the information from all cameras is merged to obtain a 3D image via triangulation as illustrated in Fig. 6. The process requires accurate knowledge of the camera geometry represented by the so-called *extrinsic*[3] and *intrinsic*[4] camera parameters [11]. The accuracy of locating a single marker in the 3D measurement volume thus depends on the 2D marker localization error in the individual camera images and an accurate knowledge of the camera geometry:

---

[3] Extrinsic camera parameters: Parameters that define the pose of an individual camera's reference frame with respect to a known reference frame. In a two-camera setup, these parameters typically describe the rigid transformation aligning the axes of the coordinate systems of the individual cameras.

[4] Intrinsic camera parameters: Parameters necessary to link the pixel coordinates of an image point with the corresponding coordinates in the individual camera's reference frame.

- 2D marker localization error: The 2D marker localization error depends on the following factors:
  - Camera properties: Marker tracking accuracy improves with increased camera resolution and improved lense quality and depends on the geometrical setup of the cameras [11].
  - Marker localization algorithm: The quality of the 2D feature detection algorithm is crucial for accurate marker localization [11].
  - Marker properties: The performance of the feature detection algorithm depends on the material properties of the markers and increases with an increasing size of the marker relative to the image plane [11].
  - Marker pose: Accurate marker localization depends highly on the pose of the marker within the measurement volume of the tracking system. As already mentioned above, the size of the marker relative to the image plane plays an important role in this context. When flat markers are utilized, the orientation of the marker panel relative to the tracking system is also crucial.
  - Marker motion: Tracking errors due to marker motion relative to the cameras (*dynamic tracking errors*) are mainly caused by end-to-end delay from the time of the measurement until the application displays or uses the data [11]. Furthermore, marker motion leads to image blur. In consequence, tracking accuracy decreases with increased speed of the tracked marker relative to the cameras [86].
  - Occlusion: Partial occlusion of a marker by other objects can lead to a shift in the estimated marker center, or the marker may not even be recognized at all.
  - Illumination conditions: Tracking accuracy can be highly dependent on illumination conditions. In passive systems, tracking error typically increases with decreasing light intensity [86]. Furthermore, anisotropic lighting behaviour may lead to a shift in the estimated fiducial center [11].
- Erroneous camara geometry: An erroneous camera geometry results in systematic tracking errors [11]. It originates from two possible error sources:
  - Erroneous camera calibration: The external and internal camera parameters must be determined initially (typically by the manufacturer). This process - referred to as camera calibration or tracking system characterization - is prone to error. A common procedure for characterizing an optical tracking system is to move markers throughout the field of measurement (FOM) in a representative manner, according to some convenient reference, whose accuracy is sufficiently better than that of the systems

being characterized [161]. The reference positions and their corresponding sensor data can then be used to determine the model parameters, typically with some appropriate fitting algorithm that minimizes the error between the transformed reference data and the sensor data.

- Change in geometry: The geometrical parameters of the cameras may change after calibration, for example due to a physical shock or changes in temperature (*thermal drift*).

Erroneous tool geometry

The pose of a tracking target (e.g., the tip of an instrument) is computed from the positions of its markers. Hence, accurate tool tracking requires exact knowledge of the tool geometry. Inaccurate tool geometry may result from the following factors:

- Erroneous tool calibration: If the measurements of a tool were extracted from a construction plan, tracking inaccuracies may result from an inaccurate realization of this plan. Alternatively, the position of the tip of the tool and (possibly) the pose of its axis relative to the markers can be determined with a calibration procedure, e.g., by a pivoting approach (cf. e.g. [11, 99]): The tool tip is placed in a fixed position and the tool is pivoted about this fixed point. The position of the tip in the tool coordinate system is then defined as the most invariant point (in a least squares sense) in the pivot motions [99]. This procedure is prone to error. Most calibration procedures involve tracking the markers of the tool to be calibrated and thus also depend on the 3D marker localization accuracy presented above.

- Change in geometry: Changes in the tool geometry after calibration also lead to an erroneous tool geometry. Needle bending during the intervention, for example, can lead to tracking inaccuracies because the tool tip of a needle-shaped instrument is extrapolated from the marker positions.

Additional factors

In general, there is both an error in tool geometry and inaccuracy in tracking the markers. The degree of influence of these two sources of error on the overall tool tracking accuracy is determined by two additional factors:

- Marker configuration: The tool tracking error depends crucially on the number and arrangement of the markers [42]. In particular, the tool tip tracking error increases with an increasing distance to the centroid of the markers. Occlusion of one or several of the markers or cameras may also increase tracking error [138].

- Tracking algorithm: The tracking device estimates the pose of the tool from the tracked marker positions. The degree of influence of the tracking error of individual markers depends on the applied tool tracking method.

4.4.2 Target registration error

In the proposed navigation approach, the position of the target is continuously estimated based on the poses of the fiducial needles. Hence, the TRE results from (1) the *FLE*, which is the error of locating the navigation aids in tracking space and in image space, and (2) the *Modelling error*, which is the error resulting from the fact that the applied deformation model does not accurately reflect reality (Fig. 20).

Fiducial localization error (FLE)

The FLE is the error of locating the navigation aids in image space and tracking space. More precisely, it is the error of locating the control points which are used to register the tracking coordinate system with the image coordinate system. As these control points are extracted from the navigation aids, the tool localization error and the control point localization error are directly related. The FLE consists of two parts:

- FLE in tracking space: The FLE in tracking space is essentially the tool tracking error (see above).

- FLE in image space: The error of locating a tool in the planning CT image can be attributed to three sources of error:
    - Erroneous image: Image distortion, breathing artefacts and metal artefacts may result in an inaccurate representation of the fiducial needle in the image.
    - Erroneous tool geometry: If the tool geometry is not known exactly, it is impossible to fit a model of the tool accurately to the image (cf. *Tracking accuracy → Erroneous tool geometry*)
    - Errors induced by localization algorithm: The FLE depends crucially on the method applied for fitting a model of the tool to the planning image. The performance of the applied algorithm depends on the image resolution, the applied metric for assessing the quality of a fit, and the applied optimizer, which may get stuck in local minima. If manual interaction is required, it also depends on the skills of the user.

The degree of influence of the FLE on the TRE depends on the number and configuration of the fiducials (cf. *Tracking error*) as well as on the target position [42].

Modelling error

The modelling error reflects the discrepancy between the true biomechanical behaviour of the tissue and the estimated behaviour represented by the deformation model. It depends essentially on the following factors:

- Biomechanical behaviour of the target organ: Capability of modelling the ordinary biomechanical behaviour of the tissue during continuous breathing.

- Tissue manipulation by fiducials: Capability of modelling the altered natural behaviour of the tissue caused by the inserted fiducial needles.

- Tissue manipulation by instrument: Capability of modelling the altered natural behaviour of the tissue caused by instrument insertion.

- Fiducial fixation: If the fiducials are not anchored within the tissue, they potentially move inside the target organ. In consequence, it may not be valid to assume that certain *fixed* points within the liver are tracked via the navigation aids.

Additional factors

In general, there is both a modelling error and a FLE. The degree of influence of these two sources of error on the TRE depends crucially on the fiducial configuration and the target position (cf. section 4.4.1).

4.4.3 User error

The user error depends primarily on the following factors (Fig. 21):

- Guidance method: The provided visualization scheme.

- Experience: The experience of the user with the system.

- Response time: The reaction time of the user.

- Operator tremor: Involuntary alternating movement of the operator that causes a jagged trajectory of the instrument.

Unfortunately, the user error is further affected by the system error; one of the main challenges related to the process of needle insertion, for instance, is the correct alignment of the instrument axis with the planned trajectory to the target. As an initial alignment cannot be corrected after partial needle insertion without withdrawing the instrument, the resulting user error depends on an accurate knowledge of the instrument geometry. In practice, it is generally impossible to isolate the error induced by inaccurate needle tracking from the operator induced error.

4.4.4 Discussion

This section described the most important sources of error associated with the proposed navigation approach. A graphical representation of the error hierarchy was developed to illustrate how individual errors are propagated. As the interplay of the individual sources of errors is highly complex, there is no straightforward method for determining the overall targeting error from the errors associated with the leave nodes. Several groups (e.g. Bauer *et al.* [10]) proposed models for predicting the tool tracking accuracy from a set of input parameters (e.g., the FLE, the fiducial configuration, the camera setup) via error propagation. Yet, these models are generally restricted to certain noise distributions (typically: zero-mean Gaussian distribution), cannot cope with systematic errors, and assume that the tool geometry is known exactly.

It is worth noting that the FRE is often used as a figure of merit for registration accuracy [146], but Fitzpatrick *et al.* [42] showed that this may be misleading: While the TRE increases with a decreasing number of fiducials and an increasing distance of the target to the centroid to the fiducials and is highly dependent on the fiducial configuration, the FRE increases with an *increasing* number of fiducials, is independent of the target position and approximately independent of the fiducial configuration [42]. In consequence, the FRE is not part of the error propagation diagram. It can, however, be used as an estimate of the FLE [100].

In summary, the overall needle insertion error depends on a variety of different sources of error. In the following chapters, the individual modules of the system are evaluated separately with the aim of quantifying the contribution of the individual sources of error to the overall error.

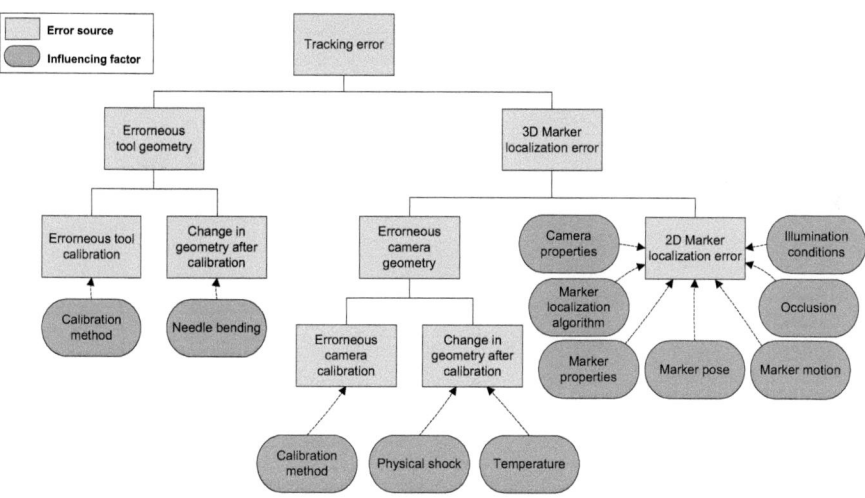

Figure 19: Hierarchical representation of the sources of error associated with the instrument and fiducial tracking error.

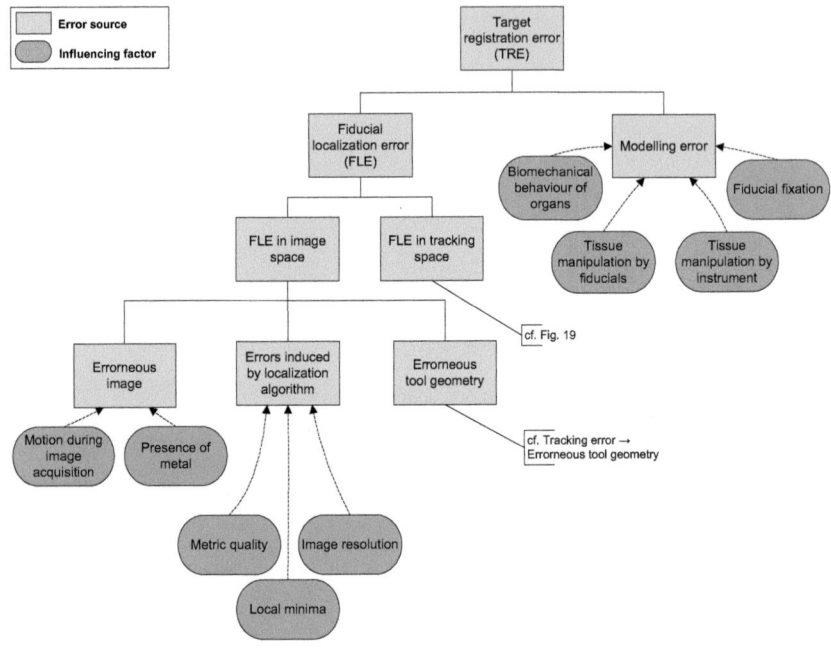

Figure 20: Hierarchical representation of the sources of error associated with the TRE.

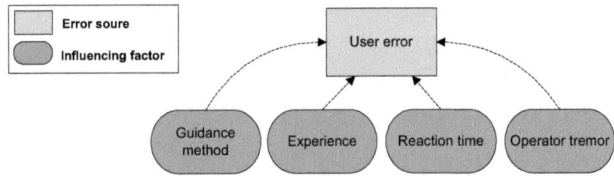

Figure 21: Factors influencing the user error.

5

RESPIRATORY LIVER MOTION SIMULATOR

> *It is inexcusable for scientists to torture animals;*
> *let them make their experiments on journalists and politicians.*
>
> — Henrik Ibsen

To reduce the number of animal experiments for validating the navigation system, a respiratory liver motion simulator was developed that allows for *ex-vivo* experiments to be conducted in real tissue (animal or human) actuated so as to mimic respiratory action. This chapter describes the design of the motion simulator (section 5.1), presents the experiments that were conducted to analyze the liver movement generated by the device (section 5.2 and 5.3) and discusses the simulator in the context of related work (section 5.4).

5.1 DESIGN

The design of the respiratory phantom is based on the constitution of the human corpus. It can be constructed at low cost and is composed of the following non-metallic components (Fig. 22):

- Two breathing bags (Vital Signs, Inc.; New Jersey, USA) representing the lobes of the lung
- A perforated plate imitating the diaphragm
- Slide rails and elastic bands for controlling the movement of the liver
- A set of components modeling the ribcage with skin
- A filling element modeling the surrounding abdominal organs
- A leak-proof box containing the individual components

Plexiglas® was chosen as basic material because of its transparency, but another synthetic material would also be adequate. Since all components are non-metallic,

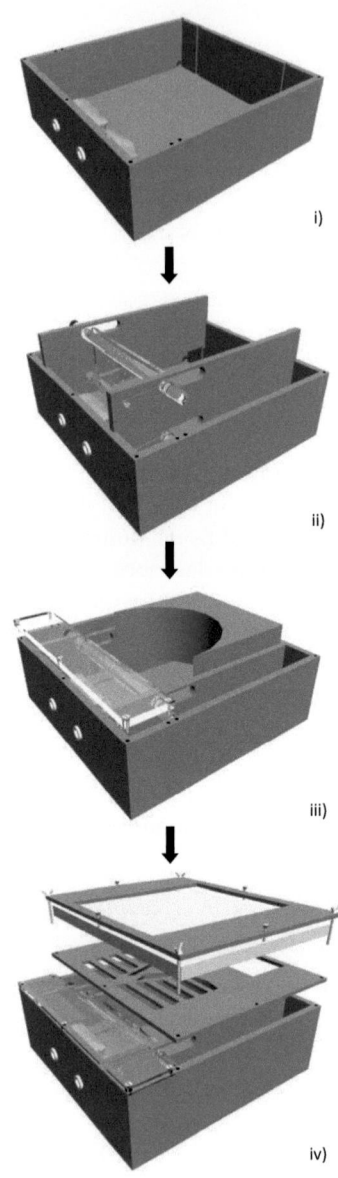

Figure 22: Schematic view of individual components of the respiratory liver motion simulator. i) Box with breathing bags, connections to lung ventilator and outlet stopcock (left corner in the back). ii) Artificial diaphragm and construction for controlling respiratory motion. iii) Lung cover and filling element. iv) Ribcage with skin. For a clearer illustration, some of the modules are not shown in their original material (Plexiglas®).

(a) CT slice (b) volume rendered image

Figure 23: CT image of the motion simulator with mounted ribcage in full expiration: Coronal plane and volume rendered image. (Reprinted with permission from Maier-Hein *et al.* [90].)

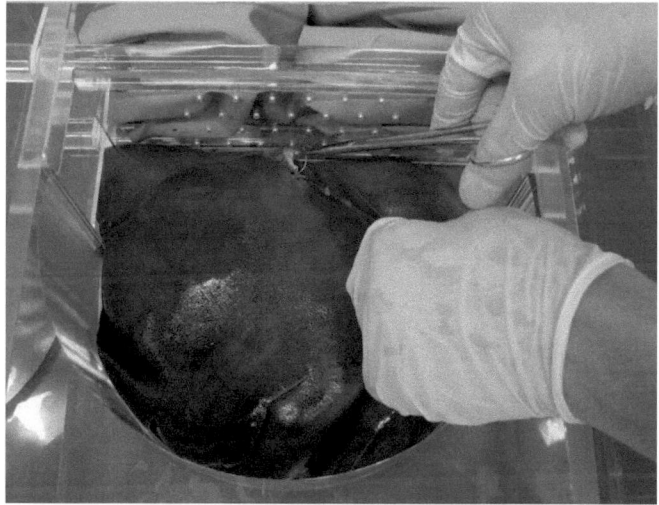

Figure 24: Sewing of a porcine liver to the motion simulator.

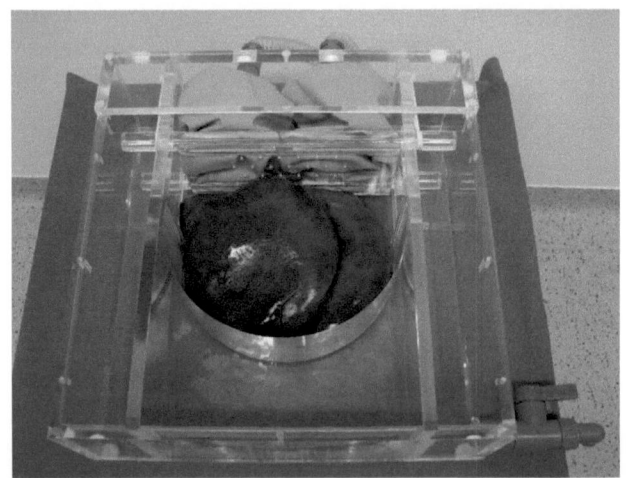

(a) full expiration

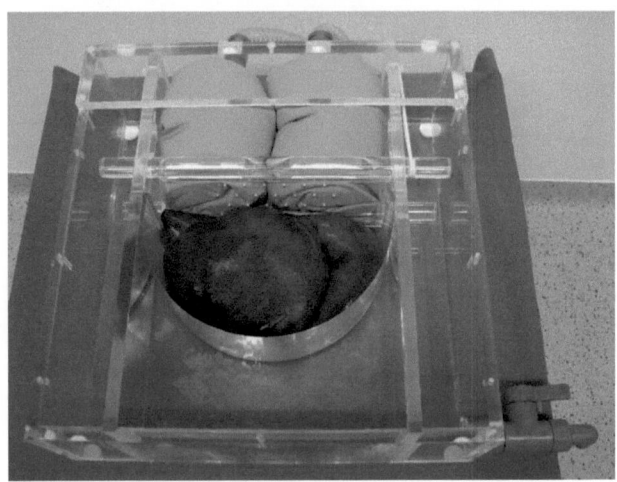

(b) full inspiration

Figure 25: Respiratory liver motion simulator without ribcage in full expiration (a) and full inspiration (b).

the motion simulator is suitable for CT and MR imaging. Figure 23 shows a CT image of the apparatus with mounted ribcage and skin in full expiration.

To use the device, it is necessary to mount an explanted human or porcine liver to the artificial diaphragm as shown in Fig. 24. Next, the simulator is connected to a lung ventilator (Servo Ventilator 900C, Siemens-Elema AB, Solna, Sweden) whose settings control the breathing pattern. When the breathing bags are filled with air, the resulting force acting on the diaphragm model causes a movement of the diaphragm and thus of the liver in cranio-caudal direction (Fig. 25 and 26). When the lungs relax, elastic bands connected to the plate via two cylinders pull the diaphragm and therewith the liver back to its original position.

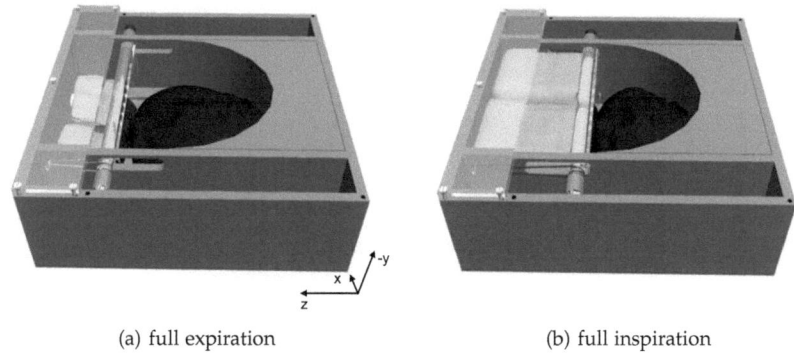

(a) full expiration   (b) full inspiration

Figure 26: Schematic view of the motion simulator without ribcage and skin in full expiration (a) and full inspiration (b).

Optionally, a ribcage with skin can be mounted to the patient model (Fig. 27). For this purpose, a piece of foam is clamped between the two "skin frames" shown in Fig 22. For experiments with an ultrasound device, the entire box can be filled with water. The modular constitution of the simulator further allows for easy cleaning.

5.2 MOTION ANALYSIS

To analyze the liver movement generated by the motion simulator three porcine livers and three human livers, explanted from patients with acute liver failure or endstage liver cirrhosis during liver transplantation, were examined. Informed consent was obtained from the patients in oral and written form. The system was tested for fixed settings of the lung ventilator (breathing rate: 16 cycles/min; inspiration pressure: 30 mbar; duration of inspiration: 33%). In order to monitor the

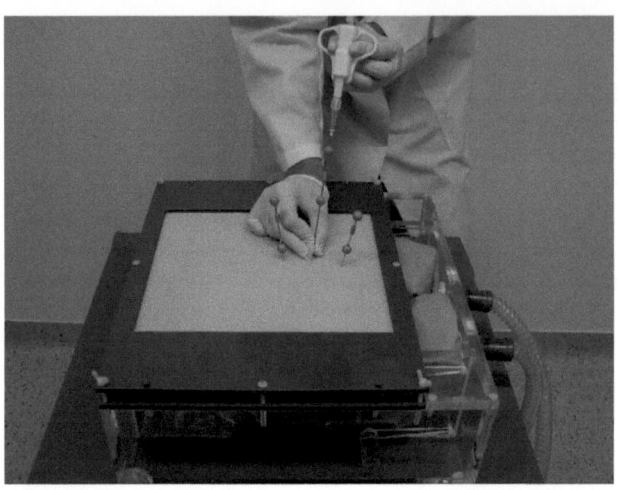

Figure 27: Performing of a biopsy in the motion simulator with mounted ribcage, skin, and liver.

liver position over time, four needles equipped with retro-reflective markers were inserted into the tissue as exemplarily shown in Figure 28 (insertion depth ≈ 3 cm). This arrangement allowed for registering liver displacement as well as tissue deformation because the needles were spread in both cranio-caudal and lateral direction. It should be pointed out that the needles had to be placed relatively close to the diaphragm because the tissue was not sufficiently thick in other parts of the liver. The Polaris® Vicra™ optical tracking system (Northern Digital Inc. (NDI); Ontario, Canada) was used to track the fiducial needles over time, and liver shift and deformation were computed from the movement of the needles. To be robust to needle placement, three needle configurations (i.e., arrangements) were examined for each liver[1]. For each configuration, the following measurements were performed:

1. *MIN:* A timer with the period of the lung ventilator was used to record the needle positions in ten consecutive end-expiration phases to analyze if the simulator brings the liver reliably back into its original position representing end-expiration.

2. *MAX:* A timer with the period of the lung ventilator was utilized for measuring the needle positions in one end-expiration phase and ten consecutive end-inspiration phases to determine the displacement of the liver between expiration and inspiration.

---
[1] in one liver, only two configurations were considered for the experiment MAX due to corrupt data.

(a) during inspiration

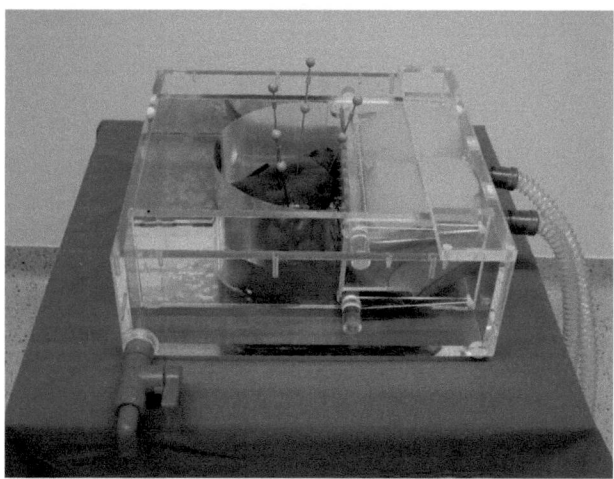

(b) full inspiration

Figure 28: Respiratory liver motion simulator with mounted porcine liver and fiducial needles during inspiration (a) and in full inspiration (b).

For each experiment, the movement of the liver along the three axes of the coordinate system of the motion simulator was determined with an optically tracked reference plate having a known orientation relative to the respiratory phantom (alignment of the edges): Upon initialization, the tracking coordinate system was registered with the coordinate system of the reference tool and all positional data was then recorded in reference coordinates. The position of the liver for sample t was defined by a set of control points on the fiducial needles: Four control points $\{P_{i1}^t \ldots P_{i4}^t\}$ with an inter-control point spacing of 1 cm were distributed along each needle i beginning at its tip, with the last control point at 3 cm approximating the liver surface. The displacement δ^t of the liver relative to the initial position ($t = 0$) was defined as:

$$\delta^t = \frac{1}{4 \cdot 4} \sum_{i=1}^{4} \sum_{l=1}^{4} \left\| \vec{p}_{il}^t - \vec{p}_{il}^0 \right\|_2 \qquad (5.1)$$

where $\vec{p}_{il}^t$ represents the vector from the origin to P_{il}^t and $\|.\|_2$ denotes the Euclidean norm. The mean displacement δ_μ averaged over all n samples of an experiment was then defined as:

$$\delta_\mu = \frac{1}{n} \sum_{t=1}^{n} \delta^t \qquad (5.2)$$

To analyze organ *deformation* (as opposed to organ shift), a rigid registration was computed for each time point as follows: Based on the least square method by Horn [58], a rigid transformation $\Phi_{0 \to t}$ was calculated from the current and initial positions of the control points. The mean distance error ϵ_{def} between corresponding control points after registration served as an approximation of liver deformation, with $\epsilon_{def} = 0$ corresponding to purely rigid movement. Formally, this can be written as:

$$\epsilon_{def}^t = \frac{1}{4 \cdot 4} \sum_{i=1}^{4} \sum_{l=1}^{4} \left\| \Phi_{0 \to t}(\vec{p}_{il}^t) - \vec{p}_{il}^0 \right\|_2 \qquad (5.3)$$

$$\epsilon_{def} = \frac{1}{n} \sum_{t=1}^{n} \epsilon_{def}^t \qquad (5.4)$$

The experiments were conducted with a preliminary version of the motion simulator. Differences of the former model to the current device concerned aesthetics only, not functionality.

5.3 RESULTS

The results of the motion analysis are shown in Tab. 3. Mean displacement between expiration and inspiration (data set MAX) was 15.0 ± 4.7 mm in the case of the porcine livers (PL) and 11.6 ± 2.7 mm for the human livers (HL) with cranio-caudal movement making up the main part (14.2 ± 4.9 mm (PL) and 8.7 ± 7.7 mm (HL)). The values of ϵ_{def} of 2.7 ± 1.4 mm (PL) and 0.9 ± 0.5 mm (HL) indicate that the livers were deformed and not only shifted rigidly. The deformation was, however, much higher in the porcine livers.

The small values obtained for the MIN experiments show that the simulator brought the livers reliably back into their original positions representing end-expiration. The displacement values and the degree of deformation varied considerably for the different livers and configurations (high standard deviation), yet the generated liver movement was generally regular; Figure 29 exemplarily visualizes the movement of the needle tips for one sample configuration. The needle tip showing the greatest displacement was placed closest to the diaphragm.

	Porcine livers		Human livers	
	MIN	MAX	MIN	MAX
Displacement				
lateral	0.0 ± 0.3	1.1 ± 2.1	0.0 ± 0.1	0.4 ± 1.0
posterior-anterior	0.1 ± 0.3	1.9 ± 3.1	0.0 ± 0.1	1.1 ± 2.1
cranio-caudal	0.3 ± 1.0	14.2 ± 4.9	0.5 ± 0.7	8.7 ± 7.7
total	0.9 ± 0.8	15.0 ± 4.7	0.7 ± 0.5	11.6 ± 2.7
Deformation	0.3 ± 0.3	2.7 ± 1.4	0.1 ± 0.1	0.9 ± 0.5

Table 3: Mean displacement (according to eq. 5.2) and mean deformation (according to eq. 5.3) in mm (± σ) of the three porcine livers and the three human livers for the experiments MIN and MAX introduced in section 5.2.

5.4 DISCUSSION

This chapter presented a liver motion simulator for *ex-vivo* experiments in a respiring patient model. According to the conducted motion analysis the movement of an explanted porcine liver mounted to the simulator is comparable to the movement of a human liver *in-vivo* (cf. Clifford et al. [28]): Mean displacement between expiration and inspiration was of the order of 10 − 15 mm, with cranio-caudal movement making up the main part. In addition, the livers showed movement due to tissue deformation. These results were obtained for a certain respiratory pattern and do not provide information about local liver movement, but they qualitatively

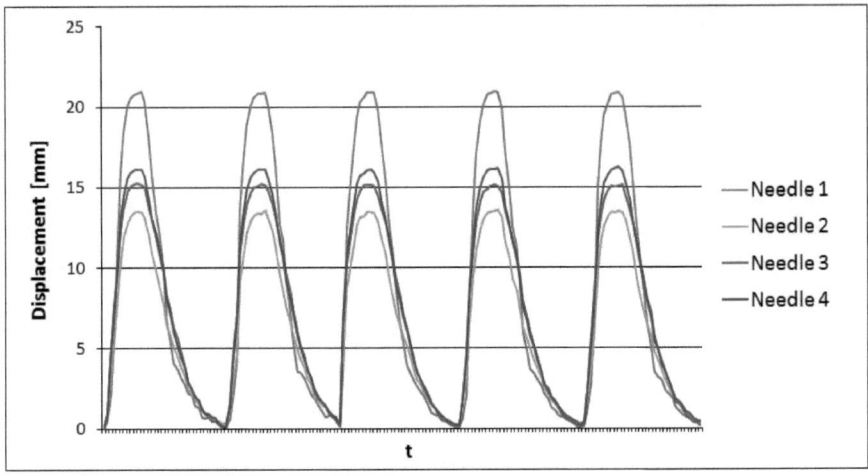

Figure 29: Visualization of the movement of the tips of the four fiducial needles over several breathing cycles for one sample configuration.

conform to previous studies on hepatic motion. Furthermore, deviations in the computed liver movement can be mainly attributed to variations in organ shape and tissue consistency as well as to the placement of the fiducial needles, which was difficult to reproduce in different livers.

The human livers underwent less organ shift than the porcine livers because of their higher volume and weight. Furthermore, the degree of tissue deformation was smaller, which can be attributed to the fact that the human livers were cirrhotic and thus less elastic than the porcine livers.

Literature on respiratory phantoms for simulating liver motion is extremely sparse. Most groups apply static phantoms to evaluate their systems (cf. section 10.1.3). Cleary *et al.* [27] developed a respiratory liver motion simulator including a synthetic liver mounted on a one degree of freedom linear motion platform. In a recent report, the authors introduced a computer-controlled pump which is coupled to a synthetic torso to produce chest wall movements and simulate natural breathing patterns [83]. *In-vitro* experiments, however, are not possible with the device. The proposed simulator has not been designed to model the entire human torso as accurately as possible but rather to provide a cost-efficient solution for simulating liver interventions prior to moving to animal experiments. It is lightweight and CT and MRI compatible. Due to the integration of a lung ventilator, the breathing pattern is controllable. The device can be constructed at low cost provided that access to standard hospital equipment is granted. It has already successfully been used for simulating liver tumor biopsies (Fig. 27) and can also potentially be used for simulation of ultrasound guided interventions and open surgery.

In conclusion, the respiratory liver motion simulator introduced in this report is considered a valuable device for reducing the number of animal experiments in the early stages of a research project. To extend the range of application of the respiratory phantom, integration of skin motion and perfusion is suggested for future work.

6

TRACKING: TOOL DESIGN, ACCURACY, AND ROBUSTNESS

Without geometry, life is pointless.

— *Anonymous*

A core component of an image-guided navigation system is the ability to track instruments in real-time during the procedure and to display them in relation to the patient's individual anatomy. Due to the high accuracy requirements for the proposed navigation application, it was decided to use an optical tracking system for this purpose (cf. section 4.1).

One of the most well-established tracking systems in clinical use is the Polaris® system (Northern Digital Inc. (NDI), Waterloo, Ontario, Canada) with passive optical markers. It emits infrared light, which is reflected by spherical markers coated with a retro-reflective material. While widely used, the system has one major disadvantage: Due to the volumetric markers and the required inter-marker distance of 5 cm, light tool design is challenging. In contrast, the recently introduced MicronTracker 2 (Claron Technology, Inc., Toronto, Ontario, Canada) is a passive system which allows for construction of relatively lightweight tools. It makes use of the available visible light illumination to locate objects marked with a painted or printed target pattern. Table 4 summarizes the properties of the two tracking systems.

This chapter compares the Polaris® system with passive markers and the MicronTracker 2, model H40, with regard to their suitability for soft tissue navigation with fiducial needles. It introduces the tools[1] developed for the two tracking systems (section 6.1), assesses the tool tip tracking accuracy and precision under typical clinical light conditions (section 6.2), and compares the robustness of the tracking systems to illumination conditions as well as to the velocity and the orientation of a tracked tool (section 6.3).

---

[1] In this chapter, the term *tool* is generally used to refer to a tracked device (fiducial needle, instrument, etc.).

	Polaris®	MicronTracker 2
General Properties		
Camera type	active[a]	passive[b]
Integration of detection algorithm	tracking system	software
Interface	RS-232/RS-422	IEEE-1394a
Maximum data rate	115 kbps	400 Mbps[c]
Operating temperature	18-23°C	18-30°C
Multi-camera support	no	yes
Tools		
Tool type	passive	passive
Maximum number of tools	6	100
Required inter-marker distance	5 cm	N/A[d]
Performance		
Marker tracking error (RMS)	0.35 mm[e]	0.20 mm[f]
Update rate (max.)	60 Hz	15 Hz
Measurement volume	large[g]	small[h]

Table 4: System specifications for the Polaris® system with passive markers and the MicronTracker 2, model H40. In the case of the MicronTracker 2, the inter-marker distance refers to the required distance between two *XPoints*.

---

[a] Active cameras emit light to locate targets.
[b] Passive cameras use available light in the visible spectrum to locate targets.
[c] A high data rate is necessary because the tracking device transfers the captured images as opposed to the poses of the tracked tools [25].
[d] According to the manufacturer, "'the maximum detection distance of an Xpoint is roughly 100 times its radius. For example, a 5 mm radius would allow detection up to 50 cm, and a 12 mm radius would provide detection up to the far limit of the FOM" [25].
[e] According to the manufacturer [161], the error was obtained by measuring a single marker at a set of specified locations throughout its pyramid volume with a coordinate measuring machine (CMM).
[f] According to the manufacturer, this value corresponds to a "single target position accuracy. For H40, $\approx 30,000$ averaged positions at distances of 40-100 cm" [25], where the term target refers to a single *XPoint*.
[g] Please refer to NDI for detailed indication of measurements.
[h] Please refer to the manufacturer specifications for detailed indication of measurements [25].

6.1 NAVIGATION TOOLS

In optical systems, the pose of tracking target (e.g., the tip of a tracked instrument) is computed from a set of features that are localizable by the tracking system. As described in section 3.2.3, the accuracy of tracking a target depends crucially on the tool design. The navigation tools used for the proposed navigation scenario should be characterized by high tracking accuracy and a light design. Unfortunately, these are conflicting requirements because tool tracking accuracy increases with the number of markers and the room taken by the markers as described in section 3.2.2. This section introduces possible tool designs for needle-based soft tissue navigation with the Polaris® system and the MicronTracker 2.

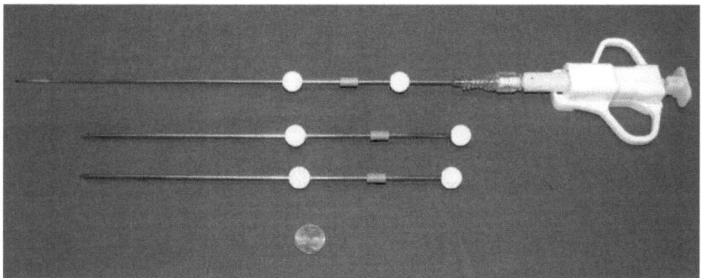

Figure 30: Custom-designed 5DoF biopsy needle and navigation aids. Different inter-marker distances (60 mm, 80 mm, 90 mm) allow for differentiation between the individual tools.

6.1.1 *Polaris tools*

The tracking algorithm of the Polaris® system requires a tool to be defined by at least three optical markers with a minimum inter-marker distance of 5 cm. This, however, leads to a big tool size and high weight. To address this issue, 5-Degrees-of-Freedom (5DoF) needle-shaped tools equipped with only two optical markers were constructed as shown in Fig. 30.

Different distances between the two markers allow for differentiation of the individual tools. When arranged symmetrically with respect to the needle axis, two markers are sufficient to determine the axis of the device, yet, it is impossible to determine its orientation. To be able to derive the tip position from the positions of the markers, a so-called *intervention plane* is defined, whose normal is always at an angle of less than 90° to all tools. The plane can be initialized by a user or be based

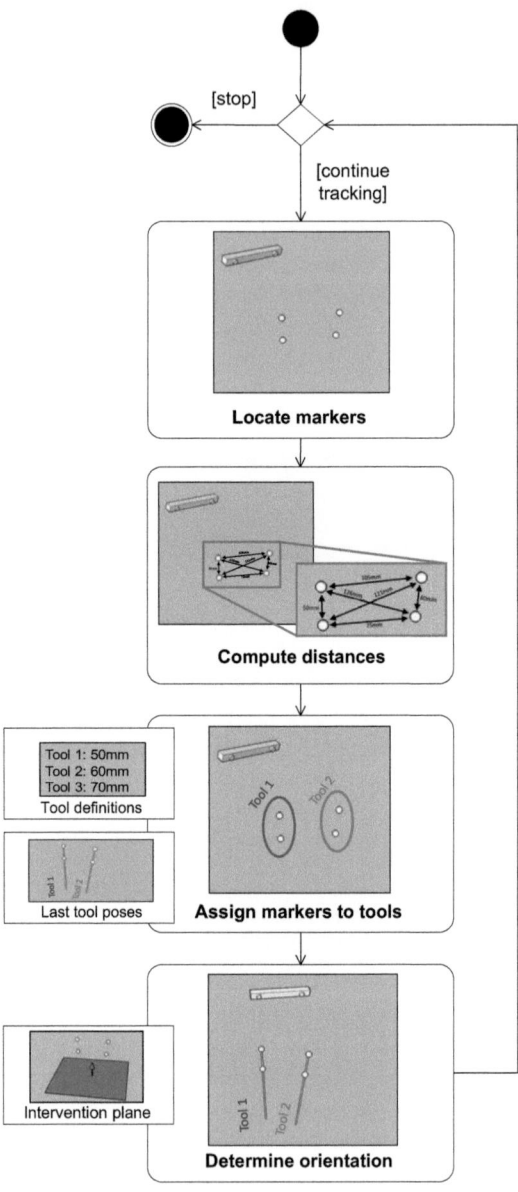

Figure 31: Tracking algorithm for the custom-designed 5DoF Polaris® tools. Individual markers are assigned to the corresponding tools in real-time. The orientation of the tools is computed from the known normal of the intervention plane.

on prior knowledge (e.g., default position of the patient relative to the tracking system) and be updated continuously based on the fiducial positions. A tracking algorithm was implemented that assigns individual markers to the corresponding tools based on the known inter-marker distances (Fig. 31). In ambiguous situations, the algorithms takes into account previous tool positions. As the 5DoF positions of the fiducial needles can be determined from the location of only two markers, this tracking approach reduces the room taken up by the tools significantly.

Unfortunately, the light design is achieved at some cost. The major disadvantage is the fact that a standard calibration procedure is not possible for 5DoF tools. Consequently, the tools must be constructed perfectly symmetrically. Deflections and errors in the construction cannot be compensated for. In addition, application of a small number of markers generally decreases tracking accuracy [42, 161].

It is worth mentioning here that the Polaris® Vicra™ system, which is an optical tracking system based on the same tracking technology as the Polaris® system and is also provided by NDI, requires an inter-marker distance of only 3 cm. However, the system has a smaller FOM, and light tool design is still challenging due to the volumetric markers.

6.1.2 MicronTracker 2 tools

In contrast to the Polaris® system, which works with volumetric markers, the MicronTracker 2 uses flat marker panels as shown in Fig. 32(b). The tracking algorithm is based on the detection of so-called *XPoints*[2], connected by imaginary *Vectors*[3] as shown in Fig. 32(b).

The fact that *XPoints* corresponding to different *Vectors* can be located close to each other allows for construction of needle-shaped 6DoF tools. For this purpose, the so-called *narrow X design* suggested by the manufacturer [25] was chosen as design pattern as shown in Fig. 32(b). Due to the lever effect, the tracking accuracy increases (theoretically) with a decreasing distance between the tip of the tool and the nearest *XPoint* and increasing lengths of the *Vectors* [25].

To calibrate the fiducial needles, a calibration device was constructed (Fig. 33) which sets the tool axis perpendicular to the calibration panel with the tip at its centroid.

---

[2] *XPoint*: One "checkerboard intersection painted on a flat surface." [25]
[3] The two imaginary straight lines crossing at an *XPoint*'s center are referred to as *XLines*. "Viewing the *Xlines* from the *XPoint* center outwards, *BW Xline* is the one with the black on the left and white on the right [...]." [25] A *Vector* is defined as two "*XPoints* arranged such that one's *BW Xline* is aligned (co-linear) with the other's *WB Xline*." [25]

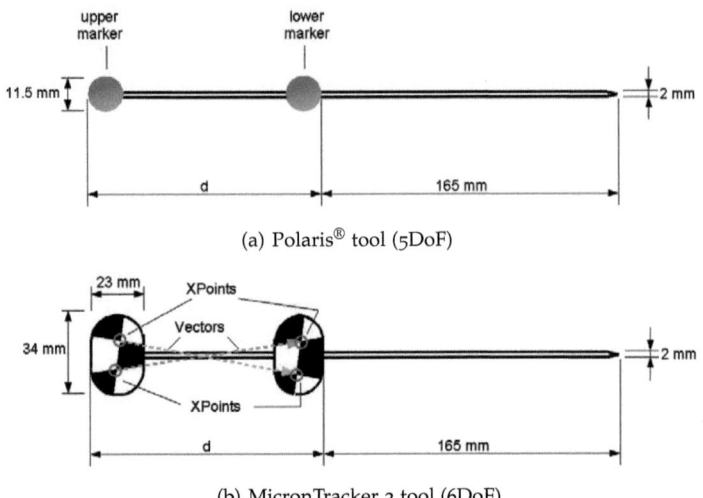

Figure 32: Schematic view of the Polaris® 5DoF fiducial needles (a) and the MicronTracker 2 6DoF fiducial needles (b). For each system, three tools (n_1, n_2, n_3) with different inter-marker distances/*Vector* lengths were constructed. The part of the needle taken up by the markers was d = 61.5 mm (n_1), d = 81.5 (n_2) and d = 101.5 (n_3) in length. In the case of the Polaris® system, these distances correspond to inter-marker distances of 50 mm, 70 mm, and 90 mm.

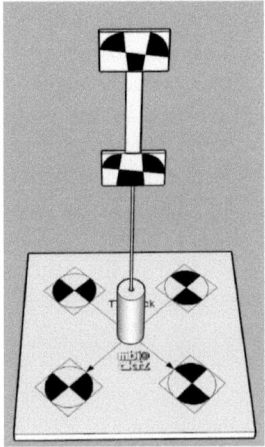

Figure 33: Calibration device for the MicronTracker 2 for computing the pose of the tip relative to the fiducial pattern. The axis of the tool is set perpendicular to the marker panel. An *angle indication* (cf. Fig. 34(b)) is used to obtain the correct orientation.

6.2 TRACKING ACCURACY AND PRECISION

Several accuracy assessment protocols and accuracy studies have been presented for both optical [69, 161] and electromagnetic [43, 62, 163] systems in the past. However, the MicronTracker 2 has not yet been evaluated in the literature. According to the manufacturer specifications, the FLE[4] (provided as RMS marker/XPoint tracking error) of the MicronTracker 2 (model H40) is lower than that of the Polaris® system as shown in Tab. 4. However, it is well-known that the RMS target tracking error is not a good indicator of tracking accuracy [161] because (1) it depends crucially on the chosen measurement volume, (2) is independent of the tool design and (3) does not take into account the pose of the object in the tracking coordinate system. To address this issue, this section determines the tool *tip* tracking accuracy for the proposed tool designs both theoretically and experimentally. Furthermore, the construction accuracy for the custom-designed 5DoF Polaris® tools is evaluated.

6.2.1 Accuracy phantom

To be able to assess the needle tip tracking accuracy within a sufficiently sized measurement volume for different tools, an *accuracy phantom* was developed, which allows for measuring a tool position at $3^3 = 27$ different positions within a tracking volume of 40 cm · 40 cm · 30 cm. This volume was chosen because it fits into the measurement volumes of both examined tracking systems and is sufficiently sized for navigated punctures of the liver. The phantom consists of a *base panel* (Fig. 34(a)) and two *height adapters* (one shown in Fig. 34(b)), which allow for the attachment of a *pipe device* (Fig. 34(b)).

6.2.2 Experiments

Estimating tracking error is generally challenging due to the lack of ground truth data [11]. To compare the accuracy of the two investigated tracking systems in the context of needle-based navigation, two studies were conducted: (1) A simulation study for predicting the tracking accuracy of the different proposed tool designs using the FLE (here: error in locating a marker/XPoint within the measurement volume of the corresponding tracking system) (*tool design*) and (2) an experimental study assessing the needle tip tracking accuracy and precision for the two examined tracking systems, within a sufficiently sized measurement volume for different tool sizes under typical clinical light conditions (*tool position and length*). In addition, the construction accuracy of the Polaris® tools was assessed (*construction accuracy*). For

---

4 In this context, the term *fiducial* refers to the passive markers in the case of the the Polaris® systems and to the *XPoints* in the case of the MicronTracker 2.

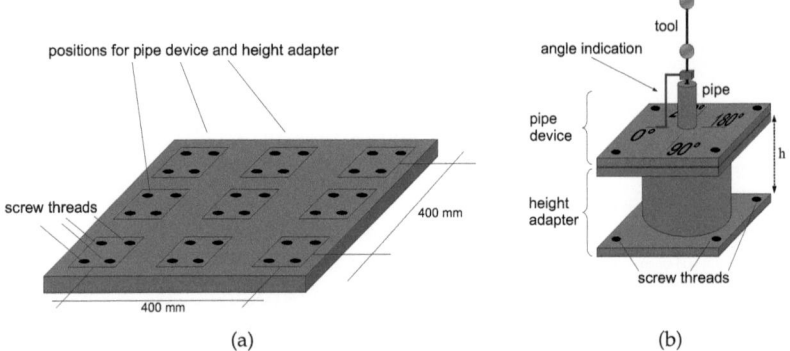

Figure 34: *Accuracy phantom: Base panel* (a) and *pipe device* with *height adapter* and tool (b). The height of the two adapters is h = 15 cm and h = 30 cm respectively. The angle indication can be used to verify the rotational symmetry of a 5DoF tool or to calibrate a 6DoF tool.

each system, three tools (n_1, n_2, n_3) with different inter-marker distances/*Vector* lengths were constructed as shown in Fig. 32. The following sections introduce the individual experiments performed for this study.

Tool design

Given a distribution of the FLE and a pose of a tool relative to the tracking coordinate system, the tracking accuracy (TRE) of a target connected rigidly to a set of Markers/*XPoints* was estimated via Monte Carlo simulations (cf. section 3.2.2) as follows:

- Polaris® tools: The tool geometry was represented by two marker positions $M^{object} = \{\vec{m}_1^{\,object}, \vec{m}_2^{\,object}\}$ and the target (i.e., the tip position) $\vec{t}^{\,object}$ in the tool coordinate system. The rigid-body transformation Φ^{ref} relating the tracking coordinate system with the tool coordinate system was used to compute the ground truth target position $\vec{t}^{\,ref} = \Phi^{ref}(\vec{t}^{\,object})$. Next, the following steps were repeated n times:

  1. The localized marker positions $\vec{m}_1^{\,sim}$ and $\vec{m}_2^{\,sim}$ were simulated by perturbing $\vec{m}_1^{\,ref}$ and $\vec{m}_2^{\,ref}$:

  $$\vec{m}_i^{\,sim} = \vec{m}_i^{\,ref} + \Delta \vec{m}_i \qquad (6.1)$$

  where $\Delta \vec{m}_i = (x_i, y_i, z_i)$ was randomly drawn from a zero-mean 3D Gaussian distribution $N(0, diag(\sigma_x^2, \sigma_y^2, \sigma_z^2))$. When an isotropic Gaussian distribution $N(0, \sigma^2 I)$ of the FLE was assumed, the following formula was applied for determining σ^2 [41].

$$\sigma = \frac{FLE}{\sqrt{3}} \qquad (6.2)$$

where the FLE is the RMS FLE provided by the manufacturer. Note in this context that the RMS of a zero-mean Gaussian distribution is equivalent to the standard deviation [11]. By default, a standard deviation of $\sigma = 0.20$ mm was chosen along each coordinate axis which corresponds to an FLE of 0.35 mm.

2. The estimated target position $\vec{t}^{sim}$ was computed from the positions of the two markers according to the implemented tracking algorithm.

3. The Euclidean distance between the true target position and the estimated tip position $\left\| \vec{t}^{ref} - \vec{t}^{sim} \right\|_2$ was stored as TRE.

- MicronTracker 2 tools: The tracking algorithm of the MicronTracker 2 for deriving the pose of a tracking target connected rigidly to the target pattern has not been published. To approximate the tracking error, a point based registration of the XPoints based on the least square method by Horn [58] was applied to derive the pose of the target from the XPoint positions. For this purpose, the tool geometry was represented by the positions of the XPoints $\vec{x}_1^{object}, \ldots, \vec{x}_4^{object}$, and the position of a target $\vec{t}^{object}$. The rigid-body transformation Φ^{ref} relating the tracking coordinate system with the tool coordinate system was used to compute the ground truth target position $\vec{t}^{ref} = \Phi^{ref}(\vec{t}^{object})$. Next, the following steps were repeated n times:

1. The localized XPoint positions $\vec{x}_1^{sim}, \ldots, \vec{x}_4^{sim}$ were simulated as in equation 6.1. By default, a standard deviation of $\sigma = 0.12$ mm was chosen in the case of isotropic Gaussian noise, which corresponds to an FLE of 0.20 mm (cf. eq. 6.2).

2. The estimated target position $\vec{t}^{sim} = \Phi^{sim}(\vec{t}^{object})$ was computed from the positions of the XPoints by finding the rigid-body transformation Φ^{sim} that minimizes the FRE according to the least square method by Horn [58] (cf. section 3.2.3).

$$FRE(\Phi^{sim}) = \sqrt{\frac{1}{4} \sum_{j=1}^{4} \left\| \vec{x}_j^{sim} - \Phi^{sim}(\vec{x}_j^{object}) \right\|_2^2} \qquad (6.3)$$

3. The Euclidean distance between the true target position and the estimated target position $\left\| \vec{t}^{ref} - \vec{t}^{sim} \right\|_2$ was stored as TRE.

In all cases, the estimated tracking error for a given target could then be computed as the RMS TRE averaged over all simulations.

To compare the tool designs of the different tracking systems, the proposed workflow was applied to the tips of all tools n_1, n_2, n_3, introduced in Fig. 32, for different standard deviations $\sigma \in [0, 0.5]$ assuming an isotropic Gaussian distribution of the FLE ($n = 100,000$). Although the FLE has been shown to be anisotropic [161, 11, 84], this approach is very common [42], because the *true* distribution of the FLE has not been reported in the literature, is difficult to model and depends upon the device applied to perform the measurements. Because an isotropic Gaussian distribution of the FLE allows neglecting the rigid-body motion relating the tool coordinate system with the tracking coordinate system [41], the pose of the tracking coordinate system was not varied throughout the experiment by setting $\Phi^{ref}(\vec{x}) = \vec{x}$.

Tool position and length

The aim of the *tool position and length* experiment was to assess the needle tip tracking accuracy and precision for the two examined tracking systems within a sufficiently sized measurement volume for different tool sizes. The experiments were conducted in the premises of a hospital (Krehl Klinik, Heidelberg) to obtain typical clinical light conditions. Prior to performing the measurements, the Micron-Tracker 2 was calibrated using a calibration tool provided by the manufacturer.

For each needle n_i and each position p_j of the accuracy phantom, introduced in section 6.2.1, the tool tip positions were recorded for a period of 30 s to obtain a set of $N = 300$ measured positions $\mathbf{M}^{ij} = \{\vec{m}_{ij}^1, \ldots, \vec{m}_{ij}^N\}$ (Fig. 35). The recorded data was then used to (1) determine the tool tip tracking accuracy within the chosen measurement volume and (2) to assess how *jitter*[5] effects the precision of tracking a tool tip in practice.

Similar as in [62], a grid matching approach was applied to quantify the tool tip tracking accuracy. For each needle n_i, the known positions in the phantom coordinate system $P^{ref} = \{\vec{r}_1, \ldots, \vec{r}_{27}\}$ and the set of (averaged) measured positions $M^i = \{\vec{m}_{i1}^\mu, \ldots, \vec{m}_{i27}^\mu\}$ were used as source and target landmarks respectively to define a landmark based rigid transform Φ_i mapping the tracking coordinate system to the phantom coordinate system according to the least square method by Horn [58]. The RMS tool tip tracking error was defined as the RMS distance between the reference positions and the transformed measured positions:

$$e_{RMS}^{grid}(n_i) = \sqrt{\frac{1}{27} \sum_{j=1}^{27} \left\| \vec{r}_j - \Phi_i(\vec{m}_{ij}^\mu) \right\|_2^2} \tag{6.4}$$

---

5 Jitter: "Momentary deviation caused by random optical or electrical noise in the image capture and analog-to-digital conversion circuitry" [25]

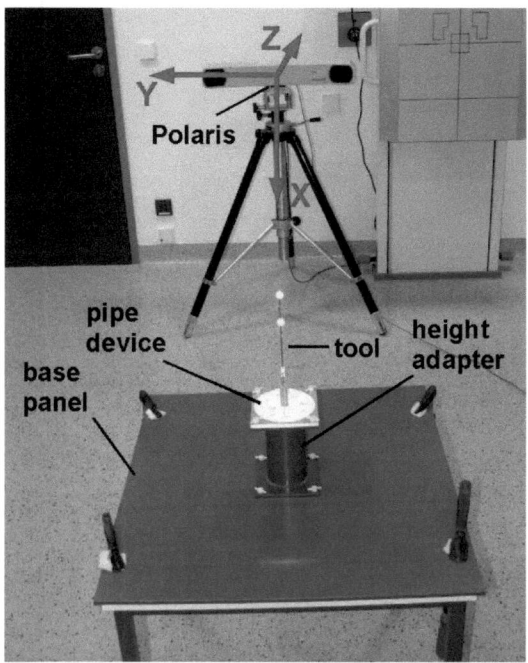

Figure 35: Experimental setup for the accuracy measurements showing the Polaris® optical tracking system and the *accuracy phantom*.

As suggested in related work [62, 69], tracking precision was quantified by *jitter*. The RMS jitter error for tool n_i and position p_j was defined as the RMS distance between the measured tip position and the mean tip position $\vec{m}_{ij}^{\mu}$:

$$\epsilon_{RMS}^{jitter}(n_i, p_j) = \sqrt{\frac{1}{N}\sum_{k=1}^{N}\left\|\vec{m}_{ij}^k - \vec{m}_{ij}^{\mu}\right\|_2^2} \qquad (6.5)$$

The *overall* RMS jitter error for tool n_i, $\epsilon_{RMS}^{jitter}(n_i)$, was obtained by additionally averaging over all positions.

Construction accuracy

In the case of the 5DoF Polaris® tools, an accurate construction relies primarily on the symmetric attachment of the markers to the axis of the needle. In order to measure the construction error for tool n_i, the following experiment was conducted:

1. The pipe device (Fig. 34(b)) was attached to the base panel (Fig. 34(a)), and the needle was inserted into the pipe.

2. For four different rotation angles $\alpha \in A = \{0°, 90°, 180°, 270°\}$ within the pipe, the position of the navigation aid was recorded for 10 sec, yielding a set of $n_R = 100$ lower marker positions $\mathbf{L}_i^\alpha = \{\vec{l}_i^{\alpha_1}, \ldots, \vec{l}_i^{\alpha_{n_R}}\}$, a set of upper marker positions $\mathbf{U}_i^\alpha = \{\vec{u}_i^{\alpha_1}, \ldots, \vec{u}_i^{\alpha_{n_R}}\}$ and a set of (extrapolated) needle tip positions $\mathbf{T}_i^\alpha = \{\vec{t}_i^{\alpha_1}, \ldots, \vec{t}_i^{\alpha_{n_R}}\}$ for each angle α. Note that the *real* needle tip remained in a constant position during the rotation due to its fixation in the pipe.

3. For each angle α the mean lower marker position $\vec{l}_i^\alpha$, the mean upper marker position $\vec{u}_i^\alpha$ and the mean tool tip position $\vec{t}_i^\alpha$ were determined.

4. The reference position (i.e., the estimated *true* tool tip position) was computed from the positions of the optical markers:

    a) The ideal lower marker position $\vec{l}_i$, and the ideal upper marker position $\vec{u}_i$ were computed as follows:

    $$\vec{l}_i = \frac{1}{4} \sum_{\alpha \in A} \vec{l}_i^\alpha \qquad (6.6)$$

    $$\vec{u}_i = \frac{1}{4} \sum_{\alpha \in A} \vec{u}_i^\alpha \qquad (6.7)$$

    Note that these positions represent a symmetric attachment of the markers to the needle axis.

    b) Let $\vec{v}$ be the normalized direction vector of the needle defined by $\vec{u}_i$ and $\vec{l}_i$. The reference tip position was computed as

    $$\vec{t}_i = \vec{u}_i + (|n_i| - r) \cdot \vec{v} \qquad (6.8)$$

    where r denotes the marker radius and $|n_i|$ denotes the length of the navigation aid n_i.

5. The RMS error was defined as the RMS distance between the measured tip position and the reference tip position:

$$\epsilon^{constr}(n_i) = \sqrt{\frac{1}{4 n_R} \sum_{\alpha \in A} \sum_{k=1}^{n_R} \|\vec{t}_i^{\alpha_k} - \vec{t}_i\|_2^2} \qquad (6.9)$$

6.2.3 Results

The results of the *tool design* experiment are shown in Fig. 36. As expected, the TRE depends crucially on the size of the tools as well as on the FLE and is better for the MicronTracker 2 tools, which provide four fiducials as opposed to two. The differences in accuracy between the individual tools decrease when the target approaches the centroid of the fiducials (Fig. 37). Depending on the noise distribution, the TRE at the centroid of the fiducials ranged from 0.1 mm to 0.6 mm.

According to the *tool position and length* experiment (Tab. 5 and Fig. 38), the tool tip tracking error increases considerably with a decreasing tool size and is better for *all* tools in the case of the Polaris® system, which suggests a more accurate camera calibration (cf. section 4.4.1). The jitter error depends crucially on the position within the tracking volume (Fig. 38) and occurs primarily in z-direction, i.e., along the view direction of tracking system. While the Micron Tracker 2 tools outperformed the Polaris® tools in the simulations, the jitter error for the MicronTracker 2 is only significantly better in the case of the largest tool, n_3.

		n_1	n_2	n_3	All
Accuracy	Polaris®	1.68	1.28	0.98	1.31 ± 0.35
	MicronTracker 2	2.52	1.66	1.55	1.91 ± 0.53
Precision	Polaris®	0.27	0.20	0.18	0.22 ± 0.05
	MicronTracker 2	0.91	0.21	0.08	0.40 ± 0.45

Table 5: Results for the *tool position and length* experiment. Mean RMS tool tip tracking error (cf. eq. 6.4) and mean RMS jitter error (cf. eq. 6.5) in mm for the needles n_1 (d = 61.5 mm), n_2 (d = 81.5 mm) and n_3 (d = 101.5 mm) averaged over all 27 tip positions. The last column lists the mean RMS error (± σ) averaged over all tools.

	n_1	n_2	n_3	All
Construction error	0.56	0.88	0.94	0.80 ± 0.20

Table 6: Results for the *construction accuracy* experiment. RMS tool tip tracking error (cf. eq. 6.9) in mm for the fiducial needles n_1 (d = 61.5 mm), n_2 (d = 81.5 mm) and n_3 (d = 101.5 mm). The last column lists the mean RMS error (± σ) averaged over all tools.

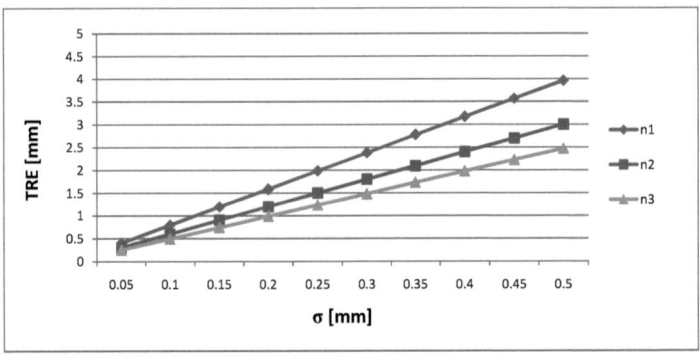

(a) Polaris

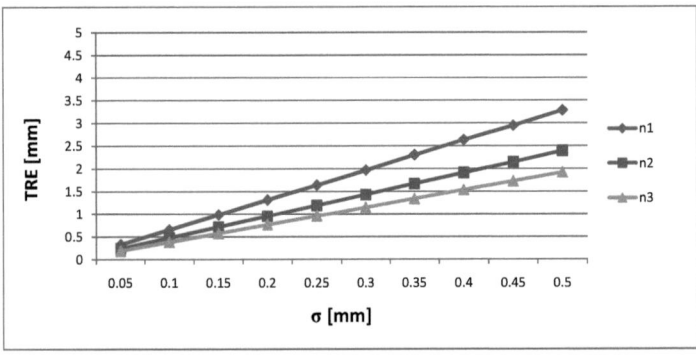

(b) MicronTracker 2

Figure 36: Results for the *tool design* experiment. Predicted RMS tool tip tracking error (in mm) for the needles n_1 (d = 61.5 mm), n_2 (d = 81.5 mm) and n_3 (d = 101.5 mm) obtained from $n = 100{,}000$ Monte Carlo simulations and a zero-mean isotropic Gaussian distribution of the FLE with different standard deviations σ along each coordinate axis (cf. section 6.2.2)

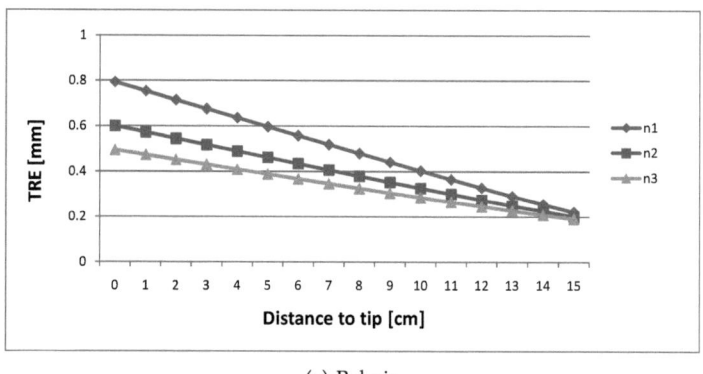

(a) Polaris

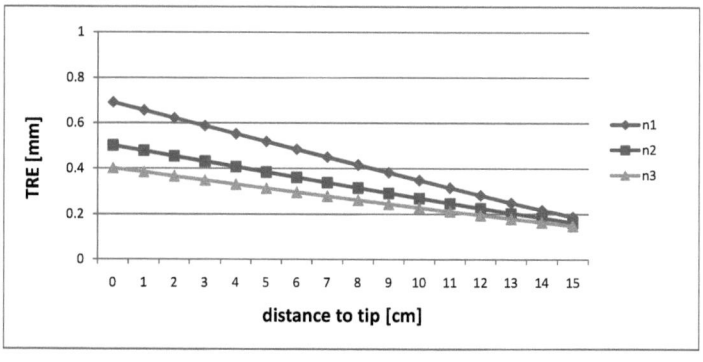

(b) MicronTracker 2

Figure 37: Predicted tracking accuracy along the needles of the navigation aids n_1 (d = 61.5 mm), n_2 (d = 81.5 mm) and n_3 (d = 101.5 mm) for a zero-mean isotropic Gaussian distribution of the FLE with a standard deviation of $\sigma =$ 0.1 mm along each coordinate axis. As the distance to the tool tip increases, the target approaches the centroid of the markers/*XPoints*.

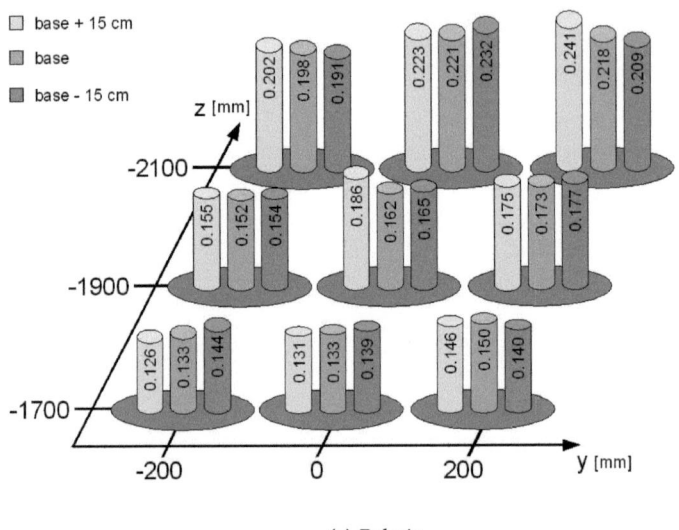

(a) Polaris

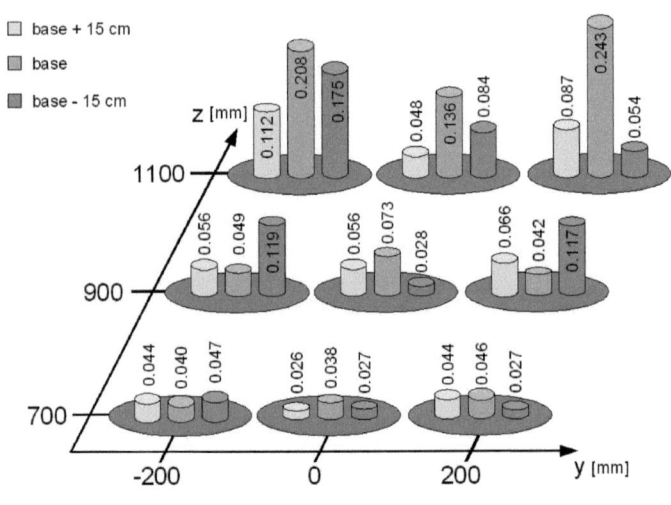

(b) MicronTracker 2

Figure 38: Static jitter error (cf. eq. 6.5) in mm for 27 tip positions of tool n_3 within the measurement volume of the Polaris® system and the MicronTracker 2. The view direction of the tracking systems was along the z-axis. The colors of the bars represent the height of the tool within the tracking volume with *base* corresponding to *marker* positions close to $x = 0$.

According to Tab. 6, the RMS tracking error resulting from an inaccurate construction of the Polaris® tools is of the order of magnitude of 0.8 mm.

As the accuracy does not increase with a decreasing tool size, it can be assumed that the construction accuracy has a higher effect on the tool tracking error than the marker tracking error - at least in the center of the FOM.

6.2.4 Discussion

This section evaluated the accuracy and precision of two optical tracking systems in the context of needle-based soft tissue navigation: The well established NDI Polaris® system with active camera and passive markers, and the MicronTracker 2 (model H40) with passive camera and passive markers. The custom-designed 5DoF Polaris® tools could be tracked accurately compared to the MicronTracker 2 tools despite the small number of markers. A theoretical simulation showed that submillimetric tool tip tracking accuracy is possible when an appropriate tool design is chosen.

Several issues deserve further discussion. To begin with, it should be noted that the proposed tool designs are not optimal with respect to the general design recommendations [158] because a small number of fiducials is applied. Using more markers, however, would have led to inappropriately large tools.

The *tool design* experiment assumed that the tool geometry was known exactly. Although this is clearly a simplification, this approach allowed for isolation of the tracking error differences resulting exclusively from the tool design. The simulations could readily be adapted to account for tool construction or calibration errors. Furthermore, the experiments assumed an isotropic Gaussian distribution of the marker tracking error because the aim of the experiment was to compare different tool designs rather than to quantify the tracking accuracy for a specific pose within the tracking volume or for different noise distributions. Future work should investigate this issue.

It is important to keep in mind that the *tool position and length* experiment was conducted in a relatively large volume within the FOM of the MicronTracker 2. A smaller volume should yield a better tracking precision and accuracy. Furthermore, the accuracy assessment was based on the tips of the tools and is thus effected by the calibration accuracy of the tools if they are not always positioned in exactly the same way relative to the phantom coordinate system. The calibration accuracy was only evaluated for the Polaris® system because the developed MicronTracker 2 tools do not allow for 360° rotation of a tool.

In conclusion, both systems are well-suited for needle-based navigation in terms of tool design, tracking accuracy, and precision.

6.3 TRACKING ROBUSTNESS

To evaluate the robustness of the Polaris® system and the MicronTracker 2, the sensititity of the two tracking systems to illumination conditions, motion, shadow, and orientation of the tools was assessed. The percentage of invalid samples[6] and the jitter error were generally used as indicators of tracking robustness.

6.3.1 Experiments

The experiments were conducted in a laboratory environment to allow for evaluation of the sensitivity of the systems to isolated factors such as light intensity. Prior to performing the measurements, the MicronTracker 2 was calibrated with the calibration tool provided by the manufacturer. The following paragraphs introduce the individual experiments performed for this study.

Luminosity

In order to determine the light sensitivity of the two tracking systems, the jitter error e_{RMS}^{jitter} (eq. 6.5) for tool n_3 (Fig. 32) was recorded at a fixed position (center of the tracking volume) for different light intensities in the range of 1 to 500 lx.

Shadow

To test the sensitivity of the two tracking systems to shadow, their performance was evaluated under favorable illumination conditions (200 lx and no shadow on the tool; Fig. 40(a)) and with one half of the tool covered by shadow (Fig. 40(b)).

Motion

To allow for assessing the sensitivity of the tracking systems to motion, a *rotation phantom* was constructed which can rotate a tool about a fixed axis of rotation such that the markers/XPoints perform a circle-shaped movement at a constant speed. Tool n_3 was mounted to the *rotation phantom*, and the position of the tool tip was recorded over several rotation cycles ($N = 300$ samples) for different speeds in the range of 2.5 cm/s to 62.5 cm/s, which correspond to rotational speeds of 0.03 rps to 0.75 rps (rps: Revolutions per second). For a given speed, the circle yielding the best fit of the recorded data according to the least square method was determined, and the tracking error e_{RMS}^{circle} was defined as the RMS distance of the data points to the computed circle. Note that although e_{RMS}^{circle} does not incorporate errors that occur along the direction of movement (in the xy-plane) it allows to *compare* the tracking error for different speeds.

---

[6] Invalid sample: A tracked tool cannot be located at all.

Orientation

In contrast to the Polaris® system, the MicronTracker 2 utilizes flat fiducials as opposed to volumetric markers. To assess how the orientation of a tool relative to the MicronTracker 2 influences tracking accuracy, the jitter error e_{RMS}^{jitter} (eq. 6.5) was determined for all tools introduced in Fig. 32 and a fixed position (center of the tracking volume) for three different angles: Orientation towards the tracking system (0°), as shown in Fig. 40(a), 22.5° rotation, and 45° rotation. Note in this context that the *XPoint/Vector* localization error of the MicronTracker 2 should be best when the tool is directly facing the tracking system because the size of the marker panel in the image planes of the camera is the largest in this case. On the other hand, Ma et al. [84] showed that in the presence of anisotropic noise, the tool tip tracking error for a given FLE is worst when the tool directly faces the camera.

6.3.2 Results

The results of the *luminosity* experiment are shown in Fig. 39. It is noticeable that the jitter error of the MicronTracker 2 increases considerably with decreasing light intensity, while the Polaris® system is insensitive to illumination conditions. When *shadow* was generated, the MicronTracker 2 tools were not located at all (Fig. 40(b)).

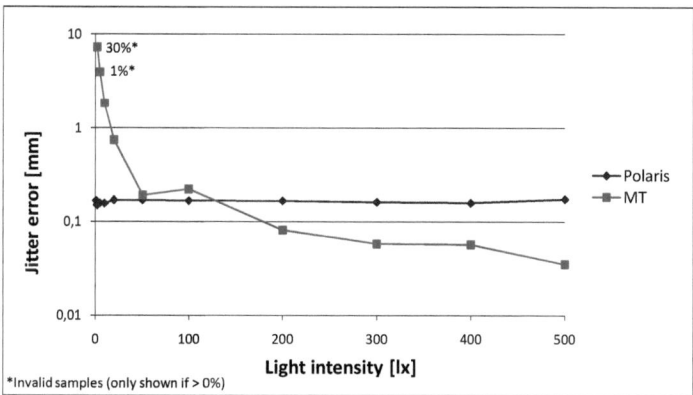

Figure 39: Results for the experiment *luminosity* showing the jitter error (cf. eq. 6.5) for the Polaris® system and the MicronTracker 2 (MT). The percentage of invalid samples (tool not located) is explicitly stated for values > 0%. At 1 lx, the tool was not recognized at all by the MicronTracker 2 (not shown in the diagram).

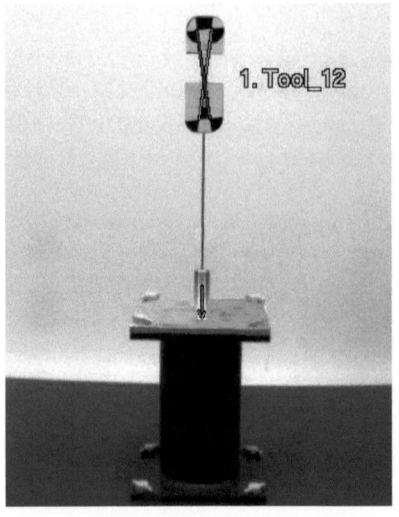 

(a) without shadow   (b) with shadow

Figure 40: Camera frames of the MicronTracker 2 showing a recognized tool (a) and an undetected tool (b) during the *shadow* experiment. The superimposed lines on the tool represented the *Vectors* located by the tracking algorithm.

According to Fig. 41, the MicronTracker 2 is highly sensitive to the *motion* of the tracked tool. Figure 42 shows two camera frames of the system for different rotational speeds of a tool mounted to the rotation phantom: At the higher speed, the captured image appears blurred. By contrast, the Polaris® system yielded high accuracy at all velocities. Figure 43 shows the measurement points for a tool (tip) speed of 52.5 m/s (or: 0.63 rps) for both tracking systems.

Finally, the jitter error increased with an increasing *angle* between the tool (i.e., the marker facet) and the view direction of the MicronTracker 2 (Fig. 44).

6.3.3 Discussion

This section compared the robustness of the Polaris® system and the Micron-Tracker 2 (model H40) with respect to illumination conditions, motion and orientation of a tool. While the Polaris® system showed robust tracking accuracy under all conditions, the MicronTracker 2 was highly sensitive to the examined factors.

The results of this chapter suggest that the two tracking systems have complementary advantages. The MicronTracker 2 allows construction of 6DoF needle-shaped tools which are well-suited as fiducial needles for navigated interventions. As a passive system, it supports multi-camera configurations in order to eliminate

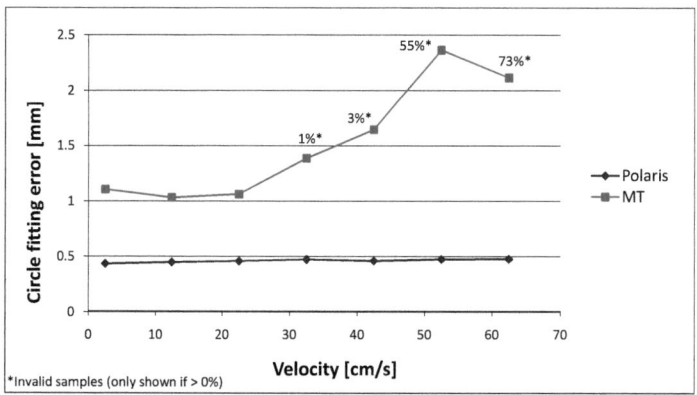

Figure 41: Results for the experiment *motion* showing the circle fitting error for the Polaris® system and the MicronTracker 2 (MT). The percentage of invalid samples (tool not located) is explicitly stated for values > 0%.

line-of-sight interruptions or to expand the FOM. The system yields good tracking accuracy under ideal conditions but is extremely sensitive to illumination conditions as well as to the velocity and the orientation of a tracked tool. If multi-camera configurations are used, the tool design should be reconsidered (*multi-facet tools* [25]) because flat markers do not accord well with multiple cameras.

The Polaris® system, on the other hand, is extremely robust with regard to the examined factors. It is a well-established system, which has shown to yield sufficient and robust tracking accuracy for a number of clinical applications. On the other hand, construction of light tools is challenging due to the required inter-marker distance of at least 5 cm (or 3 cm for the Polaris® Vicra™ system with a smaller FOM). Furthermore, it does not support multi-camera configurations.

In conclusion, the MicronTracker 2 is considered suitable for clinical applications provided that the corresponding navigation system can deal with outliers and that suitable light conditions can be guaranteed. However, if *robust* accuracy (i.e., a small *maximum* error) is relevant to the application, the Polaris® system is recommended due to its reliability.

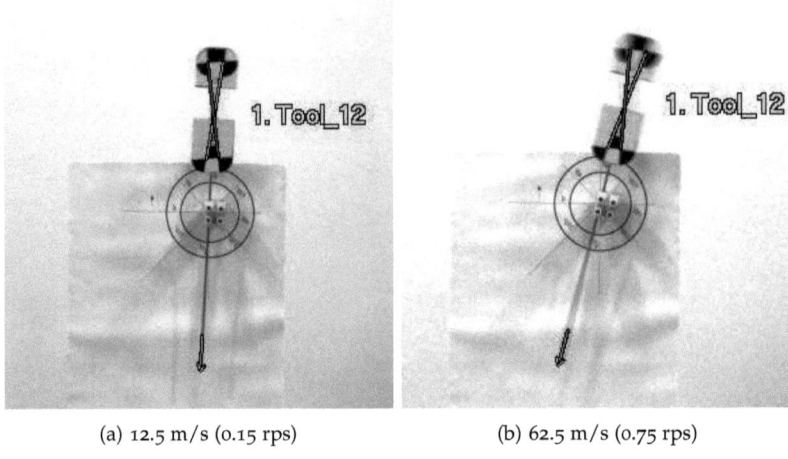

(a) 12.5 m/s (0.15 rps)   (b) 62.5 m/s (0.75 rps)

Figure 42: Camera frames of the MicronTracker 2 for different velocities of a tool mounted to the rotation phantom. At high velocities, the captured images appear blurred.

(a) Polaris®   (b) MT

Figure 43: Measurement points for a tool speed of 52.5 m/s (or: 0.63 rps) for the Polaris® system (a) and the MicronTracker 2 (MT) (b).

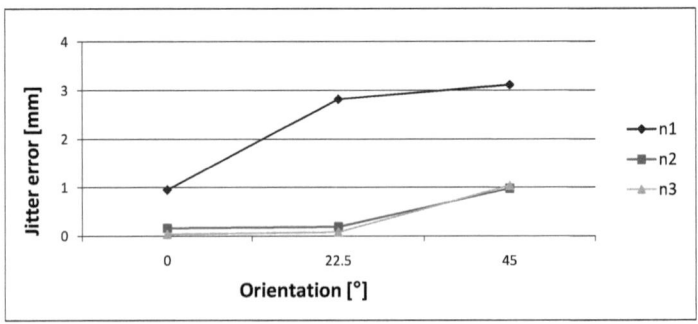

Figure 44: Results of the experiment *angle* showing the jitter error (cf. eq. 6.5) for the tools n_1 (d = 61.5 mm), n_2 (d = 81.5 mm), and n_3 (d = 101.5 mm).

7

INITIAL REGISTRATION

> *Mathematics is looking for patterns.*
> — *Richard P. Feynman, "What is science?" (1966)*

At the beginning of the intervention, the image coordinate system is aligned with the tracking coordinate system. This process involves two steps, namely (1) locating the fiducials in both spaces, and (2) finding a rigid transformation which optimally maps the fiducials onto each other to define the coordinate transformation. The FLE in tracking space was already evaluated in chapter 6. This chapter introduces the initial registration method (section 7.1) and presents and evaluates different methods for accurately locating the fiducials in image space (section 7.2). Furthermore, it estimates the TRE corresponding to the initial registration for different numbers and arrangements of the fiducials (section 7.3). It is worth mentioning in this context that the developed motion compensation method does not rely on the coordinate transformation computed in the initial registration step; it only requires the initial fiducial poses in image coordinates and the current poses in tracking coordinates as input. Computation of an initial registration, however, is useful because the associated FRE serves as an indicator of how well the current morphology of the tissue matches the morphology of the tissue during CT scan acquisition. The latter can be used (either initially or during the intervention) to decide whether a rescan is necessary (cf. section 4.2).

In the context of registration, any object with corresponding poses in the two coordinate systems to be registered may be referred to as fiducial. In this chapter, the term *navigation aid* will be used for the fiducial needles to clearly distinguish them from the tracked markers as well as from the control points extracted from the needles for the registration process.

7.1 INITIAL REGISTRATION METHOD

The method for registering the tracking coordinate system initially with the CT coordinate system works as follows:

1. *Navigation aid localization:* After planning CT acquisition, the navigation aids are located in the image with one of the methods described in section 7.2, and a set of M control points $\vec{l}_{j1}, \ldots, \vec{l}_{jM}$ is extracted from the axis of each registered needle $j \in \{1, \ldots N\}$ in image coordinates. The part of the needle covered by the control points should roughly represent the part of the needle inside the liver with $\vec{l}_{j1}$ representing the tip of the needle[1]. By default, $M = 2$ control points are used with an inter-control point spacing of 50 mm. The navigation aid poses can now be presented by a set of control points

$$L_{img}^0 = \left\{ \vec{l}_{11}, \ldots \vec{l}_{1M}, \ldots, \vec{l}_{N1}, \ldots, \vec{l}_{NM} \right\} \tag{7.1}$$

2. *Coordinate transformation:* In the second stage of the registration procedure, the navigation aids are tracked over time to identify the state within the breathing cycle which the CT was taken in. Using the same control point locations as in the previous step, a sequence (L^k) of needle poses is obtained in tracking coordinates:

$$L^k = \left\{ \vec{l}_{11}^k, \ldots \vec{l}_{1M}^k, \ldots, \vec{l}_{N1}^k, \ldots, \vec{l}_{NM}^k \right\}. \tag{7.2}$$

For each sample k, a rigid transformation $\Phi_{k \to img}$ is computed which maps the current control points L^k onto the original control points L_{img}^0 based on the least square method by Horn [58]. The coordinate transformation is then given by the transformation $\hat{\Phi} = \Phi_{\hat{k} \to img}$ that minimizes the associated FRE within the set of recorded samples:

$$\hat{k} = \arg\min_{k} FRE^k \tag{7.3}$$

$$FRE^k = \sqrt{\frac{1}{NM} \sum_{j=1}^{N} \sum_{m=1}^{M} \left\| \vec{l}_{jm} - \Phi_{k \to img}(\vec{l}_{jm}^k) \right\|_2^2} \tag{7.4}$$

where $\|.\|_2$ denotes the Euclidean norm.

Note that although the FRE is often used as a figure of merit for registration accuracy, it is not necessarily a good indicator of the TRE because - unlike the TRE - it is approximately independent of the fiducial configuration. The FRE can, however, be used to estimate the FLE, which in turn allows for predicting the TRE based on the target position and the arrangement of the fiducials [41].

---

[1] If skin markers are applied, they can be represented by either one control point (3DoF skin markers) or by three control points (6DoF skin markers).

7.2 FIDUCIAL NEEDLE LOCALIZATION

The TRE depends crucially on the accuracy of locating the fiducials in the planning CT image, i.e., on the FLE in image space (cf. Fig. 20). Accurate localization is challenging because the needle material leads to significant artifacts in the CT images as shown in Fig. 45(b). The following paragraphs describe different methods for fiducial localization and present the experiments performed to evaluate the approaches. The methods were developed for the Polaris® tools introduced in chapter 6, because the Polaris® yielded more robust tracking accuracy than the MicronTracker 2 (cf. chapter 6).

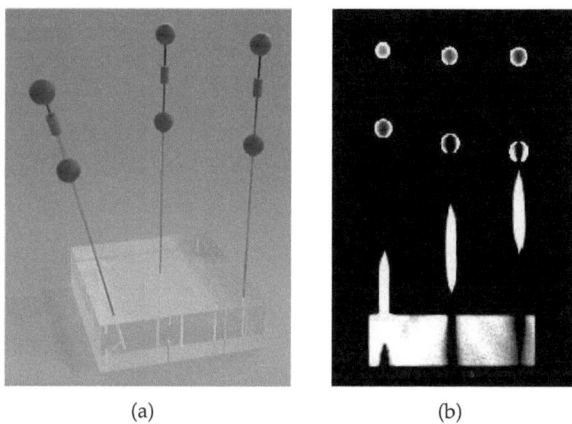

(a)   (b)

Figure 45: Registration phantom with inserted navigation aids (a) and transversal CT slice showing the metal artifacts when all needles are positioned in the scanning plane of the CT-scanner (b). The phantom is a 10 cm · 10 cm · 3 cm block of Plexiglas® with nine 2.5 cm deeply drilled holes, which form a grid with edge length 4 cm. The navigation aids have a needle diameter of 1.3 mm, inter-marker distances of 45 mm, 50 mm, and 55 mm and needle lengths of 180 mm.

7.2.1 Methods

To obtain optimal registration results, a model-to-image registration method was developed for locating a set of navigation aids accurately in a CT data set. The algorithm can be initialized with or without user interaction (*semi-automatic/fully-*

automatic method). To allow for interactive correction in difficult cases, a manual navigation aid localization method was additionally developed (*manual method*)

Fully-automatic method

The navigation aid localization method is based on the concept of model-to-image registration. Each navigation aid is modelled by a composition of a set of basic geometrical shapes. The Polaris® navigation aids, for example, are represented by a cylinder (the needle) and two spheres (the markers). Alternatively, an image of the expected appearance of a navigation aid can be provided. The parameters $\vec{p}$ to be optimized during the registration process represent a rigid transformation that maps the navigation aid coordinate system onto the image coordinate system. To quantify the registration quality of the parameters $\vec{p}$ for a given needle model j, the model is transformed to a point cloud $P_1^j, ..., P_{N_j}^j$ (extracted from the geometrical primitives or from the binary image) and the following metric M (to be minimized) is applied:

$$M(\vec{p}, j) = \sum_{k=1}^{N_j} \left| I_{img}\left(\Phi_{\vec{p}}(P_k^j)\right) - I_{ref}\left(P_k^j\right) \right| \quad (7.5)$$

where $|.|$ is the 1-norm, $\Phi_{\vec{p}}$ represents the rigid transformation defined by the parameters $\vec{p}$, $I_{img}(P)$ is the (linearly interpolated) voxel value in the CT image at point P and $I_{ref}(P)$ is the expected (linearly interpolated) voxel value in the CT image corresponding to P. If no image or only a binary image of the expected appearance of the navigation aid is provided, the metric is simplified as follows:

$$M(\vec{p}, j) = \sum_{k=1}^{N_j} I_{img}\left(\Phi_{\vec{p}}(P_k^j)\right) \quad (7.6)$$

In this case, the metric must be maximized and is based on the assumption that the navigation aids yield significantly higher Hounsfield values than the neighbouring structures and air. It essentially sums up all voxel values inside the (moving) needle model.

The workflow for fully-automatic navigation aid registration is as follows:

1. *Seed voxel finding:* The algorithm identifies all voxels within the image which exceed a predefined threshold (Hounsfield value of the needle material: 2000 Hounsfield Units (HU)).

2. *Cluster finding:* Using these seed points region growing is performed with a lower threshold (500 HU) (to include the markers) which yields a set of connected components.

3. *Cluster analysis:* Each sufficiently sized component C_{needle_i} is treated as a navigation aid candidate. In images with slice thickness larger than the radius of the needle, the partial volume effect may cause voxels corresponding to the same navigation aid to be assigned to different components. Consequently, the number of navigation aid candidates may exceed the true number of needles. In that case, a morphological closing operation followed by a morphological opening operation is applied to the image obtained from the region grower and the *cluster analysis* step is repeated, with the connected components extracted from the modified image.

4. *Needle fitting:* The following steps are then performed for each voxel cluster C_{needle_i}:

    a) *Navigation aid assignment:* Based on the center of mass of the voxel cluster C_{needle_i} and its orientation (principal component) an initial parameter set $\vec{p}_{initial}$ is computed. The needle model j yielding the best (initial) registration quality $M(\vec{p}_{initial}, j)$, according to the metric (cf. eq. 7.5), is assumed to correspond to the given voxel cluster.

    b) *Pose optimization:* Starting with the initial parameter set, a stochastic optimizer (itk::OnePlusOneEvolutionaryOptimizer [63]) is then used to minimize/maximize the metric value using a stochastic search algorithm. The final parameter set defines the pose of the navigation aid j in image space.

Semi-automatic method

The semi-automatic localization method is similar to the fully-automatic method, but the seed voxels are set by the user. This method can be applied when using a small number of needles (setting one or two seed voxels is not time-consuming), in case the fully-automatic method failed, or when a high resolution image prohibits the use of the fully-automatic method due to lack of memory (the algorithm requires a copy of the image to be held in memory).

Manual method

The manual navigation aid localization method can either be used as a stand-alone method or as an initialization step for the automatic algorithm (i.e., replacing steps 1.-3.). It requires identification of the head and tip point of a navigation aid within the image. To achieve this, the user can scroll through the CT slices of the data set and manipulate the navigation aids in two different ways. First, the location of the head and the tip of the needle model can be set to the current mouse position. Second, a model can be directly manipulated by either moving the complete navigation aid in one of the planes or by dragging only its head or tip which results in a rotation of the needle around the opposite end point. Throughout the entire procedure a fourth plane view is displayed which intersects the axis of the needle model and lies perpendicular to the scanning plane of the CT scanner (Fig. 46). This supports orientation and allows the user to judge the overall positioning.

7.2.2 Registration phantom

In order to evaluate the needle registration methods introduced in the previous section, a Plexiglas® phantom was developed that was used to compute reference needle poses in image space which the registration results were compared to (Fig. 45). Determining the pose of a navigation aid in image space with the help of the phantom requires an accurate segmentation of the Plexiglas® block. Since the block is homogeneous and surrounded by air, its surface can be extracted from the CT image with sub-voxel accuracy. The extracted surface is then registered with a point model of the block yielding a rigid transformation which - together with the known poses of the navigation aids in the phantom coordinate system - is used to determine the reference poses of the navigation aids in image space.

It should be pointed out that the positions of the *tips* of the navigation aids can be computed with high accuracy because the only error sources are:

1. The drill error which is negligible (< 0.01 mm) for the holes perpendicular to the block surface (*regular holes*). In the case of the *angular holes* the error turned out to be higher (cf. section 7.2.4).

2. The Plexiglas® segmentation error which should be smaller than the image resolution. In fact, the mean distance between the surface of the phantom (represented by a set of points) and the extracted surface after registration, which can be regarded as an indicator of the segmentation accuracy, was 0.067 ± 0.061 mm (n = 5).

In contrast, the reference positions of the *heads* could not be determined with sufficient accuracy due to the lever effect: A 1.4 mm drill adaptor was used to allow for the insertion of the needles which are only 1.3 mm in diameter. Considering the drill depth (25 mm), the needle length (180 mm) and the length of the needle tip (0.3 mm) this yields an error of the order of magnitude of 1.0 mm. However, as the Polaris® markers are clearly visible in the CT images (no metal artefacts), the head positions can be verified visually.

7.2.3 Experiments

To evaluate the proposed localization methods, three Polaris® tools were inserted into the registration phantom introduced above (cf. section 7.2.2). A Toshiba

Aquilion™ 16 CT scanner was utilized to acquire a set of five CT series using 0.5 mm slice thickness and 0.2 mm overlap. For each scan the phantom was put in a different pose (translation and rotation around all three axes of the CT coordinate system) whereas the configuration of the navigation aids within the Plexiglas® block remained constant (Fig. 45(a)). This way, a wide variety of needle poses in image space were obtained. Three different reconstructions of the original dataset were computed:

- 0.5 mm slice thickness and 0.2 mm overlap was used for an accurate Plexiglas® segmentation,

- 1.0 mm slice thickness and 0.2 mm overlap was used for navigation aid registration with a clinically realistic CT series, and

- 3.0 mm slice thickness and no overlap was used to test the performance of the registration methods with clinically "worst-case" images.

Four operators participated in the study for evaluating the proposed needle registration methods. Each operator received an introduction to the software and applied both registration methods that require human interaction to at least two sample CT series before beginning with the actual experiment.

The operator then used each method for registering the set of three needles with each of the five datasets that were reconstructed with 1.0 mm slice thickness and 0.2 mm overlap. The fully-automatic registration algorithm was additionally applied to the set of images with 3.0 mm slice thickness and no overlap. The results are presented in section 7.2.4.

7.2.4 Results

The results for the images with 1.0 mm slice thickness and 0.2 mm overlap are shown in Tab. 7. Note that only the tip positions were used for the evaluation because the refence positions for the heads were not sufficiently accurate as explained in section 7.2.3. Furthermore, the angular hole yielded worse results than the regular holes (automatic method: 0.5 ± 0.1 mm vs. 0.3 ± 0.1 mm) which suggests inaccurate drilling. It was thus excluded from the results.

It can be seen that the semi-automatic and fully-automatic method outperform the manual one with respect to both accuracy and time, yielding mean errors of 0.3 ± 0.1 mm (both algorithms). Visual inspection further showed that the models positioned by the semi-automatic and fully-automatic algorithm fitted both markers perfectly in all planes as shown by means of example in Fig. 46.

Table 8 compares the performance of the fully-automatic algorithm for two clinically possible resolutions: 1.0 mm and 3.0 mm slice thickness. The results show that the fully-automatic algorithm yields high registration accuracy even

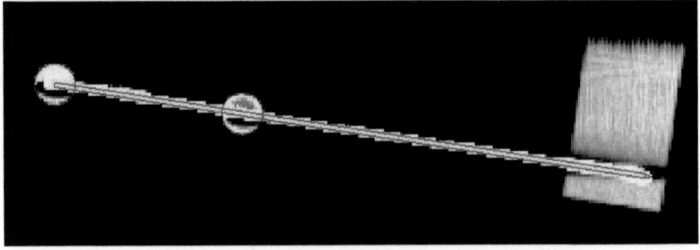

(a) 1 mm slices

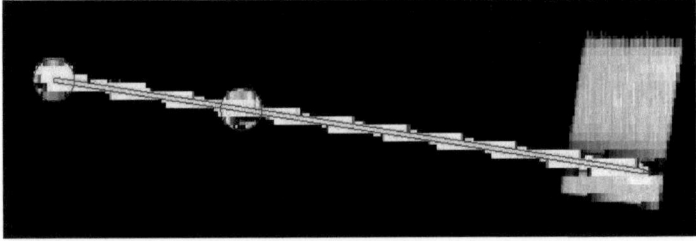

(b) 3 mm slices

Figure 46: Typical registration result of the fully-automatic method for 1.0 mm slice thickness/0.2 mm overlap (a) and for 3.0 mm slice thickness/no overlap (b). The navigation aid model (dark contour) is shown in the plane intersecting the main axis of the navigation aid which is perpendicular to the scanning plane.

for the lower resolution images. The increased distance to the reference position originates from the deviation in z-direction (i.e., the direction perpendicular to the CT scanning plane).

7.2.5 Discussion

This section presented and compared three methods for model based localization of navigation aids in CT images. The semi-automatic and automatic methods outperformed the manual method with respect to accuracy and time yielding sub-voxel accuracy and a localization time of the order of magnitude of 30 s for three needles. The registration accuracy of the algorithm depends primarily on the slice thickness of the planning CT. The lower accuracy of the manual method is partly traceable back to the fact that the users found it extremely hard to position the needle tip correctly due to the metal artifacts.

In the meantime, the algorithms have been applied to a wide variety of images. In general, the registration quality was excellent, but there are several suggestions for future work:

Method	FLE [mm]	Time [s]
Manual	1.4 ± 1.1	281 ± 90
Semi-automatic	0.3 ± 0.1	40 ± 7
Fully-automatic	0.3 ± 0.1	30 ± 2

Table 7: Fiducial localization results obtained from four users, and five images. FLE: Mean distance (± σ) of the estimated needle tip position to the reference needle tip position. Time: Mean duration (± σ) for locating three navigation aids (measured on a 2.4 GHz/2 GByte RAM machine).

Thickness/Overlap	FLE	FLE_x	FLE_y	FLE_z
1.0 mm/0.2 mm	0.3 ± 0.1	0.1 ± 0.1	0.1 ± 0.1	0.2 ± 0.1
3.0 mm/0.0 mm	1.5 ± 0.7	0.1 ± 0.1	0.1 ± 0.1	1.5 ± 0.7
$\Delta\mu$	1.2	0.0	0.0	1.3

Table 8: Comparison of registration results for different CT slice thicknesses and the fully-automatic method. FLE: Mean distance (± σ) of the estimated needle tip position to the reference needle tip position in mm. $FLE_{x|y|z}$: Mean distance (± σ) of the estimated needle tip position to the reference needle tip position in x-/y-/z-direction in mm, where z is the direction perpendicular to the CT scanning plane. $\Delta\mu$: Difference of the error means for the two resolutions in mm.

- Partial visibility: The algorithms require the entire navigation aids to be contained in the images. This problem might be overcome by dividing the metric value in equations 7.6 and 7.5 by the number of voxels that were used in the summation process.

- Connectivity: For (semi-) automatic initialization of the localization process, the needle must be visible as one connected needle cluster with large Hounsfield units and might fail in low resolution images due to partial volume effects. To address this issue, a Hough transform [64] could be applied for initializing the needle pose.

7.3 PREDICTION OF REGISTRATION ACCURACY

The main motivation for applying fiducial needles as opposed to skin markers is the ability to track points inside the target organ itself for motion compensation. But even if the morphology of the tissue during the registration process is approximately identical to the morphology of the tissue during image acquisition ("rigid body assumption"), it might be advantageous to use needles because they can be placed significantly closer to the target and thus potentially lead to a small distance of the control point centroid to the target (cf. section 3.2.3). On the other hand, skin markers potentially yield a lower FLE than fiducial needles, and their non-invasiveness allows applying a larger number. The aim of this section is to investigate this issue by comparing the expected TRE for different numbers and arrangements of fiducials via Monte Carlo simulations under the rigid body assumption.

7.3.1 Experiments

Data

To obtain realistic fiducial configurations, an *in-silico* evaluation was performed on a human CT data set. First, the skin, the liver (target organ) as well as the gallbladder, the ribs, the vena cava, the intestine, the stomach and the lungs were segmented. To obtain a set of tumor candidates T_{image}, a 3D grid with edge length 2 cm was placed into the liver as shown in Fig. 47(a). Each grid point inside the liver was added to the list of tumor candidates. Furthermore, a 2D grid with an edge length of 1 cm was projected onto the skin to obtain a set of fiducial placement candidates I.

Settings

To allow for comparing different fiducial configurations, a simulation algorithm was developed which requires making the following settings to define an experiment:

1. General settings:

    n_f: Number of fiducial needles $0 \leq n_f \leq 3$.

    n_s: Number of skin markers $0 \leq n_s \leq 8$.

    n_c: Number of configurations per tumor $\vec{t} \in T_{image}$

2. Definition of noise distributions:

    FLE_{image}^f: Error in locating a point on a fiducial needle (f) in image space. Based on the evaluation presented in section 7.2, zero-mean isotropic Gaussian distributions with $\sigma = 0.2$ mm were chosen by default along each coordinate axis (note: According to eq. 6.2, this corresponds to an FLE of approximately 0.35 mm).

    FLE_{image}^s: Error in locating a skin marker (s) in image space. By default, zero-mean isotropic Gaussian distributions with $\sigma = 0.1$ mm were chosen along each coordinate axis (note: According to eq. 6.2, this corresponds to an FLE of approximately 0.2 mm).

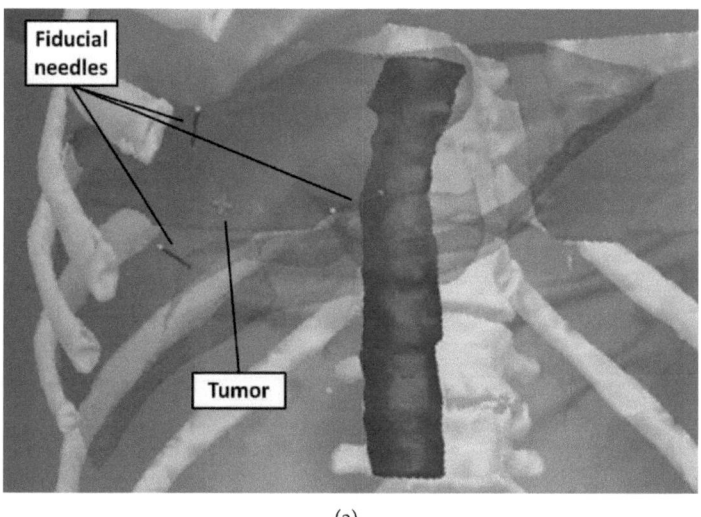

(a)

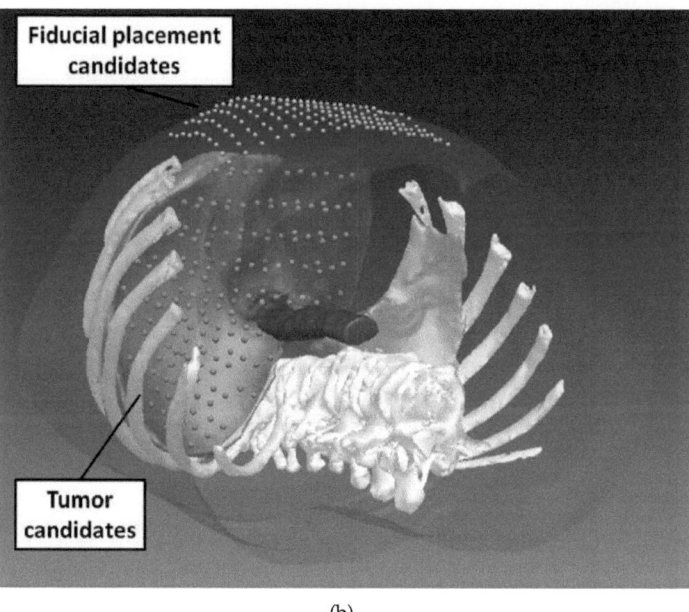

(b)

Figure 47: Screenshots of the human data set used for the *in-silico* evaluation. Tumor candidates (in the liver) and fiducial placement candidates (on the skin) (a) and example of simulated tool configuration for the precondition *enclose*(3) with the target shown as a dark cross, and the fiducial needles represented by three cylinders (b). For means of clarity, only some critical structures are visualized.

$FLE^f_{tracked}(c_i)$: Error in locating the control point c_i in tracking space. Based on the evaluation presented in section 6.2.2, zero-mean isotropic Gaussian distributions with $\sigma = 0.3$ mm and $\sigma = 0.2$ mm were chosen by default for c_1 (the tip) and c_2 (the second control point on the needle axis) along each coordinate axis (note: According to eq. 6.2, this corresponds to an FLE of approximately 0.5 mm and 0.35 mm respectively).

$FLE^s_{tracked}$: Error in locating a skin marker in tracking space. Based on the evaluation presented in section 6.2.2 (TRE in the control point centroid), zero-mean isotropic Gaussian distributions with $\sigma = 0.05$ mm were chosen by default along each coordinate axis (note: According to eq. 6.2, this corresponds to an FLE of approximately 0.1 mm).

3. Definition of preconditions on the fiducial placement:

   enclose(3) (only for $n_f = 3$): The precondition holds if and only if the volume spanned by the axes of the fiducial needles and the liver capsule is convex *and* the tumor is inside that volume (default: false).

   enclose(2) (only for $n_f = 2$): The tumor must be enclosed by the fiducial needles in cranio-caudal direction (default: false).

To obtain realistic fiducial configurations, a minimum distance of the tumor to the fiducial needles (2 cm), a maximum distance of the tumor to the tip of the fiducial needles (7 cm), a maximum distance of the skin markers to the projection of the tumor to the skin (10 cm), a minimum distance between the entry points (2 cm) and the tip points of the fiducial needles (2 cm), a minimum distance between the skin markers (3 cm), a minimum (i_{min} = 5 cm) and maximum (i_{max} = 10 cm) insertion depth of the fiducial needles as well as a maximum insertion angle of a fiducial needle relative to surface normal of the skin (α_{max} = 25°) were further defined.

Simulation Workflow

Given a set of targets T_{image}, a set of possible skin marker positions/insertion points I, a pose of the tracking system relative to the image coordinate system represented by a rigid-body transformation Φ_{ref} relating the image coordinate system with the tracking coordinate system, and a list of a-priori settings, the following workflow is repeated n_c times for each $\vec{t}_{image} \in T_{image}$:

1. Randomly generate a set $S \subset I$ of $|S| = n_s$ skin marker positions on the given grid. If the skin marker specific preconditions do not hold for S, repeat this step.

2. Randomly generate a set $E \subset I \backslash S$ of $|E| = n_f$ entry points for the fiducial needles from the given list. For each entry point, randomly generate an

insertion depth from a uniform distribution given by i_{min} and i_{max}. In addition, randomly generate an insertion angle α such that $\alpha < \alpha_{max}$. If the fiducial needles F pass critical structures or the fiducial needle specific preconditions do not hold for the generated arrangement, repeat this step.

3. Compute the ground truth control point positions in image coordinates L_{image}: Extract two control points from each fiducial needle $f \in F$ and one control point from each skin marker $s \in S$.

4. Generate the ground truth control point positions in tracking coordinates $L_{tracked}$ using the rigid-body transformation Φ_{ref}. Note that in the case of zero-mean isotropic Gaussian noise, we can assume that the TRE is independent of the rigid-body transformation relating corresponding control points [41], which allows us to set $\Phi_{ref} = I$.

5. Compute the ground truth target position in tracking coordinates $\vec{t}_{ref} = \Phi_{ref}(\vec{t}_{image})$.

6. Repeat $n = 100,000$ times

    a) Generate the perturbed control point positions in image coordinates $L_{image}^{perturbed}$ using FLE_{image}^{f} and FLE_{image}^{s}.
    b) Generate the perturbed control point positions in tracking coordinates $L_{tracked}^{perturbed}$ using $FLE_{tracked}^{f}(c_1)$, $FLE_{tracked}^{f}(c_2)$, and $FLE_{tracked}^{s}$.
    c) Determine the rigid-body transformation Φ_{sim} that minimizes the fiducial registration error according to the least square method [58] when $L_{image}^{perturbed}$ and $L_{tracked}^{perturbed}$ are used as corresponding control points.
    d) Compute the estimated target position $\vec{t}_{sim} = \Phi_{sim}(\vec{t}_{image})$.
    e) Store the Euclidean distance between the true target position and the estimated target position $\left\|\vec{t}_{ref} - \vec{t}_{sim}\right\|_2$ as TRE.

7. Store the RMS TRE obtained from n simulations.

Evaluation

In the first set of experiments, it was assumed that the morphology of the tissue during the registration process perfectly matched the morphology of the tissue during image acquisition, and the simulation workflow was applied to the following data sets:

DEFAULT: $n_f \in \{0,\ldots,3\}$, $n_s \in \{0,2,4,6,8\}$[1].

HOMOGENOUS: The same error distributions were assumed for skin markers and fiducial needles with $n_f \in \{0,\ldots,3\}$, $n_s \in \{0,2,4,6,8\}$[1]. An isotropic Gaussian error distribution with $\sigma = 0.2$ mm was chosen for the FLE in image space, while an isotropic Gaussian error distribution with $\sigma = 0.1$ mm was chosen for the FLE in tracking space (σ^2: variance along individual axes).

ENCLOSE(2): $n_f = 2$, $n_s \in \{0,2,4,6,8\}$, $enclose(2) \in \{true, false\}$.

ENCLOSE(3): $n_f = 3$, $n_s \in \{0,2,4,6,8\}$, $enclose(3) \in \{true, false\}$.

Those parameters that are not explicitly listed were set to their default values (cf. *Settings*). To allow for a comparison of the different presettings within one of the data sets, only those tumors within the list of candidates T_{image} were considered for which all preconditions (within that data set) could be fulfilled. For example, if the precondition *enclose* could not be fulfilled for a tumor close to the liver capsule, then that tumor was removed from the list of tumor candidates for all presettings in the corresponding data set ENCLOSE(3).

Several studies indicate that the liver does *not* reliably assume the same position at identical moments in the respiratory cycle [28]. In the second set of experiments, it was therefore assumed that the morphology of the liver did not perfectly match the morphology during CT acquisition but that there was a slight shift relative to the skin surface in cranio-caudal direction. In this case, the rigid transformation representing that shift in tracking coordinates was applied to the reference target position in tracking coordinates. The same transformation was applied to the *tips* of the fiducial needles reflecting the fact that they move with the target organ. In constrast, the skin entry points of the fiducial needles, as well as the skin marker positions, remained the same, and the control points were computed accordingly. The following data sets were then defined:

SHIFT(1MM): $n_f \in \{0,\ldots,3\}$, $n_s \in \{0,2,4,6,8\}$[1], $shift = 1$ mm.

SHIFT(3MM): $n_f \in \{0,\ldots,3\}$, $n_s \in \{0,2,4,6,8\}$[1], $shift = 3$ mm.

ENCLOSE(2)_SHIFT(3MM): $n_f = 2$, $n_s \in \{0,2,4,6,8\}$, $shift = 3$ mm, $enclose(2) \in \{true, false\}$.

ENCLOSE(3)_SHIFT(3MM): $n_f = 3$, $n_s \in \{0,2,4,6,8\}$, $shift = 3$ mm, $enclose(3) \in \{true, false\}$.

Again, the individual presettings of a data set ds_i were evaluated only for those targets $T_{ds_i} \subset T_{image}$ for which all preconditions could be fulfilled. The number of configurations per tumor n_c was chosen such that $n_c \cdot n_t \geq 100$, with $n_t = |T_{ds_i}|$.

---

[1] $n_f = 0$ only if $n_s \geq 4$ and $n_s = 0$ only if $n_f \geq 2$

7.3.2 Results

The simulation results are shown in Fig. 48 - Fig. 52. When the FLE was assumed to be the same for fiducial needles and skin markers (data set HOMOGENOUS; Fig. 49(a)), the TRE was substantially lower for the configurations *with* fiducial needles ($n_f > 0$). In contrast, using the default settings (data set DEFAULT; Fig. 49(b)), and thus a much lower FLE for the skin markers than for the fiducial needles, yielded the best results for $n_f = 0$. In other words, the better FLE had a higher influence on the TRE than the distance of the control point centroid to the target. The mean distance between the control point centroid to the target is shown in Fig. 48 for these experiments.

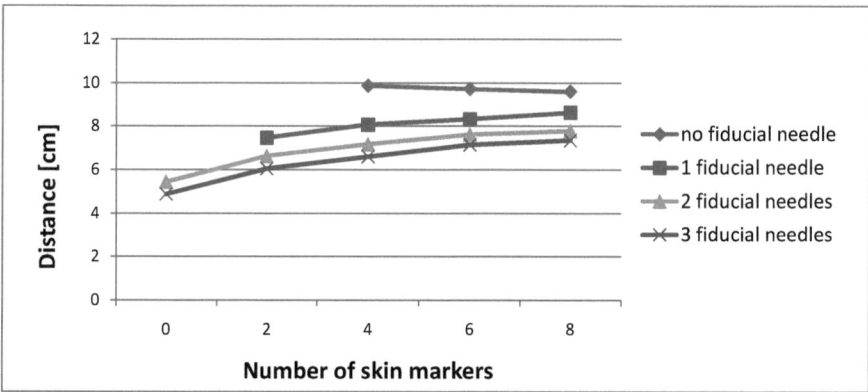

Figure 48: Mean distance between the target and the control point centroid for the data set DEFAULT introduced in section 7.3.1. The results were obtained from 104 fiducial configurations (104 targets) (note: The same configurations were used for the sets HOMOGENOUS, SHIFT(1mm), and SHIFT(3mm)).

Figure 50 shows the simulation results for the case that the liver does not perfectly reassume its pose at identical points within the breathing cycle (SHIFT(1mm) and SHIFT(3mm)). In this case, fiducial needles clearly outperformed skin markers. Adding skin markers to a given configuration even increased registration error in this case.

In the above experiments, the fiducial needles were arranged randomly in the vicinity of the target. Figure 51(a) compares the predicted TRE for the case that three fiducial needles enclose the target (cf. section 7.3.1) to the case when an arbitrary arrangement is chosen (ENCLOSE(3)). When applying no skin markers, the TRE was reduced by approximately 20% with $enclose(3) = true$ compared to *enclose* = *false*. The mean distance of the control point centroid to the target was 3.2 cm (*enclose*(3) = *false*) and 1.8 cm (*enclose*(3) = *true*) respectively. When adding skin markers, the differences in error decreased due to a decreasing difference between the distances of the control point centroids to the targets. Again, the use of skin markers led to an increase of the TRE when a slight shift of the liver was assumed (Fig. 51(b)). Similar observations were made for the enclosing arrangement of two fiducial needles (Fig. 52).

7.3.3 Discussion

This section investigated the expected TRE for different numbers and arrangements of fiducials via Monte Carlo simulations under the rigid body assumption. It could be shown that a sufficient number of skin markers can outperform fiducial needles due to the higher localization accuracy, provided that the current morphology of the tissue *perfectly* matches the morphology of the tissue during image acquisition. However, if there is only a slight shift of the liver relative to the skin surface, it is advantageous to use fiducial needles.

Several issues remain to be addressed. First, this study only investigated fiducial positions/entry points above the liver. It is, however, very common, to choose an instrument trajectory that passes between two ribs and is approximately parallel to the lateral axis of the patient. Hence, the simulation should be applied to more possible fiducial positions and more data sets. Second, in order to use the proposed method for estimating the TRE in an intervention, more realistic error distributions (e.g., anisotropic Gaussian distributions) should be used to simulate the FLE. In that case, the pose of the tracking system must also be considered. Finally, a more realistic motion model representing liver movement relative to the skin surface could be applied. It is worth mentioning in this context that we have considered giving less weight to less reliable fiducials upon rigidly registering the two perturbed point sets. Yet, due to the higher FLE of the control points on the fiducial needles, this would have decreased the influence of the needles on the computation of the target position. As a shift of the liver relative to the skin can *exclusively* be captured by the internal markers, this effect is not desirable.

In conclusion, this section demonstrated that application of fiducial needles decreases the TRE even when the morphology of the tissue during the registration process is almost identical to the morphology of the tissue during image acquisition. If an intervention requires a maximum of accuracy, fiducial needles should thus be applied even if the procedure is conducted in ventilated patients.

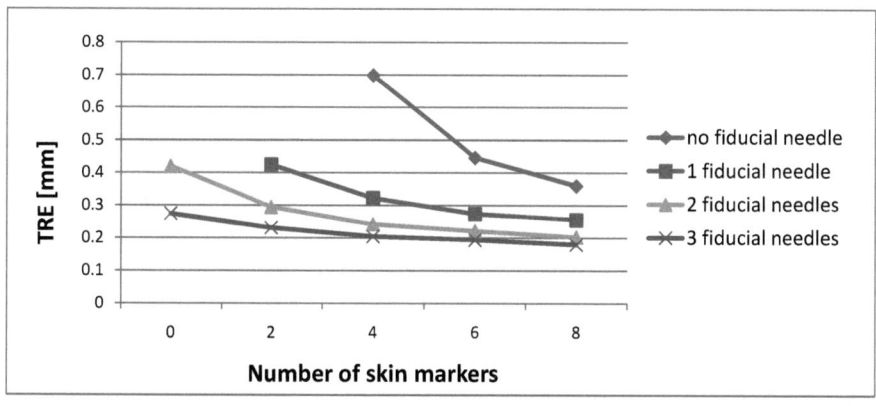

(a) HOMOGENOUS

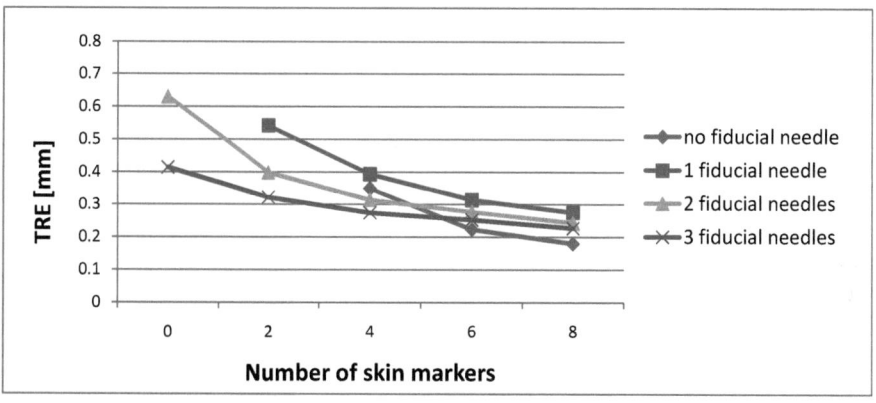

(b) DEFAULT

Figure 49: Predicted RMS TRE for the data sets DEFAULT and HOMOGENOUS introduced in section 7.3.1. The results were obtained from 104 fiducial configurations (104 targets).

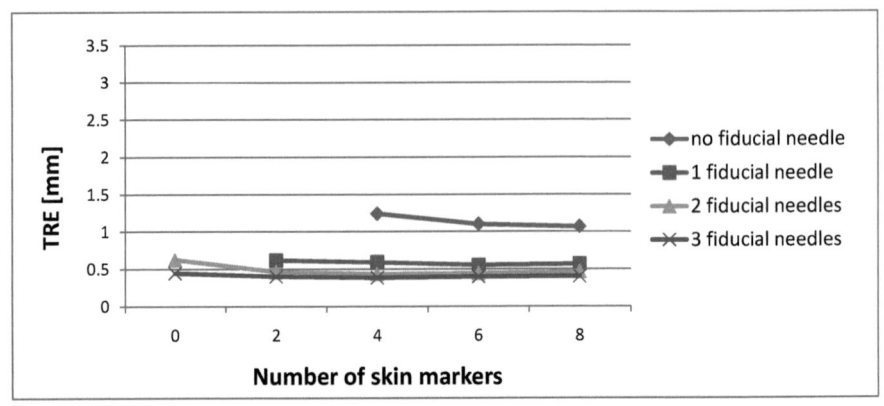

(a) SHIFT(1mm)

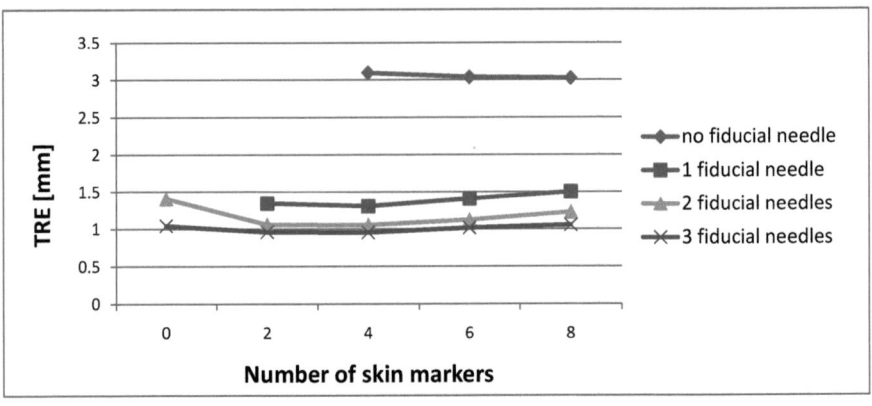

(b) SHIFT(3mm)

Figure 50: Predicted RMS TRE for the data sets SHIFT(1mm) and SHIFT(3mm) introduced in section 7.3.1. The results were obtained from 104 fiducial configurations (104 targets).

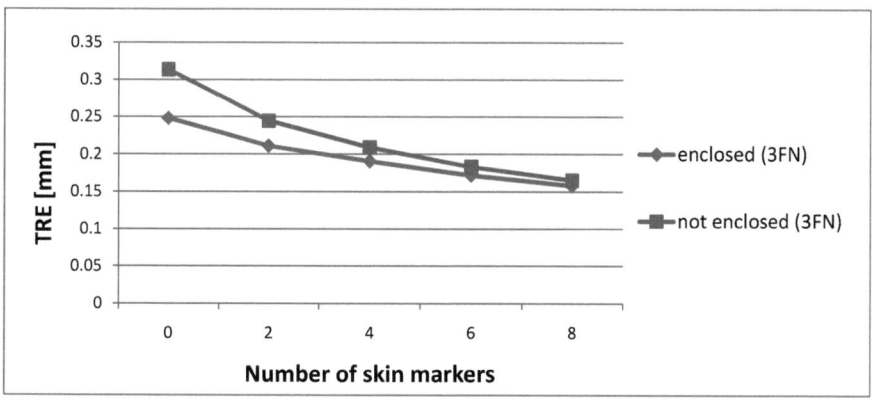

(a) ENCLOSE(3)

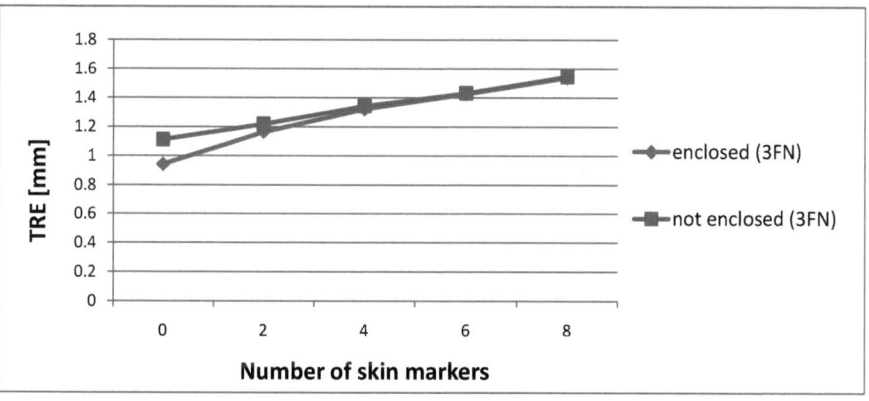

(b) ENCLOSE(3)_SHIFT(3mm)

Figure 51: Predicted RMS TRE for the data sets ENCLOSE(3) and ENCLOSE(3)_SHIFT(3mm) introduced in section 7.3.1. *Not enclosed (3FN)* refers to the case that the precondition *enclose*(3) is not required. The results were obtained from 112 fiducial configurations of 27 targets.

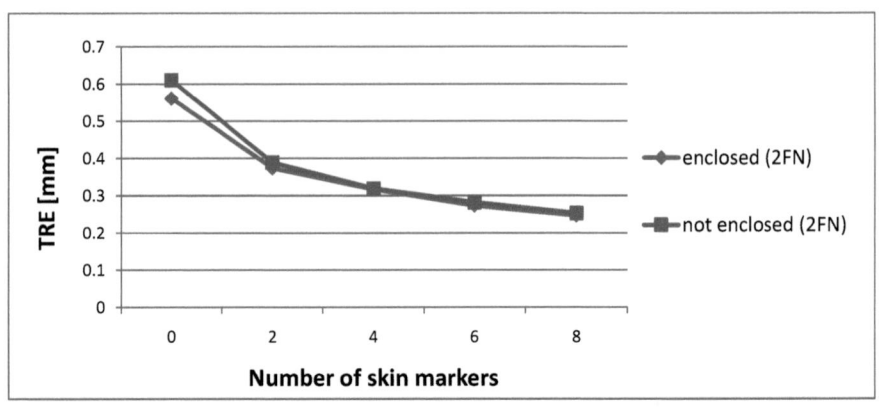

(a) ENCLOSE(2)

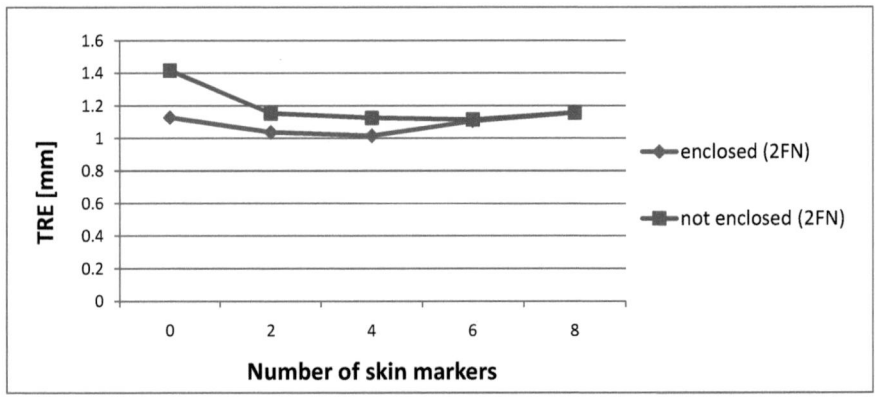

(b) ENCLOSE(2)_SHIFT(3)

Figure 52: Predicted RMS TRE for the data sets ENCLOSE(2) and EN-CLOSE(2)_SHIFT(3mm) introduced in section 7.3.1. *Not enclosed (2FN)* refers to the case that the precondition *enclose*(2) is not required. The results were obtained from 184 fiducial configurations of 92 targets.

8

MOTION COMPENSATION

> *Things should be made as simple as possible,*
> *but not any simpler.*
>
> — *Albert Einstein*

To provide high accuracy during an intervention, soft tissue navigation systems require a mechanism to compensate for intra-interventional organ shift and deformation in real-time. In this thesis, a motion compensation approach was developed which uses the initial and current poses of a set of fiducials to continuously estimate the position of a moving target. This chapter explains the basic concept of the developed method (section 8.1) and addresses the following questions:

1. What is the best method for modelling the deformation based on the fiducial poses (section 8.2)?

2. How should the fiducials be positioned for a minimal system error (section 8.3)?

3. Can fiducial needles be combined with skin markers to reduce the system error (section 8.4)?

4. What is the best combination of fiducial needles and skin markers considering the tradeoff between high accuracy and low invasiveness (section 8.5)?

5. Is it possible to perform gating based on the fiducial poses (section 8.6)?

8.1 BASIC APPROACH

The deformation model continuously estimates the position of the target or any other object initially located in the planning CT scan based on the movement of fiducial needles placed within the target region. The following section 8.1.1 briefly reviews the mathematical concepts upon which the deformation model is based and introduces the necessary notation. Section 8.1.2 presents the approach in detail.

8.1.1 Mathematical background

While affine schemes can only describe global changes in the object position, spline based approaches can capture local deformations. The spline transformations utilized for this study provide a mapping between two 3D spaces given a set of N_C pairs of corresponding control points $(\vec{p}_i, \vec{q}_i)$ ($i = \{1, \ldots, N_C\}$) [31]. The displacement $\vec{d}(\vec{x})$ at an arbitrary point $\vec{x} = (x, y, z)^T$ is computed using the following equation:

$$\vec{d}_W(\vec{x}) = \sum_{i=1}^{N_C} G(\vec{x} - \vec{p}_i)\vec{c}_i + A\vec{x} + \vec{b} \tag{8.1}$$

where $W = \left[\vec{a}_1, \vec{a}_2, \vec{a}_3, \vec{b}, \vec{c}_1, \ldots, \vec{c}_{N_C}\right]$ are the coefficients defining the spline, $A\vec{x} + \vec{b}$ represents the affine portion of the transformation ($A = [\vec{a}_1, \vec{a}_2, \vec{a}_3]$), and $G(\vec{x})$ is the basis function of the chosen spline.

In this contribution, thin-plate splines (TPS), elastic body splines (EBS), and volume splines (VS) are considered.

TPS were originally developed by Harder and Desmarais [54] and introduced to medical image analysis by Bookstein [17]. They are defined on the basis of an optimization problem [127]: The functional to be minimized represents the bending energy of a thin plate. Although this is a rather crude model with which to describe changes in anatomy, TPS have the advantage of being physically motivated and serve as a flexible deformation model.

In contrast, EBS are based on a physical model of an *elastic* material and were specifically designed for 3D [31]. They are solutions of the Navier equation, which is a partial differential equation (PDE) that describes the equilibrium displacement of an elastic, homogeneous, isotropic material subject to forces. Davis *et al.* assumed the underlying force field

$$\vec{F}(\vec{x}) = \sum_{i=1}^{N_C} \vec{f}_i(\vec{x} - \vec{p}_i) \tag{8.2}$$

and derived the EBS for different forces $\vec{f}_i(\vec{x})$ [31]. This thesis investigates two different versions of the EBS:

$$\text{EBS}(r) \; : \; \vec{f}_i(\vec{x}) = \vec{c}_i r(\vec{x}) \tag{8.3}$$
$$\text{EBS}(r^{-1}) \; : \; \vec{f}_i(\vec{x}) = \vec{c}_i r(\vec{x})^{-1} \tag{8.4}$$

where $r(\vec{x}) = \|\vec{x}\|_2$ and $\|.\|_2$ represents the Euclidean norm.

Finally, VS are a generalization of the univariate cubic interpolating splines when represented with distance functions [114].

The basis functions $G(\vec{x})$ for the different splines are as follows:

$$TPS \quad : \quad G(\vec{x}) = r(\vec{x})I \tag{8.5}$$
$$VS \quad : \quad G(\vec{x}) = r(\vec{x})^3 I \tag{8.6}$$
$$EBS(r) \quad : \quad G(\vec{x}) = (\alpha r(\vec{x})^2 I - 3\vec{x}\vec{x}^T) r(\vec{x}) \tag{8.7}$$
$$EBS(r^{-1}) \quad : \quad G(\vec{x}) = \beta r(\vec{x}) I - \frac{\vec{x}\vec{x}^T}{r(\vec{x})} \tag{8.8}$$

where I denotes the 3×3 identity matrix, and α and β are functions of the Poisson ratio $\nu = \frac{\lambda}{2(\lambda+\mu)}$ with the Lamé coefficients λ and μ and thus represent the physical properties of the given material [31].

To determine the coefficients W (cf. eq. 8.1) the interpolation condition is exploited, i.e., the spline displacements must equal the control displacements:

$$\vec{d}(\vec{p}_i) = \vec{q}_i - \vec{p}_i \tag{8.9}$$

Together with some additional flatness constraints (cf. [31]), this yields a linear system of equations for the coefficients W, which can be solved analytically [31].

The interested reader may refer to the literature for a more detailed description and comparison of the spline transformations utilized here [17, 31, 128].

8.1.2 Motion compensation method

The developed motion compensation approach is based on the concept of point based registration (cf. section 3.2.3). It requires an initialization step based on the planning CT data (*Initialization*) and an update mechanism based on the positional data obtained from the tracking system (*Real-time update*). In the first step, the fiducials are located in the planning CT image. During the intervention, a real-time deformation model is used to continuously deform the target region according to the current fiducial poses.

Initialization

The initialization of the motion compensation module requires three steps:

1. *Fiducial localization:* After planning CT acquisition, the fiducial needles are located semi-automatically in the planning CT image (cf. section 7.2), and a set of M landmarks $\vec{l}_{j1}^{img(0)}, \ldots, \vec{l}_{jM}^{img(0)}$ is extracted from the axis of each registered needle $j \in \{1, \ldots N\}$ in image coordinates. The part of the needle covered by the control points should roughly represent the part of the needle inside the liver. By default, $M = 2$ control points are used with an inter-control point spacing of 50 mm. The fiducial poses can now be presented by a set of landmarks

$$L_{img}^0 = \left\{ \vec{l}_{11}^{img(0)}, \ldots \vec{l}_{1M}^{img(0)}, \ldots, \vec{l}_{N1}^{img(0)}, \ldots, \vec{l}_{NM}^{img(0)} \right\} \tag{8.10}$$

2. *Initial coordinate transformation:* The fiducial needles are tracked over time to identify the state within the breathing cycle which the CT was taken in (cf. section 7.1). This yields a rigid transformation Φ^{init} aligning the tracking coordinate system with the CT coordinate system. The associated FRE serves as an indicator of how well the current morphology of the tissue matches the morphology of the tissue during CT scan acquisition and can be used to decide whether a rescan is necessary (cf. section 7.1).

3. *Target localization:* The target $\vec{t}^0$ is located in the planning image.

Real-time update

The deformation model is updated every 100 ms. Let $P = L_{img}^0$ be the set of initial control points ($|P| = N \cdot M$). The update algorithm for a point in time $k \geq 1$ is as follows :

1. The current pose of each fiducial j is determined by the optical tracking system and transformed to image coordinates using Φ^{init}

$$\vec{l}_{jm}^{img(k)} = \Phi^{init}(\vec{l}_{jm}^{TS(k)}) \quad m = 1\ldots M \tag{8.11}$$

It is worth noting that this step is not required. Alternatively, all computations could be performed in the tracking coordinate system. Application of the rigid transformation to the set of control points, however, is computationally inexpensive and allows visualization of the current poses of the objects relative to the initial patient's anatomy in the (original) image coordinate system.

2. The current set of control points Q^k is determined:

$$Q_j^k = \{\vec{l}_{j1}^{img(k)}, \ldots, \vec{l}_{jM}^{img(k)}\} \tag{8.12}$$

$$Q^k = \bigcup_{i=1}^{N} Q_j^k \tag{8.13}$$

3. The underlying interpolator is updated:
   - Rigid/affine transformation: If a rigid or affine transformation is applied, P and Q^k are used as corresponding control points to compute a rigid/affine transformation $\Phi_{img(0) \to img(k)}$ following the algorithm of Horn [58].
   - Spline transformation: If a spline transformation is applied, the current spline coefficients $W^k = [\vec{a}_1^k, \vec{a}_2^k, \vec{a}_3^k, \vec{b}^k, \vec{c}_1^k, \ldots, \vec{c}_{N_C}^k]$ (cf. eq. 8.1) are computed using the control point pairs $(\vec{p}_{ij}, \vec{q}_{ij}^*)$ as described in section 8.1.2.

4. The target is transformed:

- Rigid/affine transformation: If a rigid or affine transformation is applied, the resulting landmark-based transformation is utilized to transform the target point:

$$\vec{t}^k = \Phi_{img(0) \to img(k)}(\vec{t}^0) \tag{8.14}$$

- Spline transformation: If a spline transformation is applied, the current position $\vec{t}^k$ of the navigation target point $\vec{t}^0$ (original position) is determined using equation 8.1:

$$\vec{t}^k = \vec{t}^0 + \vec{d}_{W^k}(\vec{t}^0) \tag{8.15}$$

8.2 COMPARISON OF DEFORMATION MODELS

In the proposed motion compensation approach, the position of an anatomical target is interpolated from the poses of a set of reference tools with a deformation model. For an optimal performance, the model must (1) be real-time compatible and (2) reflect the physical behaviour of human tissue. In this section, the suitability of the following real-time compatible transformations (here: *Deformation models*) as basis for derived motion compensation approach was evaluated: Rigid transformations (RIGID), affine transformations (AFFINE), TPS, EBS(r), EBS(r^{-1}), and VS (cf. section 8.1.1). For this purpose, the TRE yielded by the different models was determined on a set of experiments obtained from different arrangements of three fiducial needles in two porcine and two human livers mounted to the motion simulator introduced in chapter 5. An additionally tracked needle served as the target.

8.2.1 *Experiments*

Two explanted human livers were obtained from patients that underwent liver transplantation at the Department of Surgery, University of Heidelberg, Germany. Informed consent was obtained from the patients in accordance with the Helsinki Declaration. In addition, two porcine livers were purchased at the butcher's. The set of four 5DoF Polaris® tools shown in Fig. 53 was utilized for this study with one needle serving as target and the remaining $N = 3$ needles serving as fiducial needles.

Data acquisition

For each porcine liver PL_i ($i = 1,2$) and each human liver HL_j ($j = 1,2$) used in this experiment, three different needle configurations were examined, where one configuration represents an arrangement of the four needles within the liver as exemplarily shown in Fig. 53.

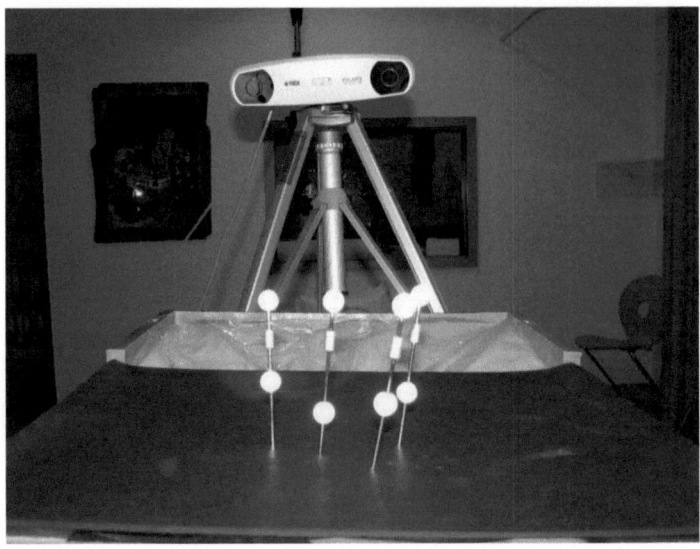

Figure 53: Sample needle configuration with three navigation aids and one target needle. The inter-marker distance of the 5DoF needles (cf. section 6.1) ranged from 45 mm to 60 mm. (Reprinted with permission from Maier-Hein et al. [89].)

For each configuration, the following workflow was conducted:

1. *Needle insertion:* The four optically trackable needles were inserted "percutaneously" into the liver, such that the target needle was surrounded by the needles serving as fiducial needles (Fig. 53).

2. *CT acquisition:* A CT scan (Somatom Sensation 16 multidetector row scanner, Siemens, Erlangen, Germany; 0.75 mm slice thickness) at end-expiration was acquired, where the state end-expiration was defined as the location with the most cranial displacement of motion within the torso model.

3. *Fiducial localization:* The semi-automatic stochastic registration algorithm introduced in section 7.2 was applied to determine the initial pose of the target needle relative to the fiducials.

4. *Data recording:* Three data sets were recorded with the Polaris® Vicra™ optical tracking system (Northern Digital Inc. (NDI); Waterloo, Ontario, Canada)

- *Continuous measurement (CONT):* Beginning in end-expiration the motion simulator was activated for a period of 30 sec and the poses of all four needles were recorded by the optical tracking system for several breathing cycles.
- *Maximal Movement (MAX):* A timer with the period of the lung ventilator was utilized for measuring the needle poses in one end-expiration phase and ten consecutive end-inspiration phases. Note that the first sample was used for registering the CT coordinate system with the tracking coordinate system as described in chapter 7. This experiment allowed for the analysis of the performance of the deformation model during maximal organ movement.
- *Minimal Movement (MIN):* A timer was used to record the needle poses in eleven consecutive end-expiration phases, to simulate an intervention which is exclusively conducted in one previously determined state in the breathing cycle. Again, the first sample was required for the registration process.

Data processing

For each experiment defined by a liver ID, a configuration ID, and a measurement type, the TRE was determined as follows:

1. *Target definition:* The original target position was defined as a set of $m = 5$ target points $T^0_{img} = \{\vec{t}_1^{img(0)}, ..., \vec{t}_m^{img(0)}\}$ with an inter-point spacing of 1 cm distributed along the registered target needle beginning at its tip. Several target points were used instead of only one, in order to account for different depths within the tissue.

2. *Coordinate transformation:* The first sample of the experiment was used to calculate the transformation Φ^{init} mapping the tracking coordinate system to the CT coordinate system (cf. section 7.1).

3. *Position estimation:* For each sample $k > 0$, a set of *measured* target points and a set of *estimated* target points in CT coordinates were determined:

    - Measured: The target needle position (recorded by the optical tracking system) was transformed to CT coordinates using $\Phi_{TS \to img}$. Next, $m = 5$ target points $T^{k,measured}_{img} = \{\vec{t}_1^{k,measured}, ..., \vec{t}_m^{k,measured}\}$ with an inter-point spacing of 1 cm were distributed along the target needle beginning at its tip.
    - Estimated: The original target points T^0_{img} were transformed to $T^{k,estimated}_{img} = \{\vec{t}_1^{k,estimated}, ..., \vec{t}_m^{k,estimated}\}$ as described in section 8.1.2. In the case of the

EBS, the Poisson ratio ν has been optimized on a training data set that is disjunctive with the set of experiments utilized for this study. The best results were achieved for $\nu = 0$.

4. *TRE calculation:* The RMS TRE was then defined as

$$TRE = \sqrt{\frac{1}{n \cdot m} \sum_{k=1}^{n} \sum_{l=1}^{m} \left\| \vec{t}_l^{k,estimated} - \vec{t}_l^{k,measured} \right\|_2^2} \qquad (8.16)$$

where n is the number of recorded samples excluding the first sample ($k = 0$), which was used for the calculation of the coordinate transformation.

In order to compute the TRE for a *set* of experiments, all determined estimation errors $\left\| \vec{t}_l^{k,estimated} - \vec{t}_l^{k,measured} \right\|_2$ for the individual experiments were put in one single vector, and the statistics were calculated over the entire vector.

In addition, the *movement* δ^{target} of the target needle was determined by replacing $\vec{t}_l^{k,estimated}$ by $\vec{t}_l^{orig}$ in eq. 8.16. For the RMS movement the following equation was thus obtained:

$$\delta_{rms}^{target} = \sqrt{\frac{1}{n \cdot m} \sum_{k=1}^{n} \sum_{l=1}^{m} \left\| \vec{t}_l^{img(0)} - \vec{t}_l^{k,measured} \right\|_2^2} \qquad (8.17)$$

8.2.2 Results

An analysis of the movement of the target needle in CT coordinates is given in Tab. 9. It can be seen, that the RMS movement δ_{rms} between expiration and inspiration (dataset MAX) was 14.9 mm in the case of the porcine livers and 10.2 mm in the case of the (heavier and less elastic) human livers and was primarily in cranio-caudal direction.

The TRE for the different transformations introduced in section 8.1.1 and the data sets CONT, MAX and MIN are shown in Tab. 10. Depending on the transformation, the TRE was in the range of 1.6 mm to 2.2 mm and of 1.2 mm to 2.0 mm for the porcine and human livers respectively when computed continuously over several breathing cycles (CONT). For the spline transformations as well as for the affine transformation, it made up approximately 15% of the RMS target movement during maximal organ deformation (MAX). The rigid transformation performed considerably worse, yielding an estimation error of over 20% relative to the target movement in all experiments. When the estimation error was exclusively computed in that state within the breathing cycle in which the CT was taken (here: End-expiration), the error difference between the rigid transformation and remaining transformations reduced drastically (MIN).

	absolute	x	y	z
Porcine livers				
CONT	9.1	1.3	0.9	8.9
MAX	14.9	2.0	1.6	14.6
MIN	1.1	0.4	0.2	1.0
Human livers				
CONT	5.4	0.7	1.5	5.2
MAX	10.2	1.0	2.6	9.9
MIN	1.3	0.4	0.5	1.1

Table 9: RMS movement of the target needle δ_{rms} (in mm) obtained from six configurations in two porcine livers and six configurations in two human livers for the three data sets CONT, MAX and MIN defined in section 8.2.1. The absolute movement as well as the movement along the lateral (x-axis in Fig. 26), posterior-anterior (y-axis in Fig. 26) and cranio-caudal (z-axis in Fig. 26) axes are shown.

In order to allow for a better comparison of the different transformations considered in this study, the TRE was further computed for the individual needle configurations in Tab. 11. The best and the worst transformations are explicitly listed. In addition, the TRE is visualized over several breathing cycles for one sample configuration in Fig. 54. Depending on the transformation and the placement of the navigation aids, the system yielded an RMS TRE in the range of 0.7 mm to 2.9 mm throughout the breathing cycle generated by the motion simulator (PL: 0.7-2.9 mm; HL: 1.0-2.4 mm). With the exception of the three configurations (PL2,C1), (PL2,C3), and (HL2,C3), the rigid transformation always yielded the worst result. A careful examination of the experimental data showed that in these cases either the navigation aids or the target needle were placed suboptimally. Figure 55 shows an example of an optimal needle placement and a misplaced target needle.

When two fiducial needles are applied, only rigid transformations can be used for motion compensation because the control points potentially lie in one common plane. In the case of the porcine livers, the error increased by 39% (CONT), 43% (MAX), and 34% (MIN) respectively when utilizing two fiducial needles as opposed to three [88].

8.2.3 Discussion

In this section, the TRE was determined for a set of real-time deformation models with a respiratory liver motion simulator. The affine transformation and the

(a) porcine livers

	RIGID	AFFINE	TPS	EBS(r)	EBS(r^{-1})	VS
CONT						
TRE	2.2	1.6	1.6	1.9	1.6	1.9
$\epsilon_{rms}/\delta_{rms}$	24%	17%	18%	21%	17%	21%
MAX						
TRE	3.3	2.2	2.3	2.8	2.2	2.7
$\epsilon_{rms}/\delta_{rms}$	22%	15%	15%	19%	15%	18%
MIN						
TRE	0.9	0.9	0.9	1.0	0.9	1.0
$\epsilon_{rms}/\delta_{rms}$	86%	80%	81%	89%	81%	88%

(b) human livers

	RIGID	AFFINE	TPS	EBS(r)	EBS(r^{-1})	VS
CONT						
TRE	2.0	1.4	1.3	1.2	1.3	1.2
$\epsilon_{rms}/\delta_{rms}$	37%	25%	24%	23%	24%	23%
MAX						
TRE	2.9	1.8	1.7	1.6	1.7	1.6
$\epsilon_{rms}/\delta_{rms}$	28%	18%	16%	15%	16%	15%
MIN						
TRE	1.2	1.0	1.0	1.0	1.0	1.0
$\epsilon_{rms}/\delta_{rms}$	88%	78%	78%	78%	79%	78%

Table 10: RMS TRE (in mm) for the different transformation types introduced in section 8.1.1 and the porcine (a) and human (b) livers. The results were obtained from six needle configurations in two livers for the three data sets CONT, MAX and MIN defined in section 8.2.1. In addition, the RMS TRE relative to the RMS movement δ_{rms} is listed in percent.

	RIGID	AFFINE	TPS	EBS (r)	EBS (r^{-1})	VS	Best	Worst
PL1,C1	2.04	1.48	1.56	1.57	1.55	1.59	AFFINE	RIGID
PL1,C2	2.86	1.82	1.90	2.19	1.83	2.29	AFFINE	RIGID
PL1,C3	2.13	0.90	0.82	0.69	0.81	0.71	EBS(r)	RIGID
PL2,C1	1.92	1.61	1.63	2.84	1.58	2.69	EBS(r^{-1})	EBS(r)
PL2,C2	1.68	1.33	1.32	1.32	1.35	1.29	VS	RIGID
PL2,C3	2.09	2.12	2.06	1.99	2.06	2.00	EBS(r)	AFFINE
HL1,C1	2.19	1.44	1.20	0.95	1.18	0.98	EBS(r)	RIGID
HL1,C2	2.37	1.06	1.07	1.10	1.07	1.09	AFFINE	RIGID
HL1,C3	2.21	1.13	1.12	1.15	1.16	1.09	VS	RIGID
HL2,C1	1.85	1.35	1.30	1.27	1.31	1.25	VS	RIGID
HL2,C2	1.92	1.78	1.75	1.66	1.74	1.69	EBS(r)	RIGID
HL2,C3	1.37	1.42	1.23	1.14	1.23	1.16	EBS(r)	AFFINE

Table 11: RMS TRE (in mm) for the data set CONT defined in section 8.2.1 and the individual fiducial needle configurations in the porcine livers (PL) and the human livers (HL). The error is shown for the different transformation types introduced in section 8.1.1, and the best and the worst transformations are explicitly listed.

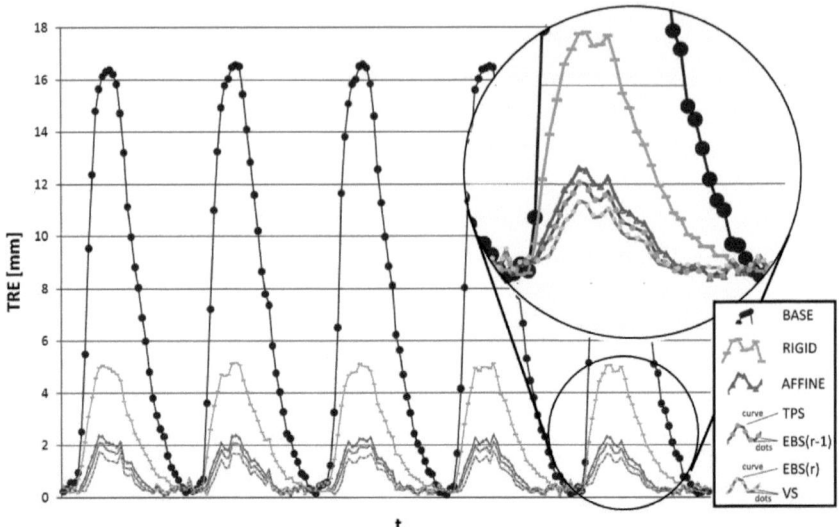

Figure 54: TRE for the tip of the target needle (in mm) over several breathing cycles for the different transformations and a typical needle configuration (PL1,C3). The movement of the target serves as base (BASE).

spline transformations (TPS, EBS, VS) performed clearly better than the rigid transformation, yielding an RMS TRE of less than 2 mm over the breathing cycle generated by the motion simulator introduced in chapter 5.

According to this study, there is no clear preference for one of the spline transformations or for the affine transformation. In fact, the non-affine part of the spline transformations was generally close to zero (i.e., $c_i \approx 0$ in eq. 8.1). Interestingly, the needle *placement* had a higher influence on the TRE than the transformation type. A possible explanation for this phenomenon is the fact that the presented motion compensation method aims to capture the motion and deformation of an *elastic* material with a set of *rigid* objects. In order to overcome this problem, the deformation model could be extended such that the volume defined by the control points on the fiducial needles remains constant over time. This would account for the incompressibility of the liver. Alternatively, one could regard the distribution of model points along the needles as noisy: When the volume spanned by the needles decreases, the inter-model point distance should increase. This could possibly be achieved by applying so-called *approximating* splines [128] which account for landmark (or control point position) errors. If the model points were distributed optimally along the needles, more distinguishing results might be obtained when

(a) favorable configuration   (b) unfavorable configuration

Figure 55: Model configuration (HL1,C1) with the target needle centered in the volume spanned by the navigation aids (a) and unfavorable configuration (PL2,C3) with a misplaced target needle (b). (Reprinted with permission from Maier-Hein *et al.* [94].)

comparing the different transformations discussed here. In addition, the parameter optimization might then yield a value for ν which is closer to the value for liver tissue (i.e., $\nu > 0$).

A possible explanation for why the affine transformation performed comparably well to the spline transformations is that a relatively small number of landmarks was used for the splines. More information could be obtained from more fiducials, which, however, would increase the invasiveness of the intervention.

An *optimal* evaluation of the deformation model would further rely on a perfectly accurate reference position over time. However, the reference target position used for this study was extracted from a *rigid* object unable to capture the elasticity of the tissue. Furthermore, the utilized needles were not firmly anchored within the liver and were thus potentially able to move relative to the tissue after insertion. Finally, the target needle possibly altered the natural movement of the liver. The use of an electromagnetic sensor as target could overcome these problems but would raise new issues such as the registration of the electromagnetic tracking system with the optical tracking system and the implantation of the target. Due to the lower tracking accuracy of electromagnetic systems compared to optical systems, the quality of the reference target position achievable with this method would probably still be worse than the one obtained in this study. The use of self-locking needles, on the other hand, could be beneficial.

Despite the drawbacks discussed above, this study was one of the first [71, 168] that has isolated the TRE from the overall targeting error of a navigation system. The performance of the system could thus be assessed independently of the provided visualization scheme and the experience of the user. Furthermore, the presented evaluation approach enables a report of the TRE against the state within the breathing cycle generated by the motion simulator.

8.3 FIDUCIAL PLACEMENT

Sections 8.2 and 7.3 showed that the fiducial placement has a high effect on the TRE. When using three fiducials, arranging the needles according to a predefined pattern is challenging considering the need to avoid critical structures and to keep a sufficient inter-needle distance. When only two navigation aids are applied, however, it is possible to stick to given rules. In this section, three different placement strategies for two needles are compared *in-vitro*.

8.3.1 Experiments

The following three placement strategies were investigated (Fig. 56):

1. *Cranio-caudal arrangement:* The two navigation aids are arranged parallel to the cranio-caudal axis of the patient. To obtain a small distance from the tumor to the centroid of the control points (cf. section 7.3), the tumor should be situated between the two needles, as shown in Fig. 56 (c_m). Since an exact placement of the navigation aids is difficult, three subcategories were defined: Left shift (c_l), exact placement (c_m) and right shift (c_r).

2. *Lateral arrangement:* The two navigation aids are arranged laterally. Ideally, the tumor should then be located between the two needles as shown in Fig. 56 (l_m). In order to account for placement error, three subcategories were defined: Shift up (l_u), exact placement (l_m), and shift down (l_d).

3. *Diagonal arrangement:* The two navigation aids are arranged diagonally, such that they can potentially capture deformation in both cranio-caudal and lateral direction. In these experiments, the inter-fiducial needle distance for this arrangement was larger than for the two other placement strategies (cf. Fig. 56), and only two subcategories were defined: Left-to-right (d_l) and right-to-left (d_r).

To allow for comparison of the three placement strategies, a porcine liver was mounted onto the motion simulator, and a 3×3 grid with a grid cell size of 4×4 cm^2 was marked onto the artificial skin (Fig. 56). One optically tracked needle was inserted through the grid cell in the middle to represent the tumor. For each arrangement shown in Fig. 56, two navigation aids were inserted through the corresponding grid cells, and the tracking system was positioned accordingly (free view of all tools). Next, the motion simulator was activated, and the poses of the three tools were recorded for 30 sec. The initial position of the target relative to the navigation aids was extracted from the first sample recorded by the optical tracking system, i.e., no CT registration was conducted, but the entire experiment was performed in tracking coordinates. As the fiducials were placed in the center

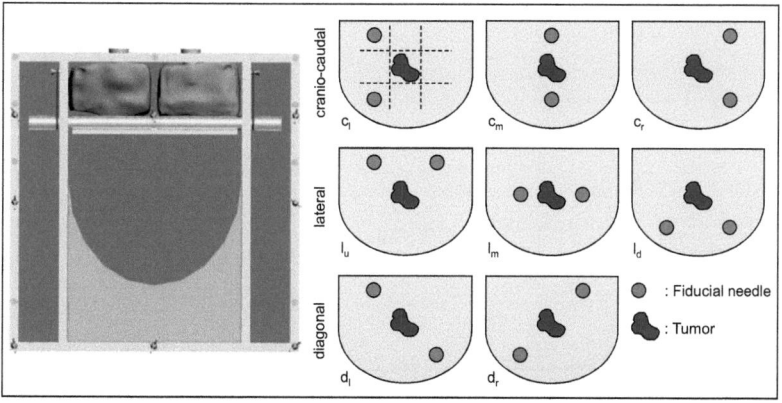

Figure 56: The three fiducial needle placement strategies and their subcategories.

of the FOM of the tracking system this potentially led to a lower FLE than that which would be achieved in practice based on the CT images. Yet, the experiment still allowed us to *compare* the different placement strategies because the absolute error was not relevant in this context.

The computation of the TRE was based on the difference between the position of the target needle according to the navigation system and its position according to the optical tracking system as described in section 8.2.1. A rigid deformation model was applied because the other models introduced in section 8.1.1 require the control points not to lie in one common plane. In order to obtain robust results, this experiment was conducted twice for each arrangement (two *passes*).

8.3.2 Results

The TRE for the different placement strategies is shown in Tab. 12. Both the cranio-caudal arrangement (RMS: 1.4 mm) and the diagonal arrangement (RMS: 1.1 mm) performed considerably better than the lateral arrangement (RMS: 2.5 mm). In case of the lateral and the cranio-caudal placement strategy, the results were particularly good when the target needle was situated between the two navigation aids.

8.3.3 Discussion

This section compared the TRE over the breathing cycle for three different placement strategies of two fiducial needles *in-vitro*. According to the results, the fiducials should be arranged such they can capture tissue motion along the cranio-caudal axis (diagonal or axial arrangement). A placement parallel to the lateral

Arrangement	TRE [mm]	δ_{rms}^{target} [mm]	$TRE/\delta_{rms}^{target}$ [%]
cranio-caudal			
c_l, pass 1	2.2	5.9	37
c_l, pass 2	1.6	4.7	34
c_m, pass 1	1.5	4.8	31
c_m, pass 2	0.8	4.7	17
c_r, pass 1	1.1	5.3	21
c_r, pass 2	1.0	5.6	18
all (cranio-caudal)	1.4	5.2	27
lateral			
l_t, pass 1	3.0	5.1	58
l_t, pass 2	3.1	4.7	67
l_m, pass 1	0.9	5.6	17
l_m, pass 2	1.1	5.6	20
l_b, pass 1	3.6	6.3	58
l_b, pass 2	3.1	4.8	64
all (lateral)	2.5	5.3	47
diagonal			
d_l, pass 1	1.4	5.2	28
d_l, pass 2	1.1	4.8	22
d_r, pass 1	1.0	5.7	17
d_r, pass 2	0.9	4.9	18
all (diagonal)	1.1	5.1	21

Table 12: RMS TRE (in mm) for the different placement strategies shown in Fig. 56 and corresponding movement δ_{rms} of the target needle. The error relative to the movement is additionally listed.

axis, on the other hand, should be avoided. The best results were achieved when the needles enclosed the tumor.

Several issues deserve further discussion. First, a rigid deformation model was applied because other models rely on a set of control points that do not lie in a common plane. The following section addresses this issue by investigating integration of skin markers when only two fiducial needles are used. Second, the TREs for this experiment were generally better than those presented in the previous section because the calculations were exclusively conducted in tracking coordinates (cf. section 8.3.1). This approach did, however, allow for comparison of the different strategies. Finally, this study was performed *in-vitro*. It can be expected that similar results would be obtained in humans *in-vivo* because it was shown experimentally in chapter 5 that the motion of a liver mounted to the motion simulator qualitatively resembles the movement of a human liver. Still, this issue remains to be investigated.

8.4 INTEGRATION OF SKIN MARKERS

According to section 8.2, non-rigid transformations yield a significantly better TRE over the breathing cycle than rigid transformations. When only two fiducial needles are applied, however, affine and spline transformations should not be used for motion compensation because they require the control points not to lie in one common plane. This section investigates integration of skin markers for improving the TRE when using two fiducial needles.

8.4.1 Experiments

This study was approved by the Committee for Animal Care and Research of the Karlsruhe Regional Council. The experiments were conducted in two anesthesized, intubated swine. The MicronTracker 2 was applied as the optical tracking system because it is based on tracking of flat target patterns and thus allows for construction of lightweight skin markers (cf. chapter 6).

Tools

The following two tool types were constructed for this experiments:

SKIN MARKERS: Thin pieces of plastic with printed target patterns as recommended by Claron Technology (Fig. 57).

FIDUCIAL NEEDLES: Commercial RFA probes (LeVeen® CoAccess™ Electrode System; Boston Scientific Corp., Marlborough, MA, USA) equipped with printed target patterns which are localizable by the tracking system. Due to the umbrella-shaped "anchors" (Fig. 57), the needles can be affixed firmly within the liver.

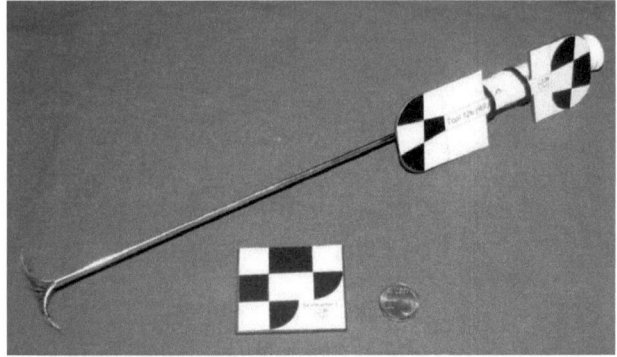

Figure 57: Fiducial needle with soft tissue anchor and skin marker constructed for the MicronTracker 2. (Reprinted with permission from Maier-Hein et al. [94].)

Data acquisition

For each swine P_i ($i = 1, 2$), three *tool configurations* C_j ($j = 1, 2, 3$) were examined, where each configuration represented an arrangement of three needles and four skin markers as shown by way of example in Fig. 58. For each configuration (P_i, C_j), the following workflow was conducted:

1. The skin markers $S = \{s_1, \ldots, s_4\}$ were attached to the skin of the swine as shown by way of example in Fig. 58.

2. Three needle-shaped tools $N = \{n_1, n_2, n_3\}$ were inserted into the liver such that they were arranged approximately parallel to the cranio-caudal axis of the swine. To prevent them from slipping out, they were affixed in the tissue via soft tissue anchors (Fig. 57).

3. A CT scan was acquired to verify that all needles were placed inside the liver.

4. Beginning in full expiration, the tool poses were recorded over seven breathing cycles.

Figure 58: Example of tool configuration. (Reprinted with permission from Maier-Hein et al. [94].)

Data processing

Processing of the recorded data for a given configuration (P_i, C_j) requires definition of a target needle $n^{target} \in N$, a set of fiducials F, and a deformation model Φ_{def} with

$$F \subset N \setminus \{n^{target}\} \cup S \text{ and } \Phi_{def}{}^1 \in \{RIGID, AFFINE, TPS\}.$$

Next, the following workflow is performed:

1. *Initialization:* The tip of n^{target} (which is extrapolated from the shaft pose) is defined as the target. To store the initial poses of all tools, a set of landmarks $L^0 = \{\vec{l}_1^0, \ldots \vec{l}_n^0\}$ is extracted from the first recorded sample (i.e., during full expiration): Three landmarks from each skin marker and two landmarks from the axis of each fiducial needle (cf. section 8.1.2). When only one fiducial needle (and no skin markers) is used for motion compensation, an additional landmark (extracted from the target pattern of the tool) is added because at least three non-collinear landmarks in total are required to define a rigid transformation. The original position of the target $\vec{t}^0$ is also stored. The deformation model Φ_{def} is then initialized with the original fiducial poses L^0. To assure robust performance, affine transformations and TPS are only applied when both skin markers and fiducial needles were used.

---

1 EBS and VS were not considered in this experiment because they yielded similar TREs as TPS according to preliminary results.

2. *Real-time estimation:* The actual intervention is represented by five breathing cycles. For each sample k, the deformation model is updated with the current control point positions $L^k = \{\vec{l}_1^k, \ldots, \vec{l}_n^k\}$, yielding the current transformation $\Phi_{def}^{0 \to k}$. Next, the target displacement δ^k, and the TRE are computed with

$$\delta^k = \left\| t^k - t^0 \right\|_2 \tag{8.18}$$

$$TRE^k = \left\| t^k - \Phi_{def}^{0 \to k}(t^0) \right\|_2 \tag{8.19}$$

For each configuration (P_i, C_j), the needle enclosed by the other two in the craniocaudal direction was defined as the target needle n^{target}. The TRE was then computed for $\Phi_{def} = RIGID$ and $n_s = 0$ (baseline) and for $\Phi_{def} \in \{RIGID, AFFINE, TPS\}$ with $n_s = 4$.

8.4.2 Results

Fig. 59 compares the performance of the motion compensation method for $n_s = 0$ and $n_s = 4$ skin markers ($n_f = 0$) for different deformation models. It can be seen that integration of skin markers improves the TRE significantly. When applying TPS with $n_s = 4$, an error reduction of 29% was achieved compared to the case that no skin markers and a rigid transformation was used. When the target needle was permuted (i.e., the target was not necessarily enclosed by the fiducials in the cranio-caudal direction), an error reduction of 37% was obtained. The performance of the rigid transformation, however, could not be improved by integration of skin markers.

8.4.3 Discussion

This study showed that skin markers can be used to improve the TRE when two fiducial needles are applied for motion compensation. System accuracy can thus be improved without increasing the invasiveness of the intervention. The drawback of this approach, on the other hand, is the fact that increasing the number of fiducials may lead to line-of-sight obstructions when applying an optical system.

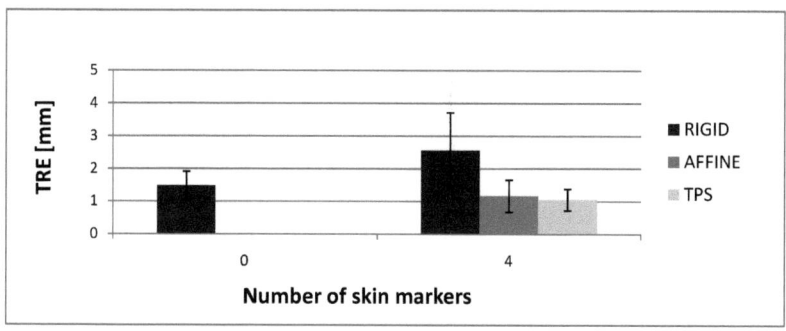

(a) enclosed targets

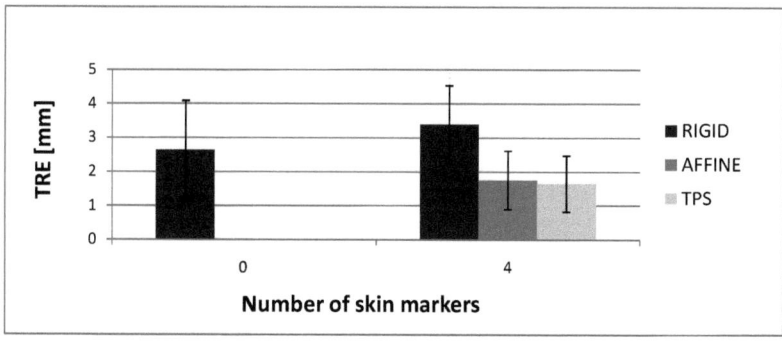

(b) all targets

Figure 59: Mean RMS TRE for $\Phi_{def} = RIGID$ and $n_s = 0$ and for $\Phi_{def} \in \{RIGID, AFFINE, TPS\}$ with $n_s = 4$ when the needle enclosed by the other two in the cranio-caudal direction was chosen (a) and for all permutations of the target needle (b).

8.5 ACCURACY VS. INVASIVENESS

When choosing the number of needles to be applied for motion compensation, there is always a tradeoff between high accuracy and low invasiveness. The last section showed that integration of skin markers improves the TRE when two fiducial needles are applied. The purpose of this study was to determine the TRE for different numbers of skin fiducials and fiducial needles *in-vivo* in order to identify an optimal fiducial configuration for a given application.

8.5.1 Experiments

This study was approved by the Committee for Animal Care and Research of the Karlsruhe Regional Council. The same data as in section 8.4.1 were used.

Data processing

To evaluate the methods on a maximum amount of data, the target needle and (if possible) the fiducials were permuted for the individual configurations. A set of experiments can be defined by three values (n_f, n_s, Φ_{def}), where $n_f < |N| = 3$ denotes the number of fiducial needles used for the real-time computation and $n_s \leq |S| = 4$ denotes the number of skin markers applied.

As the target needle and the fiducials can be permuted, this yields

$$n_c \cdot \binom{|N|}{1} \cdot \binom{|N|-1}{n_f} \cdot \binom{|S|}{n_s} = 6 \cdot 3 \cdot \binom{2}{n_f} \cdot \binom{4}{n_s} \qquad (8.20)$$

number of experiments for the selected set, where n_c is the number of configurations.

To process the recorded data for a given configuration (P_i, C_j), a target needle n^{target}, a set of fiducials F, and a transformation Φ_{def}, the workflow described in section 8.4.1 was performed.

For further analysis, each sample k was annotated with the corresponding state within the respiratory cycle $state(k) \in \{expiration, inspiration\}$. It was assumed that a fixed portion (here: 50%) of a breathing cycle corresponded to the state of expiration. Hence, the 0.5-quantil $q_{0.5}$ (i.e., the median) of δ^k_{target} was used as a threshold to classify the data, and the resulting binary curve was manually corrected by relabeling outliers (to obtain expiratory and inspiratory phases of reasonable duration). Finally, the following measures were computed:

- ϵ_{RMS}: RMS error in $\{TRE^k\}$

- $\epsilon_{RMS}(exp)$: The RMS error in $\{TRE^k | state(k) = expiration\}$

8.5.2 Results

The mean RMS TRE ϵ_{RMS} for different numbers of fiducial needles $n_f \leq 2$ and skin markers $n_s \leq 4$ during continuous breathing is shown in Fig. 60. It can be seen that the TRE decreases drastically when combining fiducial needles and skin markers as opposed to using only one fiducial type. In fact, adding one fiducial needle to a set of skin markers led to an increase in accuracy of over 50% during continuous breathing. Applying two arbitrarily placed fiducial needles for motion compensation as opposed to one, on the other hand, resulted in only a small difference.

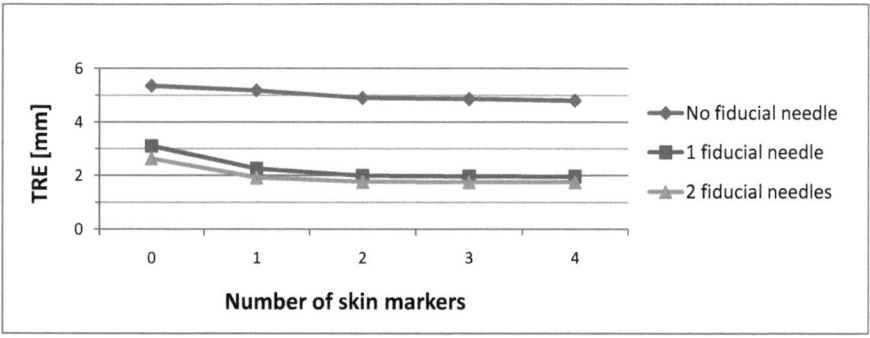

Figure 60: Mean RMS TRE for different combinations of surface markers and fiducial needles averaged over all possible permutations in two swine (cf. eq. 8.20). The corresponding transformation was affine when both fiducial needles and surface markers were used, and rigid otherwise. For $n_f = n_s = 0$, the RMS target displacement is shown.

By using all possible permutations for the target needle and the fiducial needles, the target was not generally enclosed by the other two needles in cranio-caudal direction when $n_f = 2$, reflecting the fact that cranio-caudal arrangement may not be possible when the tumor is situated close to the liver capsule or critical structures. Figure 61 lists the TRE for the case that only the most centrally located needle within the liver was used as target (i.e., the one enclosed by the other two in cranio-caudal direction). In this case, the TRE for $n_f = 2$ dropped by 34% from 1.8 ± 0.9 to 1.2 ± 0.5 (affine transformation, $n_s = 4$). Furthermore, error reductions of 12% and 20% respectively were obtained for $n_f = 0, 1$. In contrast, the location of the skin markers had no major effect on the accuracy, i.e., similar results were obtained when permuting the skin fiducials for a given n_s. According to Fig. 60, the accuracy for $n_s = 2, 3$ and 4 skin markers was comparable.

		$n_f = 0$	$n_f = 1$	$n_f = 2$
ϵ_{RMS}	RIGID	4.8 ± 1.1	3.8 ± 1.1	3.4 ± 1.2
	AFFINE	-	2.0 ± 0.9	1.8 ± 0.9
	TPS	-	2.1 ± 1.0	1.7 ± 0.8
$\epsilon_{RMS}(exp)$	RIGID	1.1 ± 0.3	0.9 ± 0.2	0.8 ± 0.2
	AFFINE	-	1.0 ± 0.4	0.9 ± 0.3
	TPS	-	1.0 ± 0.4	0.8 ± 0.3

Table 13: RMS TRE (in mm) for different transformation types and numbers n_f of fiducial needles during free breathing (ϵ_{RMS}) and at expiration only ($\epsilon_{RMS}(exp)$) averaged over all possible permutations in two swine. All skin markers were applied for motion compensation ($n_s = 4$). Note that affine transformations and TPS cannot be applied for $n_f = 0$ fiducial needles because the skin markers approximate a plane.

Table 13 compares the performance of different transformation types for different numbers n_f of fiducial needles ($n_s = 4$). While affine transformations and TPS clearly outperform rigid transformations during continuous breathing, the transformations yield comparable results when applied at expiration only. The best respective mean RMS errors for $n_f = 0, 1, 2$ fiducial needles were 4.8 ± 1.1 mm, 2.0 ± 0.9 mm, and 1.7 ± 0.8 mm during normal breathing, which corresponds to error reductions of 11%, 64%, and 70% as compared to the case when no motion compensation is performed i.e., when the target position is assumed constant. Furthermore, the use of fiducial needles improved the performance of the rigid transformation significantly (Tab. 13). At expiration, on the other hand, the lowest errors for $n_f = 0, 1, 2$ fiducial needles were similar (1.1 ± 0.3 mm, 0.9 ± 0.2 mm, and 0.8 ± 0.2 mm).

8.5.3 *Discussion*

This study investigated combining external and internal fiducials for real-time motion compensation during liver interventions. For this purpose, the TRE for different numbers of surface markers n_s and fiducial needles n_f as well as for different transformation types was compared *in-vivo*. During continuous breathing, n_f had the greatest effect on accuracy, and both affine transformations and TPS outperformed rigid transformations. In contrast, comparable results were obtained for various settings at expiration. The results of this study can be used in practice

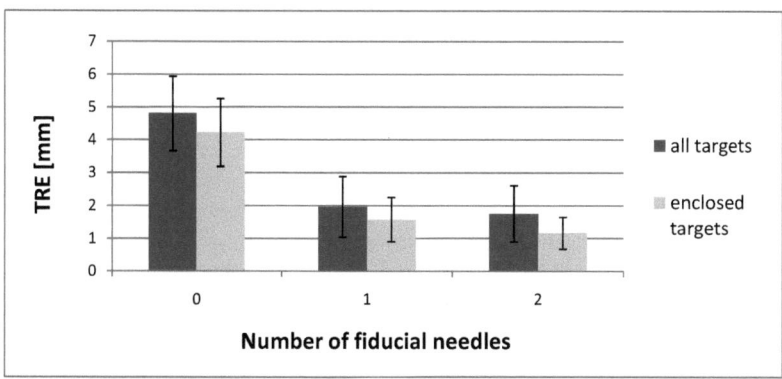

Figure 61: Mean RMS TRE for different numbers of fiducial needles ($n_s = 4$) during continuous breathing when using all permutations of targets and fiducials (*all targets*) and when using only those needles as target that were enclosed by the other two in cranio-caudal direction (*enclosed targets*). The corresponding transformation was affine for $n_f > 0$ and rigid otherwise.

to choose an appropriate set of fiducials for a given intervention, considering the tradeoff between high accuracy and low invasiveness.

Soft tissue navigation with internal markers is gaining increasing attention in the literature. One of the first motion compensation approaches based on internal markers was proposed by Schweikard et al. [133] who combined real-time tracking of skin markers with occasional detection of *implanted* internal markers based on X-ray imaging for motion compensation during radiosurgery. Another related study was performed by Zhang et al. [167], in which one electromagnetically tracked fiducial needle was used in addition to skin markers to improve registration precision during percutaneous liver punctures. However, the skin markers were not tracked and the authors did not evaluate the TRE for different numbers of surface markers and fiducial needles. Moreover, only rigid registration was performed and the tracking data was not fed into a (non-rigid) deformation model to compensate for liver motion in real-time. A study closely resembling ours has recently been published by Krücker et al. [77], who performed experiments in a swine model to investigate registration and motion correction methods in the presence of respiratory motion. The authors applied either a set of skin markers *or* a set of fiducial needles for this purpose. Similar to us, they concluded that respiratory motion can be compensated throughout the respiratory cycle when using internal fiducials. Even though the work was similar to ours, there are some major differences. First, the authors did not investigate *combining* internal and external markers for continuous motion compensation. Second, they only tracked the tips of the fiducial needles and did not feed additional points from the axes of the tools into the deformation model. Hence, they effectively used 3-Degrees-of-Freedom (3DoF) tools as opposed to 5DoF or 6DoF tools. Third, an electromagnetic tracking system was applied, which (according to the authors themselves) may have led to inaccurate tracking data due to interference with the CT scanner. Finally, the reference target needle pose was potentially inaccurate because the tools were not anchored within the tissue. Hence, the two studies, while overlapping in part, can be regarded as complementary.

This was the first study on combining internal and external markers for real-time organ motion compensation. According to the results, it is useful to combine the two fiducial types because this allows for applying non-rigid deformation models. A general recommendation is to use at least one fiducial needle and two surface markers as well as an affine deformation model for motion compensation during CT-guided liver punctures.

Several issues remain to be addressed. This study concentrated on the accuracy of the deformation model, by assuming an ideal initial registration of the tracking coordinate system with the CT coordinate system. Future work should assess the calibration accuracy of the navigation tools and of locating them in the CT image. Furthermore, the performance of the motion compensation method for more than two fiducial needles was not assessed in this experiment. In fact, it was quite cumbersome to place the needles within the tissue because the porcine livers were generally not thick and the anchors of the tools required a lot of space. In addition, it would have been challenging to track at least four fiducials and a set of skin markers concurrently, considering the requirement for enclosing the target needle by the remaining needles. Finally, the use of splines was again not beneficial compared to application of affine transformation despite the use of soft tissue anchors. A possible explanation for this phenomenon is the fact that enclosing of the target by the control points is generally not feasible when using less than three fiducial needles.

In conclusion, the results of this study could be used in practice to decide on a suitable combination of fiducials for a given intervention, considering the tradeoff between high accuracy and low invasiveness.

8.6 AUTOMATIC GATING

According to section 8.5, the TRE is substantially smaller when performing gated experiments than when assessing it during continuous breathing. The purpose of this study was to automatically detect those time slots during the intervention which correspond to the state within the breathing cycle that the CT was taken in.

8.6.1 Experiments

This study was approved by the Committee for Animal Care and Research of the Karlsruhe Regional Council. The same data as in section 8.4.1 were used.

Data processing

Initialization of the system was performed as described in section 8.4.1. Prior to the *real-time estimation* step, a *training* step was included:
For each sample k within the first two breathing cycles, a set of landmarks $L^k = \{\vec{l}_1^k, \ldots \vec{l}_n^k\}$ was extracted representing the current poses of the fiducials. Next, a rigid transformation $\Phi_{rigid}^{0 \to k}$ was computed, mapping the original landmarks L^0 onto the current landmarks L^k based on the least square method by Horn [58]. The associated FRE served as an indicator of the deformation of the tissue ($FRE_{rigid}^k = 0$: No deformation). The entire data from the *training* phase was then used to compute a threshold representing expiration:

$$FRE_{rigid}^k = \sqrt{\frac{1}{n}\sum_{i=1}^{n}\left\|\vec{l}_i^k - \Phi_{rigid}^{0 \to k}(\vec{l}_i^0)\right\|_2^2} \tag{8.21}$$

$$\theta_{rigid} = median(\{FRE_{rigid}^k\}) \tag{8.22}$$

This threshold was then used during the intervention to automatically detect the phases of expiration.

ϵ_{RMS} and $\epsilon_{RMS}(exp)$ were determined as in section section 8.5.1. In addition, the TRE for the automatically labeled states was computed:

$\epsilon_{RMS}(\theta_{rigid})$: The RMS error in $\left\{TRE^k | FRE_{rigid}^k < \theta_{rigid}\right\}$

8.6.2 Results

In general, FRE_{rigid} correlated highly with the TRE (Pearson product-moment correlation coefficient; $p < 10^2$). Furthermore, comparable results were obtained for the manually labeled states representing expiration and those classified automatically as shown in Fig. 62. It should be pointed out that (apart from several outliers) the automatically generated gating curves were identical to the manually generated ones. Surprisingly, this held even for the case when no fiducial needle was applied. Figure 63 exemplarily visualizes the TRE, the target displacement δ_{target}, and the FRE of the corresponding rigid transformation FRE_{rigid} over four breathing cycles for different numbers of fiducial needles.

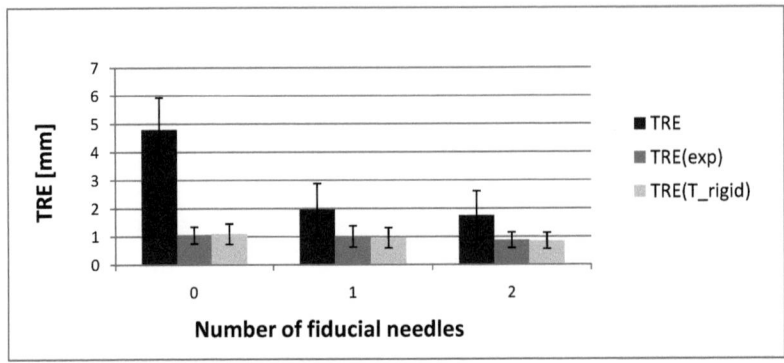

Figure 62: Mean RMS TRE for different numbers of fiducial needles during continuous breathing (TRE), at expiration (TRE(exp)) and with automatically detected favorable time slots based on the FRE (TRE(T_rigid)) as described in section 8.6.1 averaged over all possible permutations in two swine (cf. eq. 8.20). The corresponding transformation was affine for $n_f > 0$ and rigid otherwise ($n_s = 4$).

8.6.3 Discussion

This study showed that the FRE of a rigid transformation FRE_{rigid} reflecting tissue motion generally correlates highly with the TRE and can thus be used intra-interventionally as a measure of confidence for the estimation accuracy of the system.

According to the experiments, FRE_{rigid} could be used to automatically detect those time slots during the intervention which correspond to the state within the breathing cycle that the CT was taken in. It remains to be shown, however, whether continuous monitoring of the FRE can be used to support an intervention in practice. When extracting a binary gating curve from the tracking data based on FRE_{rigid}, a Kalman filter could be applied to prevent outliers from making the interventional phases too short. Still, even visualization of FRE_{rigid} by itself during an intervention could be helpful. If deep inhalation yields a higher FRE than flat inhalation, for example, the patient can be asked to adjust the breathing pattern accordingly.

In conclusion, the results of this study could be used in practice to provide an automatically generated gating curve as well as an intra-interventional measure of confidence of the accuracy of the system based on the fiducial poses.

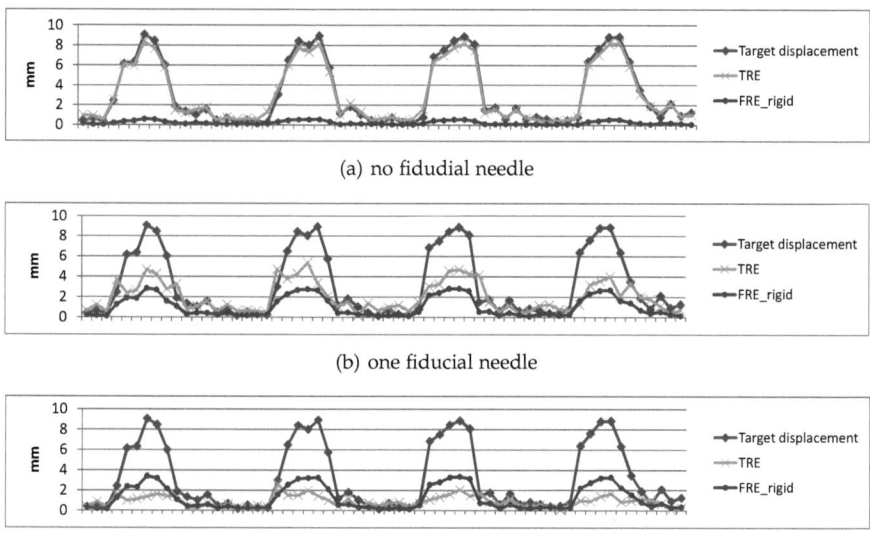

Figure 63: Sample diagrams showing the TRE, the target displacement and the FRE of the associated rigid transformation (FRE_rigid) over four breathing cycles for different numbers of fiducial needles $n_f \in \{0, 1, 2\}$. The corresponding transformation was affine for $n_f > 0$ and rigid otherwise ($n_s = 4$).

9

GUIDANCE

All information looks like noise until you break the code.

— Neal Stephenson, "Snow Crash" (1992)

An important factor to the overall performance of a navigation system is the guidance module, which presents the positional information extracted from imaging and tracking data to the operator to allow for fast and accurate transfer of the planned trajectory to the patient. As illustrated in Fig. 7, a pure 3D reconstruction of the scene is not sufficient for this purpose. This chapter introduces different visualization methods that were developed for the proposed navigation system (section 9.1), presents the experiments (section 9.2) and results (section 9.3) of a comparative study that was conducted to evaluate these methods, and concludes with a discussion of the results (section 9.4) as well as a description of the derived visualization approach (section 9.5).

9.1 VISUALIZATION METHODS

The following four different visualization schemes were designed and implemented for the proposed navigation approach:

3D OVERVIEW (OV): 3D overview of the scene which allows for user interaction and provides additional objects for facilitating the targeting process (Fig. 64).

PROJECTION VIEW (PV): Abstract view on the scene providing a three-stage guidance procedure comprising the steps (1) *tip positioning*, (2) *needle alignment*, and (3) *needle insertion*. In each step, the relevant information is extracted and presented on a 2D (projection) plane that shows the user how to move the instrument (Fig. 65 - 67).

TOOL TIP CAMERA VIEW (TT): 3D view shown from the perspective of the tip of the instrument instrument with the view direction along the needle axis (Fig. 68)

FIXED CAMERA VIEW (FC): 3D view shown from the perspective of a "virtual camera" placed above the insertion point with the view direction along the planned trajectory (Fig. 69).

The following sections describe the individual methods in detail.

9.1.1 3D Overview

The *3D Overview* shows a classical 3D reconstruction of the scene which allows for user interaction (rotation of the scene, zoom, etc.). Optionally, additional structures for facilitating the targeting process can be displayed (Fig. 64):

- Instrument elongation: An elongation of the instrument to show the direction in which the needle is pointing.

- Tip-target connection: A connecting line between the instrument tip and the target point. This line has to coincide with the elongation of the instrument for accurate targeting.

- Surgery tube: A transparent "tunnel" connecting the insertion point and the target point to visualize the planned trajectory.

The *3D Overview* is only used in combination with one or more of the remaining visualization methods.

9.1.2 Projection View

The *Projection View* is an abstract view on the scene which provides a three-stage guidance procedure adapted to the actions to be taken by the physician upon inserting the elongate instrument, namely finding the entry point (*tip positioning*), directing the instrument such as to point toward the target point (*needle alignment*) and inserting the needle towards the target (*needle insertion*). In each step, the relevant information is extracted and presented on a 2D (projection) plane that shows the user how to move the instrument:

1. *Tip positioning* (Fig. 65): The image generated in this step is meant to assist the physician in finding the predetermined entry point with the tip of the instrument. For this purpose, the tip of the instrument is projected onto a plane perpendicular to the planned trajectory as shown in Fig. 65. The physician then has to move the tip of the needle essentially parallel to the skin of the patient until the cross-mark representing the projected tip and the predetermined entry point represented by the big aiming cross coincide. Guiding arrows indicate the direction and distance the tip of the instrument

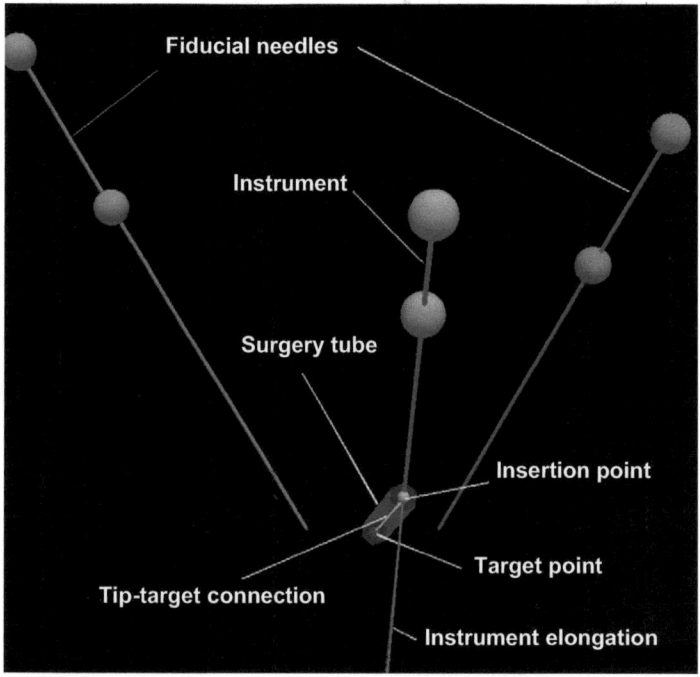

Figure 64: *3D Overview* showing the instrument, two fiducial needles, the insertion point, the target point, the *instrument elongation*, the *tip-target connection* and the planned trajectory represented by the transparent *surgery tube*.

has to be moved about the skin surface. The third dimension is easily assessed by maintaining the needle in contact with the skin. Two depth indicators provide additional help. A bar diagram indicates at which position along the predetermined trajectory the tip of the instrument currently is. If the bar of the depth indicator has reached a centre line, this indicates that the tip has reached the entry point on the skin of the patient. In addition, the depth or distance from the target point is represented by a circle of variable size surrounding the predetermined entry point: the further the tip is away from the predetermined entry point, the larger is the circle. If the needle is lowered onto the patient's skin, the circle shrinks just like a light spot of a torchlight approaching a wall. If the distance corresponding to the predetermined entry point is reached, the circle coincides with a stationary circle. Once the predetermined entry point has been found with sufficient accuracy, this is indicated by a signal (yellow signal light = insertion point reached), and the entry point finding step is completed.

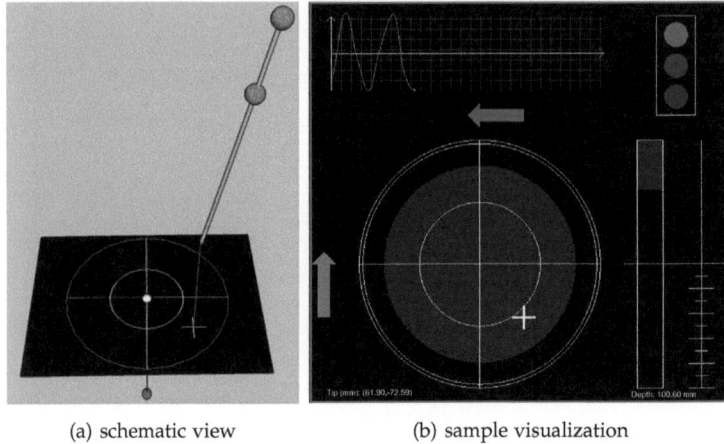

(a) schematic view (b) sample visualization

Figure 65: *Projection View* during the *tip positioning* step. Schematic view (a) and corresponding sample visualization (b). The planned trajectory is represented by a white insertion point and a dark target point.

2. *Needle alignment* (Fig. 66): Once the predetermined entry point is found, the instrument directing assisting step allows to easily tilt the elongate instrument such that its longitudinal axis is aligned with the planned trajectory. It is advantageous to perform this directing or aligning step of the elongated instrument after finding the entry point, because the instrument can be pivoted around the contact point between its tip portion and the skin without losing the entry point, which has already been located. The image displayed in this step is similar to the one shown in the previous step except that this time the *end* of the instrument is projected onto a plane orthogonal to the planned trajectory. Once the instrument is aligned with a predetermined accuracy, this is indicated by a signal (green signal light = needle aligned), and the needle may be inserted.

3. *Needle insertion* (Fig. 67): In the last step, the needle is inserted into the tissue. For this purpose, the target point is projected onto the plane that is perpendicular to the axis of the instrument and intersects the tip of the instrument. Similar as in the previous step, the user has to move the instrument such that the projected target point coincides with the center of the aiming cross, which represents the tip of the instrument. Again, depth indicators show the depth of the needle within the tissue.

In all steps within the targeting workflow, a breathing curve visualizes the movement of the (mean of the) tips of the fiducial needles along the cranio-caudal

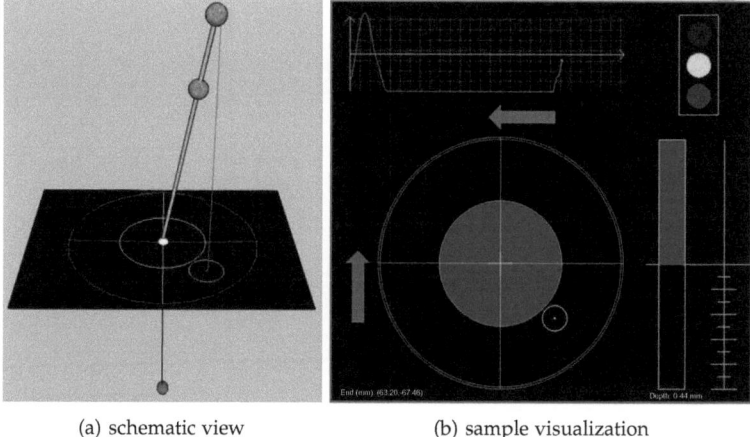

(a) schematic view (b) sample visualization

Figure 66: *Projection View* during the *needle alignment* step. Schematic view (a) and corresponding sample visualization (b). The planned trajectory is represented by a white insertion point and a dark target point.

axis of the patient (i.e., along the principal component of organ motion) as shown, for example, in Fig. 65.

9.1.3 Tool Tip Camera View

A "virtual camera" is placed into the tip of the instrument with the view direction along the axis of the instrument (Fig. 68(a)). The *view up vector* $\vec{v}$, which defines the tilt (rotation) of the camera, is computed from the normal vector $\vec{n}$ of the intervention plane (cf. section 6.1) and the view direction $\vec{d}$ of the camera as follows (Fig. 68(a)):

$$\vec{v} = (\vec{d} \times \vec{n}) \times \vec{d} \qquad (9.1)$$

$$\vec{v} = \begin{cases} +\vec{v}, & \text{if } \alpha < 90° \\ -\vec{v}, & \text{if } \alpha \geq 90° \end{cases} \qquad (9.2)$$

where α is the angle between $\vec{v}$ and $\vec{n}$ as shown in Fig. 68(a) and × denotes the cross product.

A sample visualization of the *Tool Tip Camera View* is given in Fig. 68(b): a cross in the middle of the window helps aiming at the insertion/target point, and the current depth of the tip of the instrument within the tissue is shown by a transparent depth bar. Once the insertion point has been reached, the user is given

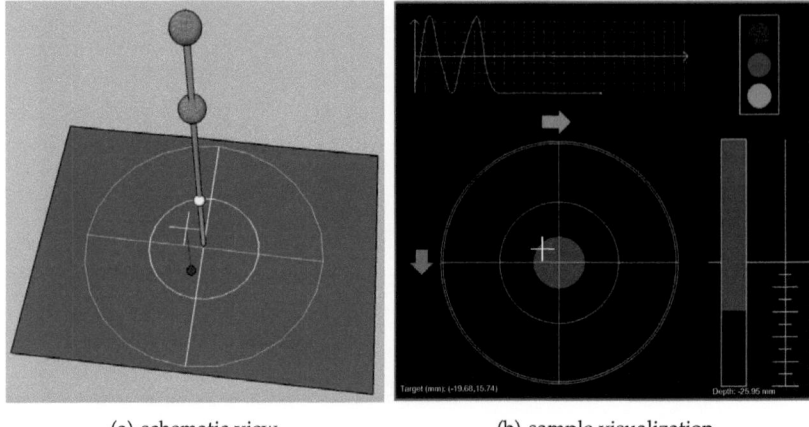

(a) schematic view   (b) sample visualization

Figure 67: *Projection View* during the *needle insertion* step. Schematic view (a) and corresponding sample visualization (b). The planned trajectory is represented by a white insertion point and a dark target point.

the impression of "flying" through a tube (*surgery tube*) representing the trajectory to the target point. Ribs, vessels, and other critical structures may be displayed in this view.

9.1.4 Fixed Camera View

The *Fixed Camera View* shows the 3D scene from the perspective of a virtual camera placed above the insertion point with the view direction along the planned trajectory (Fig. 69). User interaction with the scene is not allowed in this view. As in the *Tool Tip Camera View*, an aiming cross and a depth bar are provided. Additional structures for facilitating the targeting process can be displayed (cf. *3D Overview*).

9.2 EXPERIMENTS

The respiratory liver motion simulator presented in chapter 5 was used to evaluate the visualization methods in a realistic setup.

Six operators took part in the study.

- 2 experienced radiologists with more than 500 (R1) and 50 (R2) performed punctures respectively.

- 1 experienced surgeon with about 40 performed punctures (S1)

- 1 third year medical student (M1)
- 2 computer scientists (C1,C2)

Each participant performed a set of experiments with the goal of reaching a previously determined target point in an explanted porcine liver with an optically tracked instrument based on the visualization approaches introduced in section 9.1. Prior to each experiment, an insertion point (corresponding to a point on the artificial skin) and a target point (corresponding to a point within the porcine liver) were defined. The distance between these two points was identical (10 cm) for all experiments to provide identical conditions for the participants.

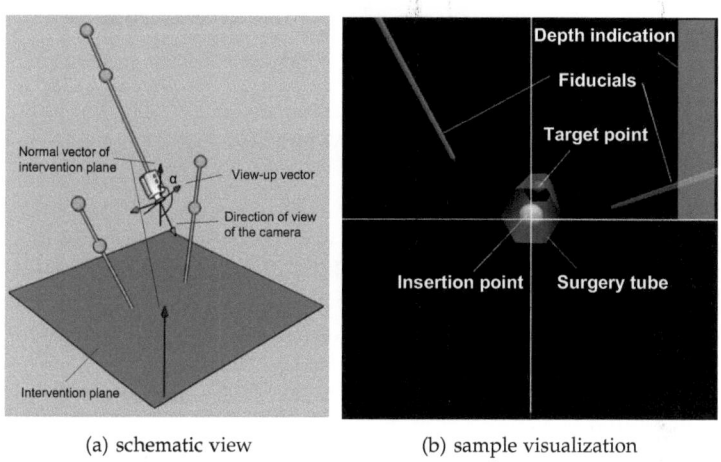

(a) schematic view   (b) sample visualization

Figure 68: Schematic view of the *Tool Tip Camera View* illustrating the computation of the view up vector (a) and sample visualization showing the target point, the insertion point, the *surgery tube*, and two fiducial needles (b).

During the targeting procedure, the proposed navigation system was used to continuously estimate the position of the moving target point from a set of two fiducial needles. The operators performed the experiments with four different views. The *Projection View*, the *Tool Tip Camera View* and the *Fixed Camera View* were used as described in the previous section. A combination of these three views with the *3D Overview* was defined as the fourth view (*Combined View*).

For each view, each operator performed six targeting experiments. The first three were performed without respiratory motion (i.e., the lung ventilator was not connected to the motion simulator), and the remaining three experiments were

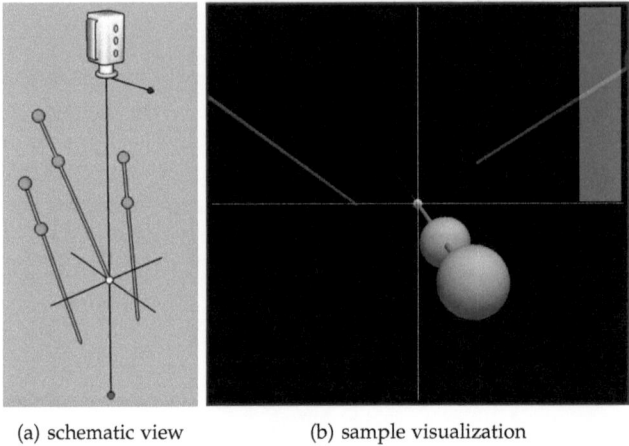

(a) schematic view   (b) sample visualization

Figure 69: Schematic view of the *Fixed Camera View* (a) and corresponding sample visualization (b). The planned trajectory is represented by a white insertion point and a dark target point.

conducted with respiratory motion. This way, the user error could be assessed with and without time pressure. The workflow for the targeting procedure was subdivided into the three steps *tip positioning, needle alignment*, and *needle insertion* described above. After each step, the operators had to verbally confirm the completion of the subtask to move to the next step. After the *tip positioning* step, the insertion point was set to the position of the tip of the instrument to isolate the errors of the different steps from each other. In the case of the experiments with respiratory motion the participants had to finish the two steps *needle alignment* and *needle insertion* within a 30 second respiratory resting period. The elapsed time was indicated by an acoustic signal. In practice, the needle insertion step could be divided into several shorter periods. Due to the missing tissue between the artificial skin and the liver, however, the insertion process could not be interrupted.

All methods were evaluated quantitatively and qualitatively. The qualitative examination was based on a questionnaire. For a quantitative evaluation, the targeting accuracy as well as the elapsed time for each step of the workflow were recorded[1]. The error of the *tip positioning* and *needle insertion* step were defined as the distance between the measured tip position of the instrument and the insertion point and target point respectively. The accuracy of *needle alignment* was defined as the angle between the axis of the instrument and the vector connecting the tool tip and the target point. It should be pointed out, that "virtual" distances provided by

---

[1] In all experiments, the time required for simulation of respiratory motion was not included.

the navigation system were measured as opposed to physical distances to isolate the system error from the user error.

9.3 RESULTS

This following paragraphs present the results of the quantitative (section 9.3.1) and qualitative (section 9.3.2) evaluation of the conducted study.

9.3.1 Quantitative evaluation

Accuracy

The targeting accuracy computed after the *needle insertion* step is given in Tab. 14 for the individual operators and views. As expected, both mean and standard deviation were persistently lower for the experiments without respiratory motion than for those with respiratory motion. The *Tool Tip Camera View* outperformed the remaining visualization schemes yielding a mean distance of 0.9 ± 0.3 mm between the needle tip and the target point averaged over the mean values of all operators. A slightly worse targeting accuracy was obtained for the *Projection View* (1.9 ± 0.9 mm) while the *Fixed Camera View* performed significantly worse (5.4 ± 0.9 mm). Interestingly, the *Combined View* was only ranked second among the four views (1.3 ± 0.7 mm). According to the paired t-test [19], the differences in accuracy for the individual views are statistically significant ($\alpha = 0.05$) with the exception of the comparison between the *Combined View* with the *Projection View* [134].

The results of the remaining steps within the workflow (*tip positioning* and *needle alignment*) are given in Tab. 15 and 16. Figure 70 further plots the targeting accuracy of the *tip positioning* and *needle insertion* step for the different visualization schemes averaged over the mean errors of the individual operators for all experiments without and with respiratory motion. The *Tool Tip Camera View* (together with the *Combined View*) yielded the best accuracy for both steps. It is worth noting that the accuracy achieved in the *tip positioning* step did not effect the accuracy of the remaining steps within the targeting workflow because the insertion point was set to the tip of the instrument upon completion of this subtask. Similarly, the *needle alignment* error was not fully propagated to the overall targeting error due to the flexibility of the skin and the lack of tissue between the liver and the skin, which allowed for correction of the instrument position after partial insertion. Despite the low overall targeting accuracy, the *needle alignment* was best performed with the *Fixed Camera View* (cf. Tab. 16).

When comparing the individual operators, it becomes clear that the computer scientists (C1 and C2), who were accustomed to the software, achieved the best targeting accuracy. The medical student (M1) with experience in computer games

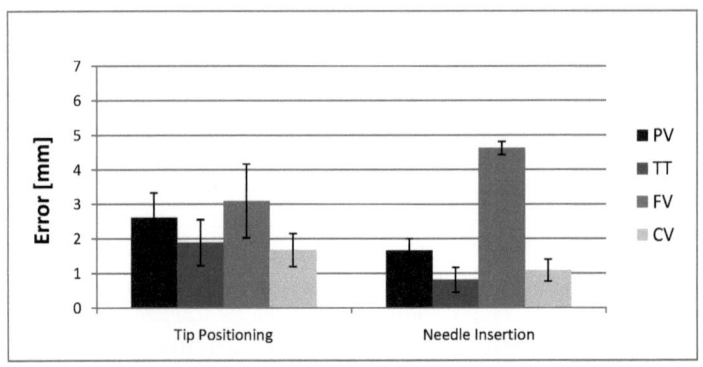

(a) without respiration

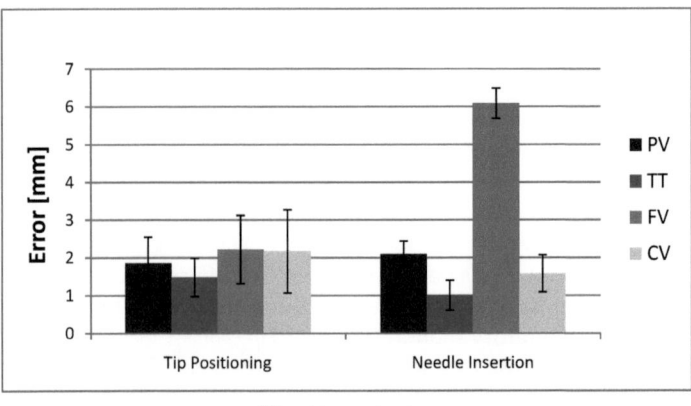

(b) with respiration

Figure 70: Mean targeting error ($\pm\ \sigma$) (in mm) for the *tip positioning* and *needle insertion* averaged over the means of the individual operators for the experiments without (a) and with (b) respiratory motion.

outperformed the physicians (R1, R2 and S1). However, there was no significant increase in accuracy in the course of the experiments for the individual operators [134].

Time

The mean time for reaching a predefined target point was 45 ± 14 sec (PV), 46 ± 9 s (TT), 33 ± 8 s (FC) and 46 ± 6 s (CV) for the experiments without respiratory motion and 30 ± 4 s (PV), 28 ± 3 s (TT), 23 ± 5 s (FC) and 30 ± 5 s (CV) for the experiments with respiratory motion. In both cases, the targeting time was averaged over the respective means of the individual operators.

Figure 71 presents the duration of the the individual steps within the workflow for the different visualization schemes averaged over all operators. The *Projection View* outperformed the remaining methods in the *tip positioning* and *needle alignment* step but was the most time-consuming method for the *needle insertion*. When both time and accuracy are considered, the *Tool Tip Camera View* is best suited for the *needle insertion* step.

Table 17 presents the results for the individual operators and visualization methods averaged over all experiments. Again, the computer scientists obtained particularly good results.

9.3.2 Qualitative evaluation

The evaluation of the questionnaire led to the following conclusions:

- All views are intuitive and provide a clear visualization of the scenery.

- The *Tool Tip Camera View* and the *Projection View* are the most suitable visualization methods for clinical use. Contrary to the *Fixed Camera View*, they are sufficiently supportive to guide the user as stand-alone views.

- The *Projection View* is particularly useful for the *tip positioning* and the *needle alignment* step. The visualization during the *needle insertion* step is not intuitive.

- The *Tool Tip Camera View* is particularly helpful for the needle insertion step.

- The *Fixed Camera View* is very intuitive and leads to fast needle insertion.

- The *3D Overview* is a helpful assistance when used in combination with the *Projection View* or the *Tool Tip Camera View*.

- The *surgery tube* is the most supportive additional structure. The *instrument elongation* and the *tip-target connection* are also helpful.

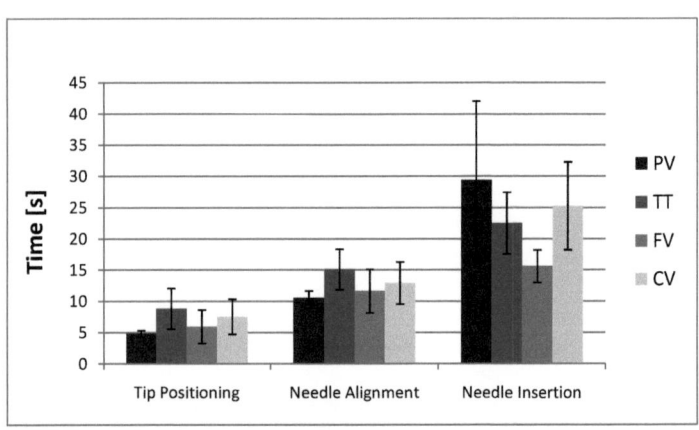

(a) without respiration

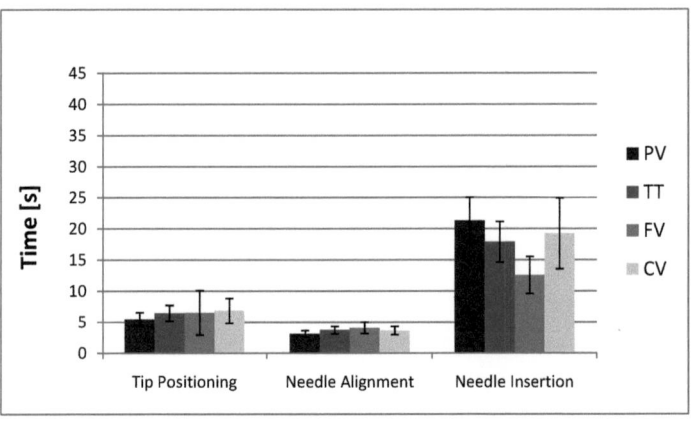

(b) with respiration

Figure 71: Time required for the individual steps within the workflow averaged over the means of the individual operators for the experiments without (a) and with (b) respiratory motion.

- In the *Combined View*, the individual windows appeared too small.
- It is difficult to pay attention to a depth indication on the side of the screen.
- Display of a breathing curve might be helpful in a clinical setting.
- Additional display of CT slices might support orientation of the operator.

More details on both the quantitative evaluation as well as on the qualitative evaluation can be found in [134].

9.4 DISCUSSION

This chapter evaluated four different visualization approaches for supporting computer-assisted soft tissue navigation both quantitatively and qualitatively. According to a recent literature research, this was the first study to evaluate a set of visualization methods for computer-guided needle insertion *in-vitro*. The results show that the user error is highly dependent on the provided visualization scheme. Although the experiments were conducted in a realistic setting, it should be noted that *in-vivo* targeting poses additional challenges to the operator. In practice, for example, an initial alignment error cannot be corrected after partial instrument insertion. In consequence, the user error measured in this study probably underestimates the true user error. The study did, however, allow for comparison of the suitability of the different visualization methods for the individual steps within the workflow. The following paragraph discuss the proposed visualization schemes and summarizes the most important advantages and disadvantages extracted from the quantitative and the qualitative evaluation.

Projection View

Unlike the other visualizations schemes, the *Projection View* reduces the available information to that which is actually needed in the individual steps within the targeting workflow. Initially, for example, only the information crucial for finding the predetermined entry point is displayed: if the physician moves the needle tip closely above the skin of the patient looking for the entry point, the search is effectively two-dimensional, while the third component, i.e., a component parallel to the predetermined trajectory is obvious for the physician, as he knows that the entry point must be on the skin of the patient. In consequence, the displayed image becomes very easy to understand and intuitive to interpret.

The method yields a high targeting accuracy but requires more time, which can mainly be attributed to the fact that the users found the provided visualization scheme not intuitive for the *needle insertion* step. Furthermore, a perfect match between the projected structure and the center of the aiming cross is hard to achieve due to the jitter of the tracking system, and the operators often hestitated in confirming sufficient accuracy for the individual steps. This might be a possible explanation of the fact that the *Fixed Camera View* yielded better results in the *needle alignment* step than the *Projection View* although the two visualization schemes are comparable in this step. Application of a Kalman filter might compensate for this disadvantage.

The advantages (+) and disadvantages (−) of the *Projection View* can be summarized as follows:

+ high targeting accuracy

+ display of relevant information only

+ suitable as stand-alone visualization for the targeting process

− high time requirements for the *needle insertion* step

− projection presented during the *needle insertion* step is not intuitive

− resolution is sometimes too low

Tool Tip Camera View

According to the performed evaluation, the *Tool Tip Camera View* is particularly suitable for the *needle insertion* step. In contrast, the *needle alignment* step can be performed more accurately with other visualization methods. Despite this, the *Tool Tip Camera View* yielded the best overall targeting accuracy which can be attributed to the fact that the orientation of the needle could be corrected during the insertion process, because of the lack of tissue between the artificial skin of the motion simulator and the liver. As in clinical practice, an initial directional misalignment cannot easily be corrected during insertion, a different visualization approach should be used for the alignment step.

The advantages (+) and disadvantages (−) of the *Tool Tip Camera View* can be summarized as follows:

+ best targeting accuracy

+ fast targeting possible

+ suitable as stand-alone visualization for the targeting process

− depth indication suboptimal

− suboptimal for the *needle alignment* process

Fixed Camera View

The relatively bad results of the *Fixed Camera View* for the needle *insertion step* can be attributed to the fact that it is relatively difficult to target the center of a point considering that the needle has its own (small) radius. This effect could be compensated by choosing a different representation of the needle.

The advantages (+) and disadvantages (−) of the *Fixed Camera View* can be summarized as follows:

+ intuitive

+ fast targeting possible

+ well suited for the *needle alignment* step

− bad overall targeting accuracy

− not well suited for the *needle insertion* step

Combined View

The *Combined View* yielded the second best targeting results of all views. The fact that it was outperformed by the *Tool Tip Camera View* can be attributed to the smaller display of the individual views as well as to the reduced attention of the operator due to an increased amount of presented information.

The advantages (+) and disadvantages (−) of the *Combined View* can be summarized as follows:

+ high targeting accuracy

+ combines the advantages of the individual visualization schemes

− individual views too small

− high time requirements

9.5 DERIVED GUIDANCE METHOD

Based on the results of the presented experiments, a three-stage visualization scheme for computer-assisted needle insertion along a predetermined trajectory was developed. The *Projection View* introduced in section 9.1.2 is applied for the *tip positioning* and *needle alignment* step while the *Tool Tip Camera View* guides the user during the *needle insertion* process (cf. Fig. 72).

Several modifications were made to the two views to address the drawbacks discussed in section 9.4. First, the projection plane presented during the *needle*

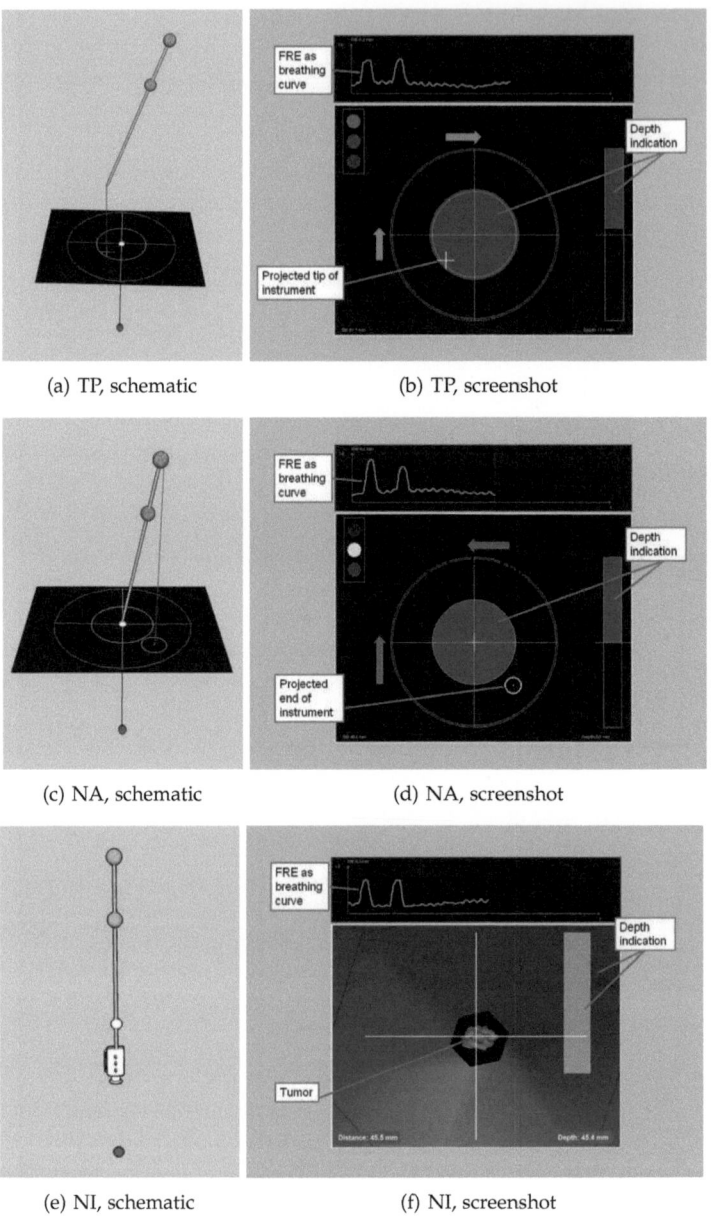

Figure 72: Three-stage visualization scheme providing separate views for the steps *tip positioning* (TP), *needle alignment* (NA) and *needle insertion* (NI).)

alignment step is set perpendicular to the vector connecting the target point and the tip of the instrument (as opposed to the planned trajectory). As by the time this step is performed, the needle tip is meant to be placed at the predetermined entry point, this vector should coincide with the planned trajectory. However, if there should be a small deviation between the actual position of the tip and the predetermined entry point, the projection vector and projection plane used allow to correct this error by adjusting the orientation of the needle accordingly.

As the depth indication is crucial for stopping the insertion of the needle at the correct position in order not to inadvertently penetrate through the tumor, an additional depth indicator was added to the *Tool Tip Camera View* (Fig. 72(f)): Once the insertion point has been reached, the position of the tip of the instrument within the *surgery tube* is indicated by a polygon-shaped structure. When the tip of the needle approaches the target point, the outer polygon (i.e., the end of the *surgery tube*) and the inner polygon approach each other, and the outer polygon touches the inner polygon just when the predetermined insertion depth is reached. This allows the user to focus the attention on the target point and the depth indication at the same time.

Finally, a breathing curve is extracted from the fiducial movement: Each time the visualization is refreshed, the least square method by Horn [58] is applied to find the best rigid transformation for mapping the current fiducial poses (represented by a set of landmarks) onto the initial fiducial poses extracted from the planning CT (represented by a set of corresponding landmarks). The associated FRE is an indicator of the deformation of the tissue and can be used to quantify how much the current state within the breathing curve resembles the state which the CT was taken in (cf. section 8.6). By continuously visualizing the FRE, a curve that reflects the breathing pattern of the patient is obtained (cf. Fig. 72).

(a) without respiration

	PV	TT	FC	CV
R1	3.9 ± 3.6	1.6 ± 0.4	7.0 ± 0.9	1.5 ± 0.1
R2	1.2 ± 1.2	1.1 ± 0.1	4.8 ± 2.1	1.6 ± 1.1
S1	0.9 ± 0.3	0.4 ± 0.2	4.1 ± 0.5	0.9 ± 0.2
M1	1.8 ± 0.4	0.7 ± 0.2	4.6 ± 0.6	0.6 ± 0.4
C1	1.0 ± 0.2	0.5 ± 0.1	4.4 ± 2.7	0.8 ± 0.2
C2	1.1 ± 0.9	0.6 ± 0.2	2.9 ± 0.1	1.1 ± 0.7
All	1.7 ± 1.1	0.8 ± 0.5	4.6 ± 1.4	1.1 ± 0.4

(b) with respiration

	PV	TT	FC	CV
R1	3.6 ± 2.9	1.0 ± 0.3	7.2 ± 3.8	2.2 ± 1.2
R2	2.0 ± 0.9	1.4 ± 0.2	5.7 ± 1.2	3.4 ± 2.7
S1	2.5 ± 1.0	1.1 ± 0.3	6.7 ± 2.2	1.2 ± 0.6
M1	1.2 ± 0.9	1.2 ± 0.7	4.9 ± 2.2	1.0 ± 0.6
C1	1.3 ± 0.5	0.9 ± 0.5	4.5 ± 1.8	0.5 ± 0.1
C2	2.0 ± 0.7	0.5 ± 0.2	7.4 ± 1.2	1.2 ± 0.3
All	2.1 ± 0.9	1.0 ± 0.3	6.1 ± 1.2	1.6 ± 1.0

(c) all

	PV	TT	FC	CV
R1	3.7 ± 2.9	1.3 ± 0.5	7.1 ± 2.5	1.8 ± 0.9
R2	1.6 ± 1.0	1.2 ± 0.2	5.3 ± 1.6	2.5 ± 2.1
S1	1.7 ± 1.1	0.8 ± 0.5	5.4 ± 2.1	1.1 ± 0.4
M1	1.5 ± 0.7	0.9 ± 0.5	4.8 ± 1.5	0.8 ± 0.5
C1	1.2 ± 0.4	0.7 ± 0.4	4.4 ± 2.1	0.7 ± 0.3
C2	1.6 ± 0.8	0.5 ± 0.2	5.1 ± 2.6	1.2 ± 0.5
All	1.9 ± 0.9	0.9 ± 0.3	5.4 ± 0.9	1.3 ± 0.7

Table 14: *Needle insertion* error (in mm) defined as the final distance between the target point and the tip of the instrument after the *needle insertion* step. For each operator, the mean error (± σ) averaged over all experiments with (a), without (b) and for all experiments (c) is given. *All* lists the mean (± σ) computed over the vector of means of the individual operators.

	PV	TT	FC	CV
R1	2.9 ± 1.2	2.0 ± 1.1	3.1 ± 1.3	2.9 ± 1.6
R2	2.6 ± 1.2	2.3 ± 1.7	2.4 ± 1.3	1.5 ± 0.9
S1	1.9 ± 0.7	1.2 ± 0.7	3.3 ± 2.7	2.1 ± 1.3
M1	1.8 ± 0.4	1.6 ± 1.0	3.2 ± 1.7	1.9 ± 1.8
C1	2.2 ± 2.2	1.7 ± 1.3	2.0 ± 1.2	1.3 ± 1.1
C2	1.9 ± 0.8	1.3 ± 1.1	2.0 ± 1.2	1.8 ± 1.0
All	2.2 ± 0.5	1.7 ± 0.4	2.7 ± 0.6	1.9 ± 0.6

Table 15: *Tip positioning* error (in mm) defined as the distance between the insertion point and the tip of the instrument after the *tip positioning* step. For each operator, the mean error (± σ) averaged over all experiments (with and without respiration) is given. *All* lists the mean (± σ) computed over the vector of means of the individual operators.

	PV	TT	FC	CV
R1	0.8 ± 0.4	0.9 ± 0.6	0.6 ± 0.2	0.9 ± 0.5
R2	1.3 ± 0.6	0.9 ± 0.5	1.0 ± 0.6	1.1 ± 0.9
S1	0.6 ± 0.4	1.0 ± 0.5	0.6 ± 0.3	0.6 ± 0.6
M1	0.7 ± 0.4	0.5 ± 0.3	0.3 ± 0.2	0.7 ± 0.5
C1	1.1 ± 0.3	1.5 ± 0.8	0.5 ± 0.2	1.0 ± 0.4
C2	0.7 ± 0.4	0.9 ± 0.2	0.7 ± 0.3	0.6 ± 0.2
All	0.9 ± 0.3	0.9 ± 0.3	0.6 ± 0.2	0.8 ± 0.2

Table 16: *Needle alignment* error (in °) defined as the angle between the planned trajectory and the needle axis after the *needle alignment* step. For each operator, the mean error (± σ) averaged over all experiments (with and without respiration) is given. *All* lists the mean (± σ) computed over the means of the individual operators.

(a) tip positioning

	PV	TT	FC	CV
R1	5 ± 1	6 ± 2	4 ± 1	6 ± 2
R2	4 ± 1	10 ± 7	7 ± 2	6 ± 1
S1	6 ± 2	9 ± 2	7 ± 4	11 ± 4
M1	5 ± 1	9 ± 2	10 ± 3	9 ± 2
C1	5 ± 1	5 ± 2	3 ± 1	5 ± 1
C2	5 ± 1	6 ± 1	7 ± 3	7 ± 2
All	5 ± 1	8 ± 2	6 ± 3	7 ± 2

(b) needle alignment

	PV	TT	FC	CV
R1	6 ± 4	8 ± 6	6 ± 4	7 ± 6
R2	8 ± 5	11 ± 12	8 ± 5	7 ± 3
S1	7 ± 4	11 ± 8	6 ± 2	11 ± 8
M1	7 ± 4	10 ± 7	11 ± 7	9 ± 7
C1	7 ± 4	8 ± 4	7 ± 3	8 ± 5
C2	6 ± 4	8 ± 5	9 ± 7	7 ± 4
All	7 ± 1	9 ± 2	8 ± 2	8 ± 2

(c) needle insertion

	PV	TT	FC	CV
R1	19 ± 4	18 ± 2	13 ± 3	23 ± 12
R2	33 ± 11	25 ± 6	11 ± 4	31 ± 9
S1	32 ± 12	18 ± 6	14 ± 2	18 ± 4
M1	20 ± 5	19 ± 2	17 ± 7	21 ± 4
C1	32 ± 13	25 ± 8	17 ± 2	26 ± 5
C2	17 ± 6	16 ± 4	13 ± 4	16 ± 5
All	25 ± 8	20 ± 4	14 ± 2	23 ± 5

Table 17: Time (in s) required for the steps *tip positioning* (a), *needle alignment* (b) and *needle insertion* (c). For each operator, the mean time (± σ) averaged over all experiments (with and without respiration) is given. *All* lists the mean (± σ) computed over the vector of means of the individual operators.

10

SYSTEM EVALUATION IN THE CLINICAL WORKFLOW

Experimental science is the queen of sciences and the goal of all speculation.

— Roger Bacon

To evaluate the performance of the developed prototype navigation system in the clinical workflow, three studies were conducted:

1. *Study I - in-vitro accuracy assessment* (section 10.1): The accuracy of the navigation system was assessed *in-vitro* with the respiratory liver motion simulator presented in chapter 5. Two operators performed 20 needle insertions in a total of four porcine livers, and the overall targeting accuracy as well as the user error were determined from control CT scans and the recorded tracking data.

2. *Study II – in-vivo accuracy assessment* (section 10.2): The accuracy of the navigation system was assessed *in-vivo* in two swine. For this purpose, the evaluation workflow developed in *study I* was applied *in-vivo*. Two medical experts and two non-experts performed 32 needle insertions in total. Based on control CT scans and the recorded tracking data, the overall targeting error, the TRE of the system and the user error were determined.

3. *Study III - navigated vs. conventional liver biopsy* (section 10.3): The conventional CT-guided liver biopsy method was compared to the navigated approach with respect to radiation exposure to the patient, accuracy and time. For this purpose, two experts performed a total of 40 biopsies (20 with each method) in five swine.

In all experiments, contrasted agar nodules were injected into the porcine livers as tumor models (Fig. 73). The following sections present the individual studies in detail.

10.1 STUDY I: IN-VITRO ACCURACY ASSESSMENT

The purpose of the *in-vitro* study was to (1) perform first experiments for evaluating the performance of the developed prototype navigation system in the clinical

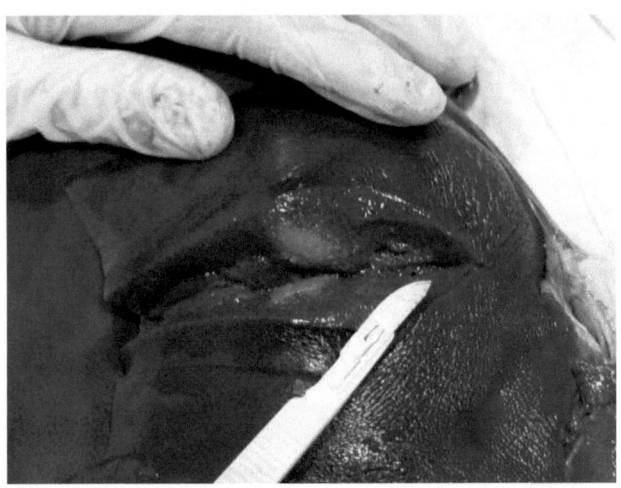

Figure 73: Agar nodule in a porcine liver. (Reprinted with permission from Maier-Hein *et al.* [92].)

workflow and (2) to develop an accuracy assessment workflow which could later be applied in an *in-vivo* study.

10.1.1 *Study design*

The approach for assessing the targeting precision of the developed navigation system is based on simulation of the clinical liver puncture workflow for porcine livers mounted onto a respiratory motion simulator. The following sections describe the workflow in detail and present the experimental conditions used in this study.

Experimental workflow

Each targeting procedure comprises four steps: *Preparation, trajectory planning, registration* and *navigation*, as well as a *post-processing* procedure. While the preparation step is conducted only once for each liver, the trajectory is planned separately for each lesion, and the remaining steps have to be repeated for each trial (i.e., every time that same nodule is targeted by one of the operators). The detailed workflow used for this study was as follows:

1. *Preparation*: Each porcine liver was prepared according to the following procedure:

    a) Based on the method proposed by Tsuchida *et al.* [148], a 5% agar dilution was prepared and mixed with contrast agent (1:15 v/v dilution).

b) Three to four agar nodules of volume 2 ml were then injected into the liver (Fig. 73). In case of a spherical lesion, a volume of 2 ml corresponds to a diameter of approximately 1.5 cm.

c) The liver was sewn to the diaphragm model (i.e., the Plexiglas® plate) of the motion simulator introduced in chapter 5.

d) Two 5DoF fiducial needles were inserted into the liver in *diagonal arrangement* (cf. section 8.3) as exemplarily shown in Fig. 74).

e) A planning CT scan of the motion simulator with the integrated porcine liver was acquired (Somatom Sensation 16 multidetector row scanner, Siemens, Erlangen, Germany). A fine resolution (0.75 mm slices) was used because the evaluation relies on accurate computation of the center of gravity of the agar nodule in both the planning CT and the control CT.

f) The motion simulator was used to simulate several breathing cycles reflecting the fact that the patients cannot hold their breaths between acquisition of the planning CT and registration.

2. *Trajectory planning*: For each lesion, a trajectory to the target was planned in the CT image as follows:

   a) The tumor was segmented semi-automatically on the basis of the graph-cut algorithm [18].

   b) The navigation target point was set to the center of gravity of the segmented tumor.

   c) An insertion point was chosen on the skin.

3. *Registration*: After trajectory planning, the initial registration was performed:

   a) The fiducial models were registered with the planning CT image by the semi-automatic algorithm described in section 7.2.

   b) The tracking coordinate system was registered with the CT coordinate system as described in section 7.1.

4. *Needle insertion*: An optically tracked instrument was used to target a given agar nodule with the navigation system. A navigation monitor provided the visualization for the targeting process according to the visualization scheme introduced in section 9.5. The targeting procedure was conducted at end-expiration with the artificial lungs relaxed. As gated experiments were performed and only two navigation aids were utilized for motion compensation, a rigid deformation model (cf. section 8.2) was chosen.

5. *Post-processing*: The targeting accuracy was determined with a control CT scan:

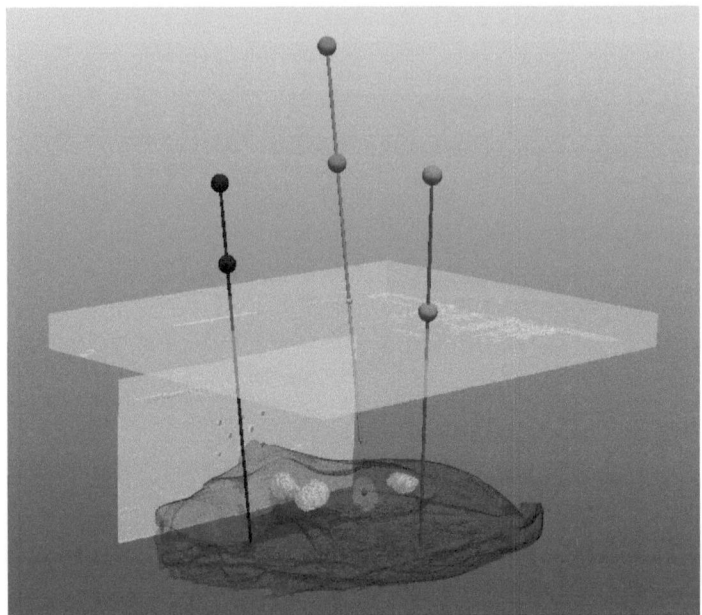

Figure 74: Reconstructed three-dimensional view of an experiment of *study I* showing the liver with four injected agar nodules, the inserted applicator, the two navigation aids, the Plexiglas® plate as diaphragm model , the artificial skin, the insertion point on the skin and the target point in one of the lesions. The inter-marker distances of the tools ranged from 50 mm to 90 mm. (Reprinted with permission from Maier-Hein *et al.* [92].)

a) Once the target was reached, the current position of the applicator was recorded. Then, the tool was released and its position was recorded again. The resulting tip "offset" was stored in image coordinates. This step was necessary because of the lack of tissue between the artificial skin (the foam) and the liver (cf. Fig. 74); once the applicator was released, the elastic skin relaxed and potentially pulled the tool several millimeters out of the liver.

b) A CT scan was acquired with the same settings as for the planning CT.

c) The tumor in the control CT image was segmented semi-automatically with the graph-cut algorithm [18].

d) The navigation target point was set to the center of gravity of the segmented tumor as reference.

e) The applicator model was registered with the control CT image by the semi-automatic algorithm described in section 7.2.

f) The position of the applicator was corrected by the offset computed in a).

g) The distance between the computed target point and the (corrected) position of the applicator tip was recorded as the overall error.

According to the proposed workflow, all lesions were punctured twice (once by each operator) based on one planning CT.

Experiments

In order to determine the overall targeting error of the proposed navigation system, one computer scientist (S1) and one fourth-year medical student (S2) conducted 20 targeting procedures in 10 tumor lesions following the workflow described above. Each participant simulated one biopsy from each lesion, and the following errors were recorded:

USER ERROR: The user error was defined as the final distance between the applicator tip (given by the tracking system) and the estimated target point position (according to the deformation model) when the target was reached.

OVERALL ERROR: The overall error was computed as described above (*post-processing*). It includes the user error, the instrument tracking error and the TRE (cf. Fig. 18). In addition, it is sensitive to changes in the applicator position between the instrument insertion step and the CT acquisition as discussed below.

10.1.2 *Results*

The proposed navigation system was successfully applied for simulating 20 liver biopsies according to the workflow described above. The applicator trajectory was generally non-parallel to the CT scanning plane, and the mean distance between the insertion point and the target point was 11.6 ± 1.0 cm.

The lesions were successfully hit in all trials with a mean FRE of 0.6 ± 0.2 mm for computation of the coordinate transformation. The mean final distance between the applicator tip and the center of gravity of the segmented agar nodule was 3.5 ± 1.1 mm averaged over all trials (Table 18).

If the first trial of subject S2 is regarded an outlier (user error: 4.0 mm) and excluded from consideration, the mean user error was of the same order of magnitude for both participants (<1 mm). The mean overall error was, however, significantly larger for S2 (4.1 ± 1.1 mm) than for S1 (2.8 ± 0.6 mm). In addition, the user error estimated with the navigation system was generally significantly smaller than the overall error, averaging only 0.8 ± 0.8 mm.

	S1	S2	S1 and S2
User error			
Mean ($\pm \sigma$)	0.5 $\pm$ 0.3	1.1 $\pm$ 1.1	0.8 $\pm$ 0.8
Median	0.4	0.7	0.6
Max	1.3	4.0	4.0
Overall error			
Mean ($\pm \sigma$)	2.8 $\pm$ 0.6	4.1 $\pm$ 1.1	3.5 $\pm$ 1.1
Median	3.0	4.2	3.3
Max	3.8	5.4	5.4

Table 18: User error and overall error for operators S1 (n = 10), S2 (n = 10) and both operators (n = 20) in mm (*study I*). The mean error ($\pm \sigma$), the median error and the maximum error for the entire set of lesions (n = 10) are listed.

10.1.3 Discussion

In-vitro evaluation of the targeting accuracy associated with the developed navigation system yielded a mean overall error of 3.5 $\pm$ 1.1 mm. The proposed evaluation approach has three key features. First, agar nodules mixed with contrast agent are used as targets, as they are clearly distinguishable from the surrounding liver tissue and can thus be segmented easily. In addition, they can be prepared such that they resemble real tumors in terms of shape and size. A second key feature is the utilization of the motion simulator as body model allowing for modelling of organ movement due to respiration, the most challenging problem in soft tissue interventions. Finally, the evaluation is performed *in-vitro*, thus allowing for experiments in moving organs, without recourse to animal experiments, which are time-consuming and expensive. According to a recent literature research, this study was the first to combine *in-vitro* experiments with simulation of respiratory motion.

The main drawback of the proposed evaluation approach is the suboptimal fixation of the applicator in the body model. Unfortunately, small movements of the tool can occur relatively easily once it has been released, because it is held in position only by a layer of foam, several millimeters of (elastic) liver tissue and the relatively soft agar nodule itself (Fig. 74). In other words, there is no assurance that the applicator will not shift further after the offset correction which potentially leads to inaccurate determination of the final applicator position and hence to an inaccurate error calculation. The large deviation between the user error and the overall error can be attributed to this phenomenon. Similarly, it is possible that the relatively large difference between the two observers with regard to the overall error was due to inaccurate determination of the applicator tip offset. The computer scientist (S1), who was more experienced in use of the system, released the applicator very carefully after each targeting and calculated the offset correction only after ensuring that the applicator had assumed its final position and showed no more movement. The other participant (S2) presumably conducted the process less carefully, causing a less accurate offset computation. In order to overcome these limitations, a real biopsy needle could be used as the applicator and the final tip position be marked with injected material. In this case, however, every nodule could only be used once.

It is worth noting, that the navigation aids were better affixed within the tissue than the instrument because they were generally inserted considerably deeper into the liver (Fig. 74) and were less effected by the resilience of the foam. As the same planning CT scan was used for *all* trials in one liver and the axes of the needles were nonparallel to each other, a shift of the navigation aids during one targeting procedure would have increased the registration error of the *next* trial. A very low FRE of only 0.6 mm on average was obtained, which suggests that the fixation of the fiducial needles was sufficient. Moreover, the overall error did not increase over time. To avoid problems related to this issue, however, the navigation aids could be attached to the skin or locked into the tissue via a soft tissue anchor.

Despite the technical problems discussed above, the obtained accuracy is high in comparison to related work. Zhang *et al.* [169] reported a success rate of 87.5% (n = 16) in two artificial tumor lesions (maximum diameter: 3.1 cm and 2.2 cm) implanted into a silicon liver mounted on a motion simulator . Subsequently, Levy *et al.* [82] evaluated the liver puncture system in a torso phantom for percutaneous intrahepatic portocaval systemic shunt. One operator performed a total of 45 punctures in vessels of different diameters and assessed the targeting accuracy with two orthogonal fluoroscopic images. The success rates were 0%, 33% and 53% for vessel diameters 3 mm, 5 mm and 7 mm respectively.

Other studies were performed in static phantoms or *in-vitro* without respiratory motion [29, 30, 151]. Das *et al.* [30] evaluated the feasibility and performance of an AR visualization prototype for virtual CT-guided interventional procedures in a multimodality abdominal phantom. With the aid of AR guidance, three radiologists performed 30 simulated biopsies of liver lesions of different sizes, and the position of the needle tip relative to the lesion was verified with US and CT. The authors reported a mean user error of 2.4 mm, an overall error of 3.5 mm and a system error of 2.1 mm (the standard deviation was not reported). Wacker *et al.* [151] also performed phantom experiments without respiratory motion to evaluate an AR navigation system in combination with a 1.5-T closed-bore MR imager. The phantoms used for simulating needle biopsies consisted of round buckets filled with gel, into which 20 hollow plastic tubes, 6 mm in diameter and height, were embedded as targets. The position of the needle tip in AR and MR space was compared in multiple imaging planes, and a mean targeting error of 2.6 mm (n = 20) was reported. Crocetti *et al.* [29] evaluated a fiducial based navigation system *in-vitro* in calf livers with radiopaque 1.5 mm lead pellets introduced into the tissue serving as targets. The authors reported a mean needle to target distance of 1.9 ± 0.7 mm (n = 24).

In conclusion, the proposed workflow demonstrated its suitability for *in-vitro* evaluation of image-guided systems. The overall targeting error yielded by the prototype system is sufficiently low for clinical use.

10.2 STUDY II: IN-VIVO ACCURACY ASSESSMENT

The purpose of *study II* was to assess the accuracy of the proposed navigation system *in-vivo*. To obtain a meaningful error analysis, the TRE and the user error were determined in addition to the overall error.

10.2.1 Study design

This study was approved by the Committee for Animal Care and Research of the Karlsruhe regional council. Like in Banovac *et al.* [6], the accuracy of the proposed navigation system was assessed by performing a total of 32 liver needle insertions in two 30 kg domestic swine (P1,P2) using hepatic agar nodules as artificial tumors. Two medical experts (E1,E2) with experience in CT-guided interventions (> 50 punctures each) and two fourth year medical students, which will be referred to as non-experts (NE1,NE2), performed eight interventions each. The following sections present the experimental conditions and describe the workflow in detail.

Animal Preparation

Each animal was prepared for the intervention according to the following procedure. The swine was anesthetized, endotracheally intubated and monitored throughout the experiments. A laparatomy was performed to inject four 2 ml agar nodules (5% agar dilution mixed with contrast agent (1:15 v/v dilution)) into the liver parenchyma using a 13 G venipuncture needle (cf. Fig. 75). Depending on the anatomy of the target liver and the location of the incision, the nodules were injected either into the medial segment of the left hepatic lobe or into the medial segment of the right hepatic lobe, avoiding critical structures such as large vessels and the gall bladder. A CT scan of the abdomen confirmed the size and location of the sphere-shaped nodules (diameter: 1-2 cm). On completion of the experiments, the anesthesized animal was killed by venous injection of 2 mmol/kg potassium chlorid to induce asystole.

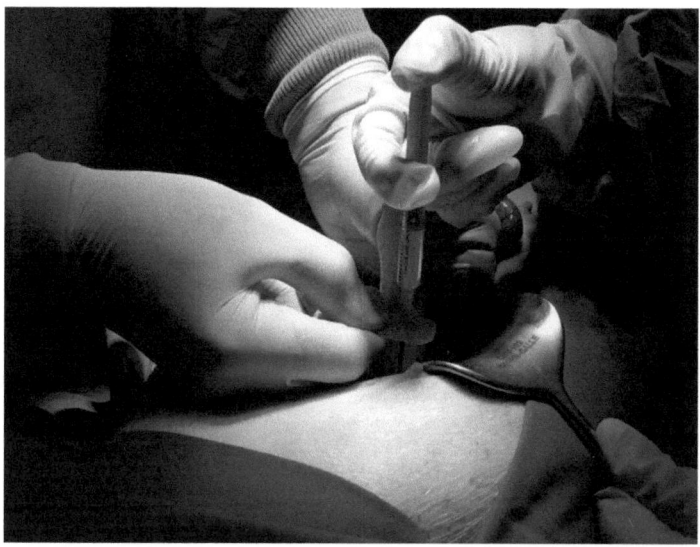

Figure 75: Injection of contrasted agar nodules into the liver of a swine.

Experimental Workflow

In each swine, one expert and one non-expert targeted each of the four lesions twice (two *passes*). For each pass, an ultrasound (US) device was used to insert the navigation aids such that they were arranged along the cranio-caudal axis of the animal and did not intersect a lesion. Custom-designed silicon patches (Fig. 76), which provide high friction compared to porcine skin, were used to affix the needles to the skin and thus prevented them from slipping out. Both operators then targeted the set of four lesions according to the following procedure. Pre-procedural expiratory CT scans of the animal were acquired (Toshiba Aquilion 16 slice multidetector CT scanner, Toshiba, Tokyo, Japan; 1 mm slice thickness) showing the entire set of lesions and both navigation aids. The steps *registration*, *path planning* and *needle insertion* were then performed as described in section 10.1.1. During needle insertion, the swine was held in expiration for 20 seconds intervals. Once the operator was satisfied with the instrument position, a control CT scan was acquired with the same settings as for the planning scan. Note that one planning CT scan was used for four needle insertions performed by one operator (i.e., for one pass). Furthermore, one fiducial needle configuration was used for both the expert and the non-expert to obtain comparable experimental conditions. In P1, the non-expert inserted the fiducial needles both times and in P2, the expert inserted the needles. In all second passes, the lesions were targeted in reverse order. Tables 21 and 22 list the experiments in chronological order.

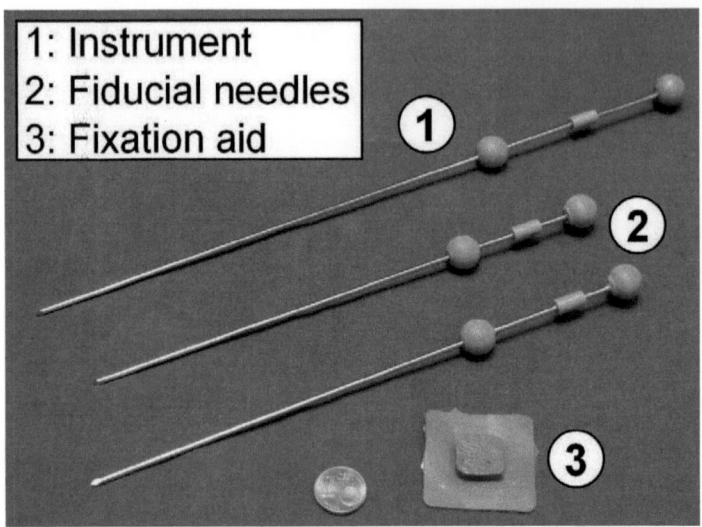

Figure 76: Navigation tools for *study III*. Instrument (1) and navigation aids (2) with a needle radius of 1 mm and inter-marker distances ranging from 45 mm to 75 mm. The fixation aid (3) is composed of silicon and prevents the fiducial needles from slipping out. (Reprinted with permission from Maier-Hein *et al.* [96].)

Accuracy assessment

The majority of accuracy studies on guidance systems for needle punctures evaluate the overall targeting error, i.e., the distance between a reference target position and the final position of the tip of an inserted instrument in post-procedural images. Unfortunately, this error depends crucially on the provided visualization scheme and the experience of the user. To be able to quantify the contribution of different sources of error, the user error and the TRE were also determined:

USER ERROR: The user error was defined as the distance between the tip of the instrument and the planned target point according to the navigation system prior to the control CT acquisition. The associated FRE of the corresponding rigid transformation (cf. section 8.1.2), which will be referred to as FRE^{user}, can be computed with eq. 7.4.

TRE: The TRE, which is the distance between the true target position and the estimated target position, was approximated from the two CT scans as follows: First, the fiducial needles were registered with the control CT scan with the algorithm described in section 7.2.1. Next, a set of control points were

	Limitations
User error	• affected by inaccurate tool geometry
TRE	• inaccurate lesion segmentation
	• contrast agent (for locating lesions) diminishes over time
	• Registered needles as opposed to tracked needles are used to estimate the target position
Overall error	• inaccurate registration of the instrument to the control CT scan (e.g., due to oscillation of the tool during image acquisition)
	• inaccurate lesion segmentation
	• contrast agent (for locating lesions) diminishes over time
	• instrument may move prior to or during control CT acquisition

Table 19: Limitations in computation of the user error, the TRE and the overall error defined in section 10.2.1 (*study II*). The sources causing theses errors are discussed in section 4.4.

extracted from the registered needles (cf. section 8.1), and a point-based rigid registration of the two CT scans was performed with these landmarks. The resulting rigid transformation $\Phi_{control}$ was then applied to transform the navigation target point t_0 computed in the planning CT scan to the control CT scan, and the TRE was defined as:

$$TRE = \left\| \vec{t}_{control} - \Phi_{control}(\vec{t}_0) \right\|_2 \qquad (10.1)$$

where $\vec{t}_{control}$ was the center of gravity of the segmented lesion in the control CT scan and $\|\cdot\|_2$ denotes the Euclidean norm. The associated FRE, which will be referred to as $FRE^{control}$, was also stored. Note that the true TRE originates from the tracked fiducial needles as opposed to the registered needle positions.

OVERALL ERROR: The overall targeting error, or CT error, was defined as the distance between the tip of the inserted instrument and the center of gravity of the lesion in the control CT scan. To compute the error, the instrument model was registered to the control CT scan with the semi-automatic approach described in section 7.2, and the lesion was segmented semi-automatically with the graph-cut algorithm [18].

The sources contributing to the individual errors were already discussed in section 4.4. The limitations in assessing them with the proposed workflow are given in Tab. 19. Note that although the overall error can be approximated by the user error and the TRE, the individual components cannot be related because they were computed on different images.

10.2.2 Results

The proposed navigation system was applied for 32 needle insertions according to the workflow described above. The lesions were hit in 97% of all trials (31 out of 32) with a mean user error of 2.4 ± 2.1 mm, a mean TRE of 2.1 ± 1.1 mm and a mean overall error of 3.7 ± 2.3 mm averaged over all trials (Tab. 20). When the needle insertion was conducted immediately after the planning CT acquisition (first trial after CT acquisition), the TRE and the overall targeting error dropped to 1.7 ± 1.4 mm (n = 8) and 2.3 ± 1.0 (n = 8) respectively. The results of the individual trials are shown separately for the two swine in Tab. 21 and 22 respectively. The non-experts obtained better results than the medical experts with mean user errors of 1.6 ± 1.2 mm compared to 3.2 ± 2.4 mm. Figure 77 shows an example of an inserted instrument in a control CT scan.

The mean trajectory length was 5 ± 3 cm ranging from 1 cm to 11 cm. Despite the leverage effect, the targeting error did *not* increase with an increasing depth of the lesion, as shown in Fig. 78.

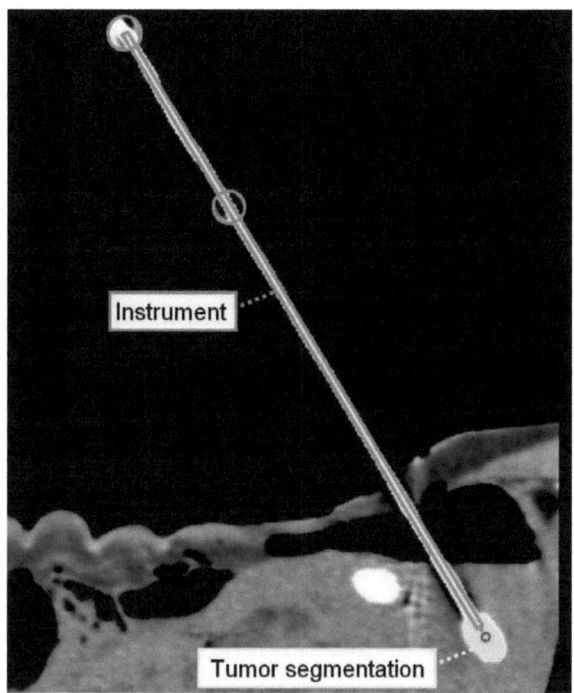

Figure 77: Control CT scan showing the registered instrument, the segmented lesion within the liver and the center of gravity of the lesion (dark circle). (Reprinted with permission from Maier-Hein et al. [96].)

The shift of the tumor relative to the navigation aids, which was computed from the registered images in the control CT coordinate system (cf. section 10.2.1), occured primarily in anterior-posterior direction, which corresponds to the y-axis of the image coordinate system. An example is shown in Fig. 79. Similarly, the direction of the error vector measured in the control CT scan was not (necessarily) along the needle axis but also in anterior-posterior direction with a mean y-component of +1.9 mm, reflecting a shift downwards.

The mean time for performing four needle insertions based on one planning CT scan (i.e., for one pass) was 57 ± 19 min with a mean setup time of 27 min, which comprises the times for *fiducial insertion* (24 ± 15 min), *planning CT acquisition* (1 ± 0 min) and *registration* (2 ± 1 min). The mean time for path planning and targeting was 5 ± 4 min and 2 ± 1 min respectively. Apart from the fiducial insertion step, experts and non-experts obtained comparable results (Tab. 23).

	TRE	$FRE^{control}$	User error	FRE^{user}	Overall error
Mean ($\pm \sigma$)	2.1 ± 1.1	0.7 ± 0.4	2.4 ± 2.1	0.9 ± 0.4	3.7 ± 2.3
RMS	2.4	0.8	3.1	0.9	4.3
Median	1.9	0.6	1.7	0.7	3.4
Max	5.4	1.9	11.0	1.7	11.6

Table 20: Error statistics (all in mm) computed on the entire set of 32 trials according to the definitions in section 10.2.1. The mean error ($\pm \sigma$), the RMS error, the median error and the maximum error for all experiments in *study II* are listed (n = 32).

10.2.3 Discussion

Evaluation of the developed prototype navigation system yielded a mean user error of 2.4 ± 2.1 mm, a TRE of 2.1 ± 1.1 mm and an overall targeting error of 3.7 ± 2.3 mm averaged over 32 needle insertions performed by four operators in two swine. Breaking the overall error down into multiple components made it possible to quantify the contribution of different error sources.

According to Tab. 24, the proposed system is highly accurate in comparison with related work. This can mainly be attributed to the application of needle-shaped fiducials for registration and motion compensation. Furthermore, optical tracking is known to be considerably more accurate than electromagnetic tracking. The user error is presumably also comparatively low - unfortunately, it has not been assessed in other studies (Tab. 24).

Study design for *in-vivo* accuracy assessment of guidance systems is challenging, and many different approaches have been investigated. Zhang et al. [169] injected contrasted agar nodules into the livers of two ventilated swine. The targeting error (median: 8.3 mm) was determined from fluoroscopic images in anterior-posterior and lateral views. As these images were only two-dimensional, the target registration error (TRE) could not be determined with this approach. Fichtinger et al. [40] conducted experiments in ventilated swine cadavers and used stainless-steel staples as targets. The overall targeting error (6.4 ± 1.8 mm) was determined from control CT scans. As the navigation system was based on 2D image overlay (the instruments were not tracked), there was no quantitative positional information throughout the procedure and the user error could thus not be determined. Khan et al. [72] evaluated their navigation system in human cadavers, with three different targets: A predefined position within the ascending aorta, a calcified plaque in an artery, and the tip of a port catheter. The overall error (8.4 ± 1.8 mm) was determined from control CT scans, but the user error and the TRE were not reported. Nicolau et al. [113] evaluated the system on six patients who underwent radiofrequency ablation of the liver. The final position of the inserted instrument

	TRE	$FRE^{control}$	User error	FRE^{user}	Overall error
NE1, pass 1					
L1	0.6	0.3	0.7	0.9	1.0
L2	2.0	0.6	3.3	1.2	6.1
L3	2.7	0.4	0.9	0.8	3.3
L4	3.7	1.6	1.2	1.6	4.4
E1, pass 1					
L1	1.2	0.4	4.6	0.7	5.8
L2	1.4	0.8	3.4	1.1	6.1
L3	2.9	0.3	4.4	0.7	3.8
L4	1.8	0.9	2.0	1.7	3.4
NE1, pass 2					
L4	2.4	0.5	1.7	1.1	2.9
L3	1.5	0.6	1.5	0.8	3.4
L2	3.2	0.9	3.9	0.6	3.8
L1	3.3	0.9	3.1	1.3	3.2
E1, pass 2					
L4	2.3	0.7	4.7	0.6	5.0
L3	1.7	0.3	4.1	0.4	6.3
L2	2.4	0.9	11.0	0.6	11.6
L1	2.2	0.4	3.3	0.6	5.2
Expert	2.0 ± 0.6	0.6 ± 0.3	4.7 ± 2.7	0.8 ± 0.4	5.9 ± 2.5
Non-Expert	2.4 ± 1.0	0.7 ± 0.4	2.0 ± 1.2	1.0 ± 0.3	3.5 ± 1.4
Both	2.2 ± 0.8	0.7 ± 0.4	3.4 ± 2.5	0.9 ± 0.4	4.7 ± 2.3

Table 21: TRE with corresponding FRE, user error with corresponding FRE and overall targeting error (all in mm) as defined in section 10.2.1 (*study II*) for the individual trials (Lx: Lesion ID) of expert 1 (E1) and non-expert 1 (NE1) in swine 1 (P1). The mean errors ($\pm \sigma$) for the experts (n = 16), the non-experts (n = 16) and all operators (n = 32) are also reported.

	TRE	$FRE^{control}$	User error	FRE^{user}	Overall error
E2, pass 1					
L1	3.0	1.3	2.1	1.2	0.6
L2	1.8	0.9	2.6	1.4	3.3
L3	4.1	1.6	2.1	1.5	3.7
L4	5.4	1.9	0.9	1.4	7.1
NE2, pass 1					
L1	1.2	0.3	0.6	0.6	0.9
L2	1.5	0.6	3.7	0.4	2.7
L3	1.3	0.6	0.9	0.5	2.2
L4	1.9	0.6	0.9	0.7	3.0
E2, pass 2					
L4	1.0	0.2	1.8	0.3	0.7
L3	0.6	0.2	1.3	0.5	2.5
L2	1.7	0.6	1.7	0.6	3.9
L1	0.9	0.8	1.6	0.5	2.9
NE2, pass 2					
L4	1.5	0.7	1.0	0.7	1.8
L3	0.5	1.1	0.9	1.1	1.6
L2	2.8	0.8	0.8	0.9	0.7
L1	2.5	0.5	0.5	0.8	3.9
Expert	2.3 ± 1.7	0.9 ± 0.6	1.7 ± 0.5	0.9 ± 0.5	3.1 ± 2.1
Non-Expert	1.6 ± 0.7	0.7 ± 0.2	1.2 ± 1.0	0.7 ± 0.2	2.1 ± 1.1
Both	2.0 ± 1.3	0.8 ± 0.5	1.5 ± 0.8	0.8 ± 0.4	2.6 ± 1.7

Table 22: TRE with corresponding FRE, user error with corresponding FRE and overall targeting error (all in mm) as defined in section 10.2.1 (*study II*) for the individual trials (Lx: Lesion ID) of the expert 2 (E2) and non-expert 2 (NE2) in swine 2 (P2). The mean errors (± σ) for the experts (n = 16), the non-experts (n = 16) and all operators (n = 32) are also reported.

	Experts	Non-experts	All
Fiducial insertion	14 ± 5	33 ± 16	24 ± 15
Planning-CT	1 ± 0	1 ± 0	1 ± 0
Registration	2 ± 1	2 ± 1	2 ± 1
Path planning	5 ± 3	5 ± 4	5 ± 4
Targeting	2 ± 1	2 ± 1	2 ± 1

Table 23: Mean duration (± σ) (in min) of the individual steps of the navigation workflow for the experts (n = 16), the non-experts (n = 16) and averaged over all operators (n = 16) for *study II*.

was ascertained from a control CT scan, which was registered rigidly with the planning CT scan based on the segmented liver surfaces. Both the tracked needle position and the real needle position were transformed to the planning CT scan and the distance between the tips of the needles were defined as the system error (mean: 4.3 mm). As the tracking information was not used to guide the needle placement, neither the user error nor the overall targeting error could be reported. Similarly, Krücker *et al.* [78] defined different anatomical targets in 19 patients and reported the *tracking error* (3.5 ± 1.9 mm and 5.8 ± 2.6 mm without/with previous instrument positions) as the distance between the virtual needle position superimposed onto the control CT scan and the true needle position ascertained from the image. The registration of the planning CT scan with the control CT scan was based on surface markers serving as landmarks for a point-based registration. Again, the user error and the overall targeting error could not be reported because the navigation system had not been used to guide needle placement. Wacker *et al.* [151] used the pancreatic tail (n = 3), the gallbladder (n = 3), a renal calyx (n = 2) and a central bile duct (n = 2) as targets in three swine, and one author performed ten puncture attempts (one in each target). The overall targeting error (9.6 ± 4.9 mm) was obtained from verification MR scans but the user error, the TRE and the system error were not reported.

One purpose of this study was to assess the contribution of different error sources to the overall targeting error. To achieve this, a modification of the approach proposed by Zhang *et al.* [169] was applied, yet control CT scans were used for instrument verification as opposed to 2D fluoruscopic images. A limitation of the proposed evaluation approach is the lack of fixation of the instrument within the lesion. In fact, all participants in this study reported a shift of the instrument once they released it to allow for the control CT scan acquisition, which led to a relatively large user error (and thus overall error) in several cases. Despite the fact that the operators were allowed to reposition the instrument until they were satisfied with the result, optimal positioning was not always possible due to the weight of the

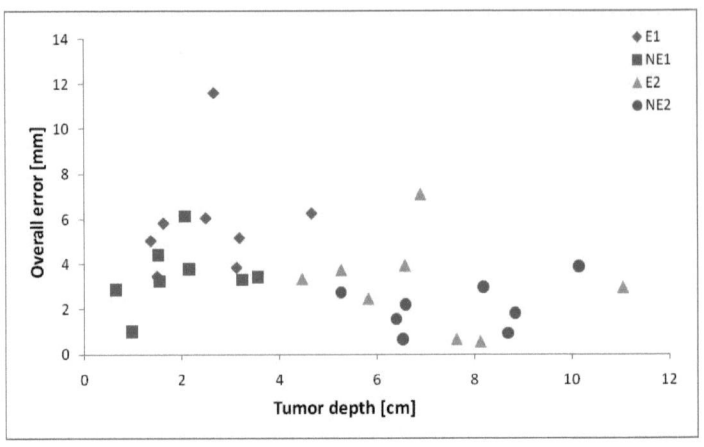

Figure 78: Overall targeting error plotted against tumor depth (*study II*).

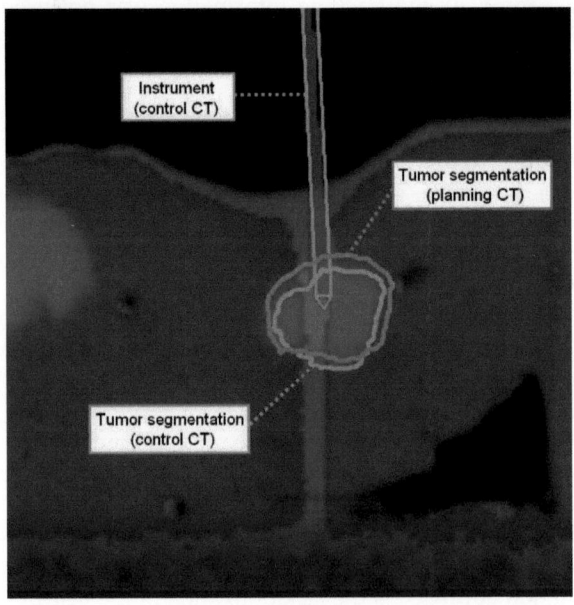

Figure 79: Planning CT scan registered to the control CT scan showing the shift of the tumor due to instrument insertion (*study II*). The segmentations of the lesions are shown as dark contours. (Reprinted with permission from Maier-Hein et al. [96].)

instrument, which tended to pull the needle partly out of the liver when the trajectory was short. One lesion (P1,L2), for instance, was situated so close to the liver capsule that the instrument did not even stay within the liver parenchyma which led to high user errors of up to 12 mm. Note that this phenomenon is a possible explanation for the fact that short trajectories sometimes yielded lower accuracy: The deeper the lesion, the better the fixation of the needle. Unfortunately, the anatomy of the porcine livers did not always allow for implantation of deeply located lesions. Anchoring the instrument within the liver itself was considered to address this issue, yet, the soft tissue anchor would have potentially destroyed the lesion and thus not have allowed multiple needle insertions. Needle movement is generally a problem for both conventional and computer-assisted needle insertions, however, it has not been discussed in related studies.

Surprisingly, the non-experts performed better than the experts with a user error of 1.6 ± 1.2 mm compared to 3.2 ± 2.4 mm. A possible explanation for this phenomenon is the fact that the experts are accustomed to inserting the needle very quickly. The non-experts, on the other hand, had to learn the procedure without any prior knowledge and were thus more amenable to the navigated method. This issue will be investigated in the future.

Although gated experiments were performed, the TRE was significantly larger than zero, indicating tumor shift and/or deformation that was not captured by the fiducials. As the needle insertions that were conducted immediately after the planning CT acquisition yielded better accuracy than the remaining ones, this can be attributed to the manipulation of the tissue by repeated needle insertions. Furthermore, the instrument was reused many times and thus potentially caused more tissue deformation than a sharp needle would have caused. Registration of the planning CT scan with the control CT scan showed that the tumor shifted primarily in anterior-posterior direction - not (necessarily) along the direction of the instrument. This displacement could possibly have been captured by the fiducial needles if they had been affixed within the liver itself and not on the skin, which, however, would have raised new issues in the context of tool design and risk of injury.

The operators performed four needle insertions based on only one planning CT, reflecting the fact that needle repositioning is very common during RFA procedures to completely destroy a tumor. When the needle insertion was conducted immediately after the planning CT acquisition, the error dropped significantly. Therefore, the tradeoff between accuracy and time should be considered when deciding on an optimal number of planning CTs in practice.

The time for inserting the fiducial needles via ultrasound was relatively long (24 min) especially for the non-experts (33 min) who had no experience in punctures. This can partly be attributed to the fact that the operators were not familiar with the anatomy of the swine. Furthermore, one fiducial needle configuration was used for targeting all four lesions, which had to be considered when planning the fiducial insertion. Still, intervention time was not the focus of this study. In a second *in-vivo* study (cf. section 10.3), an average procedure time of 20 min (n = 20) was obtained.

In conclusion, the proposed liver navigation system allows for accurate needle placement into hepatic tumors in ventilated swine based on only one planning CT scan. The advantages and shortcomings of the proposed approach in comparison to related work are discussed in chapter 11.

10.3 STUDY III: NAVIGATED VS. CONVENTIONAL LIVER BIOPSY

The purpose of the second *in-vivo* study was to compare the conventional CT-guided liver biopsy method with the navigated approach with respect to radiation exposure to the patient, accuracy and time.

10.3.1 Study design

This study was approved by the Committee for Animal Care and Research of the Karlsruhe regional council. A total of 40 liver biopsies were performed in five 22-29 kg domestic swine ($P_1,\ldots,P_5$) using contrasted blue-colored hepatic agar nodules as artificial tumors. A radiologist (E1) with a high level of experience in punctures (> 500) applied the conventional liver biopsy method to a total of 20 targets in the five swine. Another medical expert (E2) with experience in CT-guided interventions (> 50 punctures) used the developed navigation system to target the same nodules. A semi-automatic biopsy gun with integrated coaxial needle (BioCut™ Integral 16 G×25 cm) was used for tissue extraction (cf. Fig. 30). The following sections present the experimental conditions and describe the workflow in detail.

Animal Preparation

The animals were prepared according to the procedure described in section 10.2.1. In this study, however, 0.5 ml agar nodules were utilized as artificial tumors (note: In the case of sphere-shaped lesions, a volume of 0.5 ml corresponds to a diameter of approximately 5 mm). Furthermore, some blue color was added to the agar mixture to be able to distinguish the lesions clearly from liver parenchyma when extracting tissue (cf. Fig. 80(f)).

Experimental Workflow

In each swine, both operators targeted a set of four lesions once. Prior to the experiments, an orientation CT scan was acquired to verify that all tumors were inside the liver. The four nodules whose shape most closely resembled spheres

Authors	Fiducials	Trials	System error	TRE	User error	Overall error
Banovac et al. [6]	4 SM, 1 FN	n = 32	-	-	-	$8.3^a \pm 3.7$
Fichtinger et al. [40]	-	n = 22	-	-	-	6.4 ± 1.8
Khan et al. [72]	9 SM	n = 42	-	-	-	8.4 ± 1.8
Krücker et al. [78]	5-7 SM	n = 61	5.8 ± 2.6	-	-	-
Krücker et al. [78]	5-7 SM, 1-8 PIP	n = 59	3.5 ± 1.9	-	-	-
Maier-Hein et al. [96]	2 FN	n = 32	-	2.1 ± 1.1	2.4 ± 2.1	3.7 ± 2.3
Nicolau et al. [113]	6 - 15 SM	n = 6	$4.3 \pm n/a$	-	-	-
Wacker et al. [151]	1 RF	n = 10	-	-	-	9.6 ± 4.9

Table 24: Selection of *in-vivo* accuracy studies for computer-assisted needle placement in the liver. All errors are given as mean ($\pm \sigma$) in mm. SM: Skin marker, FN: Fiducial needle, PIP: Previous instrument position, RF: Reference frame. Generally, not all parameters were assessed, as indicated by "-". For Krücker et al. [78] the system error represents the error which the authors referred to as tracking error (cf. section 10.2.3).

---

a Banovac et al. [6] reported the median as opposed to the mean targeting error.

were chosen as targets[1]. In P1 and P2, E1 was the first to target all lesions. In P3 to P5, E2 began with the experiments. The order was randomized.

In the case of the conventional method, the workflow for targeting a lesion comprised the following steps (cf. Fig. 80):

1. *Preparation:*
    a) *Orientation CT acquisition:* A pre-procedural expiratory CT scan of the animal was acquired (Toshiba Aquilion 16 slice multidetector CT scanner, Toshiba, Tokyo, Japan; 3 mm slice thickness) to locate the tumor.
    b) *Mounting of needles:* A set of one way cannula was placed above the tumor region as shown in Fig. 80(a).
    c) *Planning CT acquisition:* A second CT scan (same settings as in a)) was acquired showing the thin needles (cannula) as small dots on the individual transversal CT slices.
    d) *Path planning:* A trajectory to the target was planned by selecting (1) a transversal CT slice, (2) the mid-point between two fiducial needles on that slice as insertion point, (3) an in-plane insertion angle and (4) an insertion depth. If necessary, the out-of-plane angle was additionally estimated. As in clinical practice, the chosen angle was copied from the monitor as shown in Fig. 80(b).

2. *Targeting*
    a) *Insertion point localization:* The insertion point was located by identifying the chosen transversal CT slice via a laser beam and marking the midpoint between the two chosen needles within that slice (cf. Fig. 80(c)). For this purpose, the swine was held in expiration.
    b) *Needle alignment:* The instrument was aligned with the planned trajectory. For this purpose, an assistant continuously compared the planned in-plane insertion angle with the actual angle of the instrument as shown in Fig. 80(d).
    c) *Needle insertion:* The needle was gradually advanced and/or redirected while its position was reassessed with control CT scans until the desired needle position was obtained[2]. The swine was held in expiration for 20 seconds intervals for this purpose. It is worth mentioning that in some cases, a thin needle was used instead of the instrument to initially locate the correct path. Once the trajectory was correct according to a control CT scan, the actual instrument was inserted.

---

1 In P1, only three lesions were used because one of the chosen nodules was extremely small, and the contrast agent diminished over time. To compensate for this, five nodules were punctured in P4.
2 The instrument required a placement of the tip of the needle several millimeters before the tumor - not in the center of the lesion.

d) *Tissue extraction:* Once the operator was satisfied with the instrument position, he used a semi-automatic biopsy gun to extract a tissue probe (cf. Fig. 80(e)). If blue-colored agar representing tumor tissue had been extracted (cf. Fig. 80(f)), the trial was complete. Otherwise, the workflow was repeated beginning from step *planning CT acquisition, path planning, needle alignment, needle insertion,* or *tissue extraction.*

As the fiducial needles were removed after each successful biopsy, the individual experiments can be regarded independent of each other.

The workflow for the navigated method was as follows:

1. *Preparation:* The workflow for preparing the needle insertion was the same as in *study II* (cf. section 10.2.1), comprising the steps *planning of fiducial insertion, fiducial insertion, CT acquisition, path planning* and *initial registration.*

   a) *Needle insertion:* Guided by the navigation monitor, the operator used the optically tracked semi-automatic biopsy gun (cf. Fig. 80(f)) to target the lesion. For this purpose, the swine was held in expiration for 20 seconds intervals. The target point was defined as the point on the planned trajectory with a distance of 5 mm to the center of the lesion.

   b) *Tissue extraction:* The operator used the instrument to extract a tissue sample. If blue-colored agar (cf. Fig. 80(f)) was in the notch of the instrument, the trial was complete. Otherwise, the workflow had to be repeated from the step *CT acquisition, path planning,* or *needle insertion* (chosen by the operator).

Evaluation

To compare the conventional CT-guided biopsy method with the navigated method, the following parameters were evaluated:

RADIATION EXPOSURE: The number of CT scans required for a successfull biopsy served as an indicator for the radiation exposure to the patient. Note that the actual radiation exposure depends on many parameters including the physical properties of the CT scanner, the chosen slice thickness and the acquired volume. Unfortunately, different persons were responsible for operation of the CT scanner in this study, and the acquired image volume was not always set to an optimal size to minimize the radiation dose. In consequence, reporting of the radiation dose would lead to misleading values.

ACCURACY: Two parameters were recorded as indicators for the accuracy of the respective method:

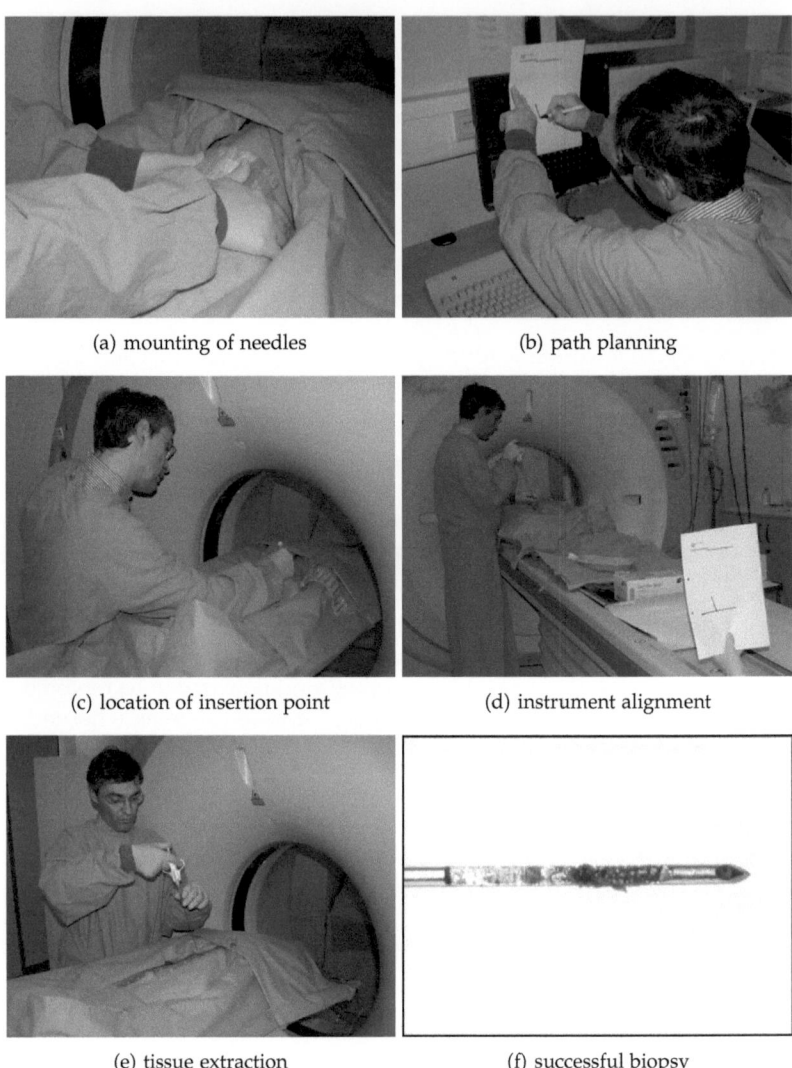

Figure 80: Workflow for conventional CT-guided liver biopsies in *study III* (cf. Fig. 5). After CT acquisition, a set of needles is placed above the tumor region (a). Next, a second CT scan is acquired, which is used to plan a trajectory to the target (b). The insertion point is located (c), and the instrument is aligned with the planned trajectory (d). Finally, the needle is gradually advanced and/or redirected while its position is reassessed with control CT scans until the desired needle position is obtained. Once the operator is satisfied with the instrument position, a tissue sample is extracted (e). A successful completion of a biopsy requires blue-colored agar in the notch of the instrument (f).

- For each trial, the number of repositionings of the biopsy needle until a positive biopsy was obtained was recorded. In the case of the navigated method, a negative biopsy always required another needle insertion, hence, the number of repositionings was generally equal to (#*attempts* − 1) for each trial, where #*attempts* denotes the number of tissue extractions. In the case of the conventional method, the value was generally equal to the number obtained by subtracting the two planning CTs from the total number of CT scans acquired.
- The number of tissue extractions until a positive biopsy was obtained was also recorded. The *hit rate* was defined as:

$$\text{hit rate} = \frac{1}{\#attempts} \quad (10.2)$$

TIME: Total procedure time as well as the duration of the individual steps within the biopsy workflow were recorded to compare the methods with respect to time requirements.

To test whether there is a statistically significant difference in the means of the individual parameters for the two methods, a two-sided Wilcoxon rank-sum test was performed with $\alpha = 0.05$.

10.3.2 Results

All 20 lesions were successfully punctured with both the navigated and the conventional method. No complications occurred during navigated instrument insertion while two complications resulted from conventional CT-guided needle insertion: Puncture of the right inferior lobe of the lung and of a big vessel.

The mean trajectory length was 6 ± 3 cm for both methods. As shown in Fig. 81(a), the number of CT scans required for a successful completion of the intervention was 6.1 ± 3.8 and 1.2 ± 0.4 for the conventional and navigated method respectively. The corresponding mean number of repositionings of the instrument[3] was 3.2 ± 3.8 (conventional) and 0.2 ± 0.5 (navigated). While the lesions were generally hit at the first attempt with the navigated method, the number of repositionings of the instruments varied considerable in the case of the conventional method and generally incrased with an increasing needle trajectory (cf. Fig. 82).

In three cases, the navigated method required more than one CT scan either due to an unfavorable placement of the fiducial needles (two cases) or due to a negative biopsy. The additional times resulting from these adjustments were included in the overall procedure time as *operating errors* as shown in Tab. 26.

---

[3] In the case of the conventional method, the number of repositionings may refer to the actual biopsy needle or the (thinner) navigation needle that was used to locate the correct trajectory (cf. section 10.3.1)

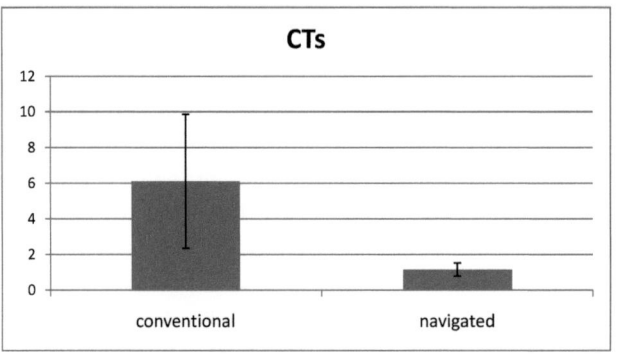

(a) number of CT scans

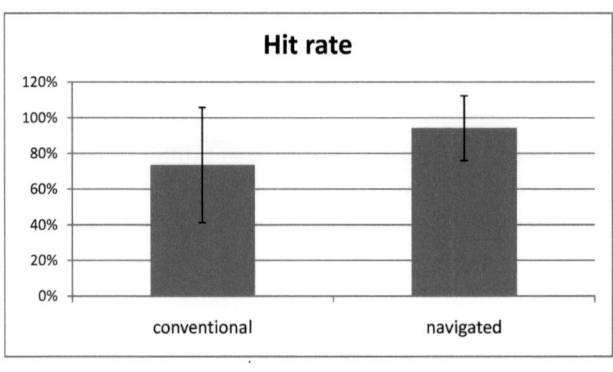

(b) hit rate

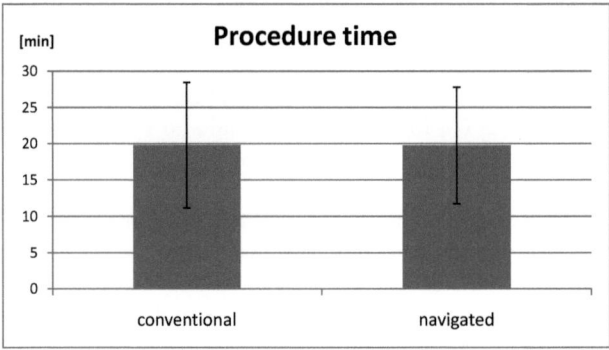

(c) procedure time

Figure 81: Number of CT scans required for a successful liver biopsy (a), hit rate according to eq. 10.2 (b) and overall procedure time (c) for *study III*. The mean ($\pm\ \sigma$) for all parameters is shown for both the conventional (n = 20) and the navigated method (n = 20).

	Duration conventional	Duration navigated
Orientation CT	6 ± 0^4	-
Planning	1 ± 1	2 ± 2
Mounting of fiducials	1 ± 0	6 ± 3
Planning-CT	1 ± 0	1 ± 0
Path planning	1 ± 1	6 ± 4
Registration	-	2 ± 2
Total preparation time	9 ± 1	17 ± 7

Table 25: Mean duration ($\pm \sigma$) (in min) of the individual steps within the workflow for preparing the actual targeting procedure for both the conventional (n = 20) and the navigated method (n = 20) (*study III*).

The mean number of tissue extractions per lesion was 2.3 ± 2.9 in the case of the conventional method and 1.2 ± 0.5 in the case of the navigated method, which corresponds to hit rates (cf. eq. 10.2) of 74 ± 32 % and 94 ± 18 % respectively (cf. Fig. 81(b)).

According to Fig. 81(c), procedure times were comparable for both methods (20 min). However, the preparation time was much longer in the case of the navigated method as shown in Tab. 25. The most time-consuming steps in the workflow were the *fiducial insertion* (6 ± 3 min) and the *path planning* (6 ± 4 min). The actual *targeting* (2 ± 1 min) was much faster compared to the conventional method (11 ± 9 min) (cf. Tab. 26).

Figure 83 shows the learning curves for the steps *preparation* and *targeting*. The time required for preparing the needle insertion could be decreased significantly in the course of the study in the case of the navigated method. For the conventional method, it was mainly the *targeting* step which improved over time.

According to the Wilcoxon rank sum test, the differences in number of CT scans, number of repositionings of the needle and hit rate are statistically significant ($p < 0.05$).

10.3.3 Discussion

The purpose of this study was to compare the conventional CT-guided liver biopsy method with the navigated approach with respect to radiation exposure to the patient, accuracy and time. According to the results, the navigated method outperformed the conventional method, reducing the mean number of repositionings of the needle by 95 % (conventional: 3.2 ± 3.8; navigated: of 0.2 ± 0.5) and the mean number of CT scans by 81 % (conventional: 6.1 ± 3.8; navigated: 1.2 ± 0.4). The mean hit rate was 74 ± 32 % (conventional) compared to 94 ± 18 % (navigated)

	Navigated	Conventional
Preparation	17 ± 7	9 ± 1
Targeting	2 ± 1	11 ± 9
Operating errors	1 ± 4	-
Overall	20 ± 8	20 ± 9

Table 26: Mean duration (± σ) (in min) for the steps *preparation* and *targeting* described in section 10.3.1 (*study II*) for both the conventional (n = 20) and the navigated method (n = 20). In the case of the navigated method, the operating errors (cf. section 10.3.2) are additionally listed.

for liver lesions with a diameter of approximately 5 mm (n = 20). Procedure times were comparable (conventional: 20 ± 9 min; navigated: 20 ± 8 min).

For both methods, the procedure time decreased in the course of the study. In the case of the navigated method, this can be attributed to the fact that the operator became more familiar with the anatomy of the swine as well as with the navigation system, which led to decreasing time requirements for *fiducial insertion* and *path planning*. In fact, procedure times were significantly smaller than in *study II* (cf. Tab. 23). In that study, the same operator had needed 14 ± 5 for the combined step *planning of fiducial insertion* (*study III*: 2 ± 2 min) and *fiducial insertion* (*study III*: 6 ± 3 min). It should be considered, however, that one fiducial configuration was used for targeting four lesions instead of one in *study II*.

In the case of the conventional method, the duration of the *targeting* step decreased significantly in the course of the experiments. A possible explanation for this is the fact that the expert used a different instrument in clinical routine and gradually became familiarized with the provided needle. In fact, he needed significantly more CT scans (11 ± 3) and attempts for tissue extraction (Hit rate: 23 ± 23 %) in the first swine than in the remaining animals (CTs: 4 ± 3; Hit rate: 82 ± 25 %).

It should be pointed out that the performance of the navigation system compared to the conventional method could not be tested in cases that are challenging for the conventional method because the needle trajectories were generally in-plane and relatively short (6 ± 3 cm). This can be attributed to the fact that the porcine livers were relatively flat. Furthermore, the experiments were conducted in ventilated swine because animals cannot cooperate with breath-hold instructions. In a clinical setting, needle insertion is more challenging in non-ventilated patients. In this case, a non-rigid deformation model for the navigated method might be necessary to obtain high accuracy over the entire breathing cycle.

The performance of the navigation system could be further optimized for clinical use. First, the biopsy needles were far too long considering the short trajectories that were chosen. Hence, the tool tip tracking error (caused by the lever effect and needle bending) and thus the overall targeting error could have been reduced by applying shorter instruments. Furthermore, the whole targeting procedure was based on only one planning CT. In practice, a control CT scan could be acquired when the target has been reached before starting with the actual therapeutic or diagnostic procedure to assure correct needle placement. On the other hand, this would increase intervention time and radiation exposure to the patient.

While navigated needle insertion is a very active field of research (cf. chapter 3), literature on *in-vivo* comparison of navigated insertion methods with conventional methods is sparse. Banovac et al. [7] compared the conventional fluoroscopy guided needle insertion technique with an electromagnetically guided approach (cf. Tab. 1). Seven punctures of a 2 ml agar lesion were conducted with each method in one swine. All trials with the navigated method were completed with a single insertion, whereas 2.9 passes on average were required for the conventional method. Overall targeting accuracy, determined from control CT scans, was approximately 7-8 mm and 6-7 mm for the conventional and navigated method respectively[5]. Khan et al. [72] compared the puncture accuracy of the conventional CT-guided technique with a navigated approach (cf. Tab. 1) in a human cadaver. The authors reported an overall targeting accuracy of 8.9 ± 1.7 mm (n = 42) and of 8.4 ± 1.8 mm (n = 42) for the conventional and the navigated method respectively. According to these studies, the accuracy of the navigation system presented in this work is high both in comparison to related work and to the conventional needle insertion method.

In conclusion, the proposed liver navigation system outperformed the conventional method with respect to radiation exposure to the patient and accuracy without increasing intervention time. The advantages and shortcomings of the proposed approach in comparison to the conventional method are further discussed in chapter 11.

---

[5] Only bar charts are provided, and the exact numbers are not stated.

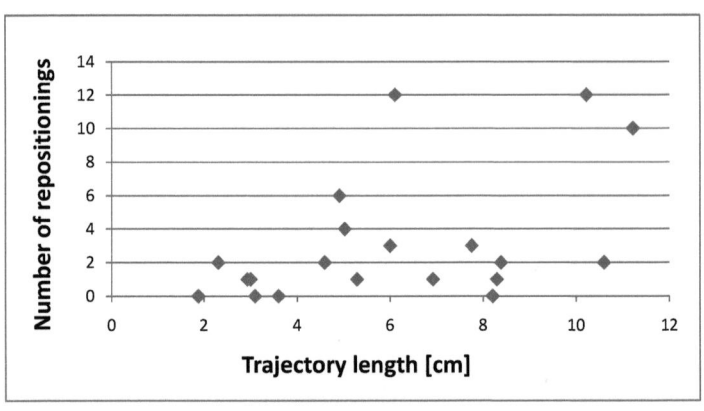

(a) conventional

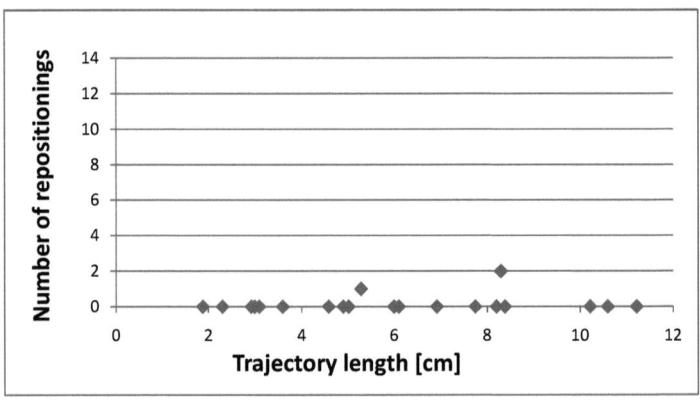

(b) navigated

Figure 82: Number of repositionings of the needle plotted against trajectory length for the conventional method (n = 20) (a) and the navigated method (n = 20) (b) in *study III*.

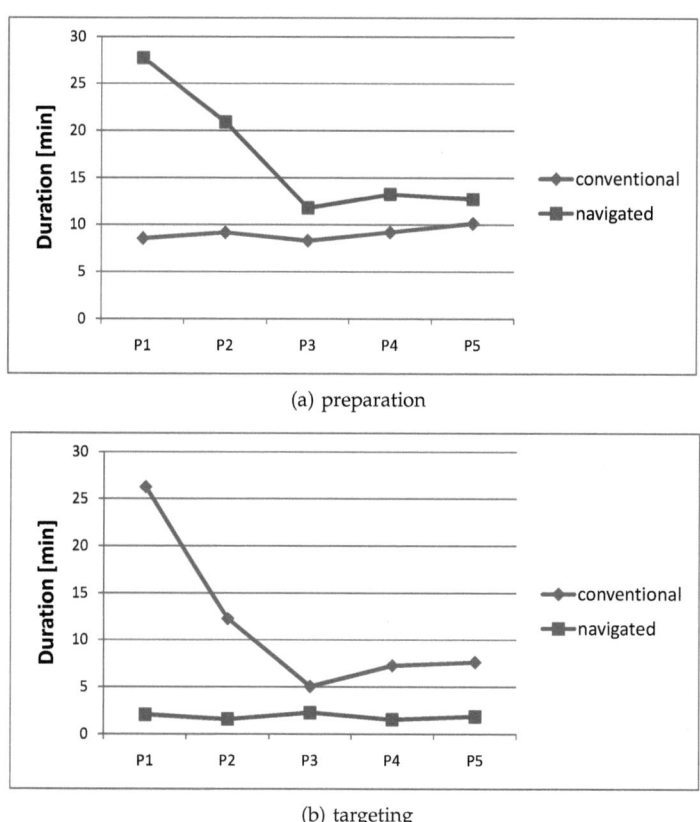

Figure 83: Learning curves for the steps *preparation* and *targeting* described in section 10.3.1 (*study III*). For each swine P_i, the mean duration averaged over all lesions is plotted for both the conventional and the navigated method.

11

DISCUSSION

> *Because the people who are crazy enough*
> *to think they can change the world,*
> *are the ones who do.*
>
> — Jack Kerouac

This thesis proposed a novel approach to computer-assisted needle insertion for percutaneous abdominal interventions. The concept was implemented and evaluated by means of percutaneous liver punctures, but is readily applicable to other organs and procedures. The individual modules of the developed navigation system as well as the studies for evaluating the proposed concepts were already discussed in detail in the corresponding chapters. This chapter discusses the navigation method in the context of related work and the state of the art in clinical practice.

Minimally invasive image-guided procedures for cancer diagnosis and therapy often require insertion of an elongate instrument into the tumor with a high degree of accuracy. In thermal ablation procedures, for example, placement of the instrument in the tumor center must be achieved with consideration of the exact zone of ablation relative to tumor margins and adjacent vital structures [28]. In biopsy procedures, accurate needle placement at the tumor margin, rather than in the necrotic center, may be required. Finally, accurate percutaneous needle placement in intrahepatic biliary ducts typically requires an accuracy of few millimeters over the needle trajectory course of several centimeters [28]. In general, the effectiveness and success of a treatment or of a diagnosis is highly dependent on the accuracy of the percutaneous insertion [1]. In the future, accuracy requirements will even further expand as targets for therapy become smaller due to improved image resolution and new forms of treatment such as gene therapy [28].

Recent developments in medical image processing and enhanced computer performance have paved the way for computer-assisted diagnosis and therapy. In clinical routine, however, image-guided systems are still restricted to bony or sufficiently rigid structures because they assume a constant target position throughout the intervention [166]. Transfer of existing navigation techniques to soft tissue organs is challenging for several reasons. First, soft tissue organs exhibit significant movement and deformation due to respiratory motion and manipulation by surgical instruments. In consequence, the position of the tumor relative to anatomical reference points changes continuously. Second, most systems rely on a simple image display technique, showing conventional axial, sagittal, and coronal views of pre-interventional static images in addition to a virtual 3D view, with tools displaced in relation to the (static) anatomy. This approach requires all anatomical structures to have the same (rigid) motion [166]. Furthermore, accurate targeting based on the standard views is challenging, especially when in-plane needle insertion is impossible. In consequence, motion compensation and guidance can be regarded as two key issues in soft tissue navigation.

Current research has turned its focus to procedures in soft tissue organs which can deform between different procedure steps (e.g. prostate), or throughout them (e.g. liver) [166]. One growing area of research aims at addressing the continuous organ movement resulting from cyclic respiratory and cardiac motion with patient specific models learnt in a pre-interventional training phase based on 4D data [16, 71]. Other methods are based on calibrating a tracked real-time imaging modality such as ultrasound in order to visualize surgical instruments in relation to the changing patient's anatomy [8, 39, 56]. Pre-interventional segmentations of the patient's anatomy can be transferred to the patient via image to image registration [156]. Unfortunately, most of the proposed approaches are not yet fast and robust enough to be integrated into an image-guided system. Furthermore, relatively little attention has so far been paid to the development of appropriate guidance methods. To date, the best *in-vivo* targeting accuracy reported for computer-assisted needle insertion was still above 5 mm.

To address these issues, this thesis proposed and evaluated a novel real-time navigation approach, based on fiducial needles, which yields high accuracy throughout the breathing cycle. The main advantage of the method is the fact that it is highly accurate (cf. Tab. 24) and does not rely on a regular breathing pattern. It can be applied to freely breathing patients, and the accuracy can be regulated by choosing the number of fiducials based on the size and location of the target. In addition, the workflow implied by the method is relatively close to that of the current clinical needle insertion workflow today because the applied imaging modality is the same and no special guidance hardware, such as a head-mounted display, is needed.

The high accuracy associated with the proposed concept can primarily be attributed to the application of fiducial needles. The fact that this initially increases the invasiveness of the intervention could be seen as the main limitation. However, as the method does not require repeated redirecting and advancing of the instrument (cf. section 10.3.2), the use of needles for motion compensation can be justified. Another disadvantage could be seen in the fact that optical tracking systems, though more accurate than other tracking systems (cf. section 3.2.2), impose the line-of-sight constraint on the tracked tools and require the use of needles thick enough to avoid bending, which is not accounted for. However, the

Advantages:
+ high accuracy
+ applicability to freely breathing patients
+ accuracy adjustable by choosing the number of fiducial needles
+ low user error
+ no special hardware (such as head-mounted display) for guidance
+ close to the conventional needle insertion workflow
Limitations:
− initial increase of invasiveness due to fiducial insertion
− associated with radiation exposure to the patient
− optical tracking imposes line-of-sight constraint

Table 27: Advantages (+) and limitations (−) of the proposed navigation concept in comparison to state of the art work.

outstanding accuracy and robustness of optical systems compensates for these shortcomings. Finally, it could be argued that the applied imaging modality (CT) is associated with ionizing radiation. CT was chosen in this work because the alternatives are associated with low image quality (US) or high costs (MR) (cf. section 3.2.1). However, the proposed approach is readily adaptable to other imaging modalities because only the fiducial localization module would need to be replaced. Table 27 summarizes the advantages and disadvantages of the proposed approach in comparison to state of the art work.

Clinical acceptance of a novel method requires evidenced benefits to the patient and/or the institution offering it. The main advantage of the system proposed here is that it can be applied in cases where traditional image guidance is not feasible, i.e., when the tumor is too small, in-plane needle insertion is not possible or patients cannot cooperate with respiratory instructions for breath-hold approaches. Due to its high targeting accuracy, the navigation system is suitable for targeting small lesions that are located deeply within the tissue and thus potentially allows for treatment of patients that could not have been treated before.

The ability to navigate on the basis of previously acquired CT data allows the procedure to be performed without radiation exposure to the interventionalist, while real-time images are still provided by the navigation system. In fact, the experiments presented in section 10.3 demonstrate that accurate needle placement can be achieved with only one planning CT scan, leading to low radiation exposure to the patient as well.

Furthermore, the image data that the navigation is based on may be acquired during distinct phases of contrast material enhancement because only one CT scan is acquired for accurate needle insertion. This aids in the targeting of lesions that are only visible during certain perfusion phases and also helps avoid vascular structures. As the needle can be inserted accurately in one pass, the risk of complications from multiple needle passes is also reduced.

Another important advantage of the navigation system is its flexibility with respect to the trajectory to the target and the applied instruments. As it is based on 3D imaging data, in-plane instrument insertion is not required, and the system performs equally well for out-of-plane paths. Also, needle insertion does not have to be performed within the narrow gantry, which improves manageability and allows for the use of instruments of arbitrary length. These aspects allow for choosing optimal trajectories in terms of proximity to critical structures, insertion angle and length and thus potentially decrease procedure times and complication rates.

Finally, according to the operators that used the system, navigated needle insertion was easy to learn, and even operators with no clinical experience in punctures obtained a high targeting accuracy. In consequence, it can be expected that little operator training would be required in clinical routine, and medical experts could concentrate on other interventions that cannot be conducted by less experienced physicians.

In comparison to the conventional method, the primary disadvantage of the navigated needle insertion method can be seen in the initial increase of invasiveness due to fiducial insertion. As already stated above, the use of needles can be justified by the fact that the proposed method does not require repeated insertion of the instrument for accurate targeting. Another limitation of the proposed approach could be seen in the introduction and setup of additional hardware in the interventional suite, which introduces additional preparation times and makes integration into the clinical workflow challenging. On the other hand, even the prototype navigation system yielded procedure times similar to the conventional procedure. It can be expected that a commercialized system would enable even shorter intervention times, thus reducing hospital costs. Table 28 summarizes the advantages and limitations of the proposed navigation concept in the context of clinical practice today.

Several issues remain to be addressed to ensure that the proposed approach will ultimately benefit patient care. Many details were already discussed in the respective chapters. The following paragraphs summarize the most important suggestions for future work.

FIDUCIAL INSERTION: So far, the process of fiducial insertion was the most time-consuming step within the workflow. It is based on US to minimize the use of ionizing radiation but has two major drawbacks: First, two imaging modalities are required by the navigation system which potentially increases costs and intervention time. Second, the planning CT that the fiducial insertion is

Advantages:
+ applicability to small targets due to high accuracy
+ in-plane needle insertion not required
+ no gating required
+ real-time feedback
+ low radiation dose to the patient
+ no radiation dose to the operator
+ no extensive training required
+ contrast agent only required once
+ no needle insertion in narrow gantry required
+ fewer needle insertions and thus potentially fewer complication rates
+ no extensive operator training
Limitations:
− initial increase of invasiveness
− additional hardware required

Table 28: Advantages (+) and limitations (−) of the proposed navigation concept in comparison to the conventional CT-guided needle insertion method.

based on may not reflect the current anatomical picture because it may have been taken numerous days before the intervention. An alternative approach that remains to be investigated is to utilize skin markers for accurate fiducial insertion: at the beginning of the intervention, the external fiducials are affixed to the skin of the patient, and a low resolution planning CT is done. Based on this CT, an optimal fiducial configuration is planned, and the fiducial needle(s) are inserted with the aid of the navigation system. Note that this insertion does not require a high degree of accuracy. The actual targeting is then performed with a maximum of accuracy because of the favorable fiducial configuration. Whether this method could be performed sufficiently fast remains to be investigated.

FIDUCIAL CONFIGURATION: According to chapters 7 and 8, the fiducial configuration has a high effect on the targeting accuracy. System accuracy could be further increased by automatically determining an optimal number and arrangement of the fiducials based on the size and location of the target. Furthermore, the performance of the system in the clinical workflow should be investigated for a combination of fiducial needles and skin markers as suggested in section 8.5.

TOOL CONSTRUCTION: Although the developed prototype system performed well in the clinical workflow, it may not yet be tested on patients without further improvements. One reason for this is the fact that the applied tools are not sterilizable. Furthermore, even more effort should be put into the tool design. While using soft tissue anchors appears beneficial from the technical point of view, it remains to be seen whether the tissue injury caused by the anchor is acceptable. Similarly, the needle diameter should be maximal from a technical point of view (to ensure that no bending occurs), but on the other hand, small needles potentially cause less tissue injury and are thus more suitable from a medical point of view. Some hope still lies in the improvement of the robustness of electromagnetic systems which allow for using smaller needle diameters because the sensors can be integrated into the tips of the instruments.

PATH PLANNING: Planning a trajectory to the target is one of the most time-consuming steps within the workflow making up approximately 30% of the intervention time (cf. section 10.3). So far, the trajectory is planned manually and depends crucially on the experience of the operator. (Semi-) automatic path planning (cf. e.g. [150]) might decrease intervention time and at the same time reduce the risk of injuring critical structures.

ROBOT INTEGRATION: Although a lot of effort has been invested in the guidance module, the user error is still relatively large compared to the overall error (cf. section 10.3). To address this issue, a robot could be applied for the needle insertion process as proposed in [98, 153].

APPLICATION TO OTHER PROCEDURES: The developed approach has so far only been applied to liver biopsies. Future studies should investigate its performance for ablation therapy, transjugular intrahepatic portosystemic shunt (TIPS) [1]. and other procedures that require accurate targeting of an anatomical strucure. Furthermore, the proposed motion compensation approach could potentially be applied in radiotherapy treatment. In this case, high accuracy over the breathing cycle would be required, thus suggesting application of a non-rigid deformation model. Furthermore, the tracking data would need to be fed into a prediction model to take into account system latency.

Still, transfer of the proposed concept to clinical practice will remain challenging. In fact, most clinical studies tend to favor image-guided systems over the traditional approach in terms of accuracy or radiation exposure as described in [166]. Even though, the majority of systems have not yet entered clinical routine. This can be attributed to three main factors. First, image-guided systems, though more accurate, are often associated with more costs due to expensive equipment and/or longer procedure times. Second, the proposed systems still lack integration in the clinical workflow and are generally provided as stand-alone solutions. Finally, novel technical solutions lack widespread acceptance on the part of the physicians who are often reluctant to change their habits.

To address these problems, a lot of effort has been expended in this work to ensure that the human factors issues relating to the use of technical equipment in the operating room are adequately addressed. As an image-guided system should not add time or complication to a procedure but be unobtrusive and simple to operate, a guidance mechanism was developed in close cooperation with medical partners which allows for fast transfer of a planned trajectory to the patient and does not require special hardware such as a head-mounted display. The derived method received strong acceptance on the part of the physicians that used the system so far. In addition, the navigation software can be run as a plugin in a commercialized PACS workstation software in order for data management to be handled with a minimum of user interaction (cf. section 4.3). Evaluation of the prototype system in a clinical setting further showed that integration in the clinical workflow is possible.

Regardless of the evidenced benefits of the proposed approach, widespread acceptance of the novel method can only be achieved if image-guided systems generally become standard tools for routine procedures. To achieve this, new technologies must be effectively integrated with hospital information systems.

---

[1] TIPS: Angiographic procedure performed under fluoroscopic guidance wherein a wire mesh stent is placed within the liver to decompress the portal circulation directly into the hepatic vein [103]

The concepts proposed in this thesis could then be applied to a wide variety of procedures including thermal ablation therapies, needle biopsy and gene delivery and thus contribute to a better treatment standard in clinical routine.

12

SUMMARY

> *The true way to render ourselves happy*
> *is to love our work and find in it our pleasure.*
>
> — Françoise de Motteville

Clinical practice is increasingly replacing traditional open surgical procedures with minimally invasive techniques for cancer diagnosis and therapy. These procedures typically require insertion of an elongate instrument into the organ of interest with a high degree of accuracy. In general, the success of a treatment or of a diagnosis is highly dependent on the accuracy of instrument insertion [1]. While intra-operative navigation has been proven to be highly effective in interventions on bony or sufficiently rigid structures such as the spine and the brain, computer aided soft tissue procedures are still limited to non-invasive diagnostics and surgical planning. This can be attributed to the fact that image-guided systems generally rely on the assumption that pre-operatively acquired images used to guide the intervention accurately represent the morphology of the tissue during the procedure [166]. In soft tissue interventions, however, the target organ can be subject to considerable organ shift and deformation caused by respiration [28], heartbeat [76], patient movement and manipulation by surgical instruments [149]. In consequence, the established navigation systems designed for rigid structures cannot be applied in these procedures, and soft tissue navigation remains a subject of ongoing research [166].

The main objective of this work was to design, implement, and evaluate a clinically applicable concept for computer-assisted percutaneous needle insertion into soft tissue featuring high accuracy during continuous breathing and an efficient guidance concept that requires a minimum of operator training. This chapter summarizes the contributions of this thesis (section 12.1) and presents the primary conclusions derived from this work (section 12.2).

12.1 SUMMARY OF CONTRIBUTIONS

The proposed approach estimates the position of an abdominal target (e.g., a tumor) continuously from a set of tracked fiducial needles. Prior to the intervention, the needles are inserted in the vicinity of the target, and a planning CT scan is acquired. Localization of the needles and the target in the planning image yields the initial poses of the fiducials relative to the target. During the intervention, the fiducial needles are continuously located by a tracking system, and a real-time deformation model is used to update the target position accordingly. To allow for fast and accurate needle insertion, a navigation monitor guides the physician towards the moving target.

As the liver is one of the most common sites for metastatic disease and at the same time one of the organs most affected by respiratory motion, the developed concept was implemented by means of example for percutaneous liver punctures but is readily applicable to other abdominal organs and procedures.

The overall needle insertion error associated with the presented approach depends on a variety of factors including the instrument tracking error, the user error, the fiducial localization error and the modelling error. To allow for a detailed error analysis, the developed prototypical system was evaluated in two stages. First, the system modules were evaluated separately to quantify the individual errors contributing to the overall error. Next, the system was evaluated in the clinical workflow to compare the needle-based navigation concept to state of the art work as well as to the conventional CT-guided needle insertion method with respect to accuracy, radiation exposure to the patient and procedure time. The following paragraphs summarize the results of this work.

RESPIRATORY LIVER MOTION SIMULATOR: To reduce the number of animal experiments for evaluating the proposed approach, a respiratory liver motion simulator was developed for conducting *ex-vivo* experiments in a respiring patient model [90, 91]. The simulator consists of a model of the human torso which allows for mounting of an explanted human or porcine liver to an artificial diaphragm. It can be connected to a lung ventilator for simulation of respiratory motion and is CT and MRI compatible. To analyze the liver movement generated by the simulator, the movement of a set of porcine and human livers mounted to the phantom was monitored via tracked needles inserted into the livers. Mean displacement between expiration and inspiration was in the range of 10 to 15 mm with cranio-caudal movement making up the main part. In addition, the livers showed movement due to deformation of the tissue. According to the literature [28], the liver movement generated by the motion simulator is comparable to the movement of a human liver *in-vivo*.

TRACKING: The fiducial needles used for motion compensation should be trackable with high accuracy and at the same time not handicap the operator. To optimize tracking accuracy, two commercially available optical tracking systems were evaluated with regard to their suitability for needle-based soft tissue navigation: The Polaris® system and the MicronTracker 2. For this purpose, different tool designs were developed and compared both experimentally and theoretically via error propagation methods [86]. Furthermore, the sensitivity of the tracking systems to the pose of the tools within the measurement volume, illumination conditions and motion was assessed [86]. According to the experiments, the well-established Polaris® system is well suited for needle-based navigation, yielding submillimeter tracking accuracy for custom-designed 5DoF tools with a light design. Furthermore, tracking accuracy was highly robust to illumination conditions and motion. In contrast, the MicronTracker 2 was very sensitive to the examined factors but has the distinct advantage of allowing for construction of lightweight 6DoF tools.

REGISTRATION: To allow for visualization of surgical instruments in relation to the patient's anatomy, the image coordinate system must be continuously registered with the tracking coordinate system based on the fiducial positions. This process requires accurate localization of the navigation aids in both coordinate systems. To automatically locate fiducial needles in CT images with high accuracy, a novel localization algorithm was developed which applies a stochastic optimizer to fit geometrical models of the navigations aids into the image. A phantom study yielded a localization error of 0.3 mm on 1 mm CT slices [87]. The main motivation for applying fiducial needles as opposed to skin markers is the ability to track reference points inside the target organ itself for capturing organ movement. An *in-silico* evaluation further suggests that even if the morphology of the tissue at the time of registration is approximately identical to the morphology of the tissue during image acquisition ("rigid body assumption"), it is advantageous to use needles because they can be placed significantly closer to the target and capture even small shifts of the target organ. Hence, needle-shaped fiducials outperform skin markers even in gated experiments.

MOTION COMPENSATION: To allow for application of the navigation approach in freely breathing patients that cannot cooperate with breath-hold instructions, a motion compensation method was developed, which yields high accuracy during continuous breathing. In an *in-vitro* study, the suitability of several real-time deformation models as base for the motion compensation was compared [88, 89]. For this purpose, explanted porcine and human livers were mounted to a motion simulator that moved and deformed the livers in a realistic manner. Depending on the fiducial configuration and the applied transformation, an RMS TRE in the range of 0.7 mm to 2.9 mm throughout the breathing cycle generated by the motion simulator was obtained. Affine transformations and spline transformations performed comparably well (overall RMS $<$ 2 mm) and were considerably better than rigid transformations.

FIDUCIAL PLACEMENT: As the TRE depends crucially on the arrangement of the fiducials, this thesis further investigated appropriate fiducial placement strategies. To minimize the system error, the distance of the target to the centroid of the control points extracted from the fiducials should be minimized. When three needles are applied, the target should be contained in the volume spanned by the needles (cf. section 7.3). When applying two fiducial needles, a needle placement along the principal direction of movement is advantageous with the needles enclosing the target in that direction [89].

REDUCTION OF INVASIVENESS: When choosing the number of needles to be applied for motion compensation, there is always a tradeoff between high accuracy and low invasiveness. An *in-vivo* study investigated combining external and internal fiducials for real-time motion compensation to reduce the invasiveness, while keeping sufficient accuracy for a given intervention [94]. For this purpose, the TRE for different numbers of surface markers n_s and fiducial needles n_f, as well as for different transformation types, was compared *in-vivo* with an inserted needle serving as target. During continuous breathing, n_f had the greatest effect on accuracy, yielding mean RMS errors 4.8 mm ($n_f = 0$), 2.0 mm ($n_f = 1$) and 1.7 mm ($n_f = 2$) with $n_s = 4$. These values correspond to error reductions of 11%, 64% and 70% compared to the case when no motion compensation is performed, i.e., when the target position is assumed constant. The results of the study can be used in practice to select a suitable combination of fiducials for a given tumor size and location, considering the tradeoff between high accuracy and low invasiveness.

AUTOMATIC GATING: In general, the TRE decreases in those time slots during the intervention which correspond to the state within the breathing cycle that the CT was taken in. To exploit this observation, an automatic gating scheme based on the fiducial poses was developed. It was shown that the FRE of a rigid transformation reflecting tissue motion generally correlates strongly with the TRE and can be used to provide an intra-interventional measure of confidence for the accuracy of the system [94]. Based on this measure, optimal time slots for the needle insertion can be detected automatically.

GUIDANCE An important factor to the overall performance of a navigation system is the user error, which depends crucially on the provided guidance method. To minimize this error, different visualization schemes for targeting of an anatomical structure with a needle-shaped instrument were developed and compared [134, 135]. Based on an *in-vitro* evaluation of the proposed methods, a three-stage visualization scheme for clinical use was derived [93, 96]. Depending on the state within the targeting workflow (*tip positioning, needle alignment, needle insertion*), an appropriate view on the scene is generated from the image and the tracking data, showing the user how to move the instrument to transfer a planned trajectory accurately to the patient.

ACCURACY ASSESSMENT IN THE CLINICAL WORKFLOW: Two studies were conducted to assess the needle insertion accuracy associated with the proposed approach. In the first study, the accuracy of the navigation system was assessed *in-vitro* with the developed respiratory liver motion simulator [92]. Two operators, who performed 20 needle insertions in a total of four porcine livers, obtained an overall targeting accuracy of 3.5 ± 1.1 mm determined with control CT scans. In a second study, the accuracy of the system was assessed *in-vivo* in two swine [96]. Two medical experts with experience in CT-guided interventions and two non-experts used the navigation system to perform 32 needle insertions into contrasted agar nodules (radius: 5-10 mm) injected into the livers of two ventilated swine. The lesions were hit in 97% of all trials with a mean user error of 2.4 ± 2.1 mm, a mean TRE of 2.1 ± 1.1 mm and a mean overall targeting error of 3.7 ± 2.3 mm. The non-experts achieved significantly better results than the experts with an overall error of 2.8 ± 1.4 mm compared to 4.5 ± 2.7 mm. In both animals, the operators performed four needle insertions based on only one planning CT, reflecting the fact that needle repositioning is very common during RFA procedures to completely destroy a tumor. When the needle insertion was conducted immediately after the planning CT acquisition, the TRE and the overall targeting error dropped to 1.7 ± 1.4 mm (n = 8) and 2.3 ± 1.0 (n = 8) respectively.

COMPARISON TO CONVENTIONAL NEEDLE INSERTION METHOD: To evaluate the clinical applicability of the proposed approach, the navigated needle insertion method was compared to the conventional CT-guided liver biopsy method with respect to radiation exposure to the patient, accuracy and time. For this purpose, two experts performed a total of 40 biopsies (20 with each method) of liver lesions with a diameter of approximately 5 mm in five swine. According to the results, the navigated method outperformed the conventional method, reducing the mean number of repositionings of the needle by 95 % (conventional: 3.2 ± 3.8; navigated: of 0.2 ± 0.5) and the mean number of CT scans by 81 % (conventional: 6.1 ± 3.8; navigated: 1.2 ± 0.4). Procedure times were comparable for both methods (conventional: 20 ± 9 min; navigated: 20 ± 8 min).

12.2 CONCLUSIONS

In this thesis, new concepts for computer-assisted soft tissue interventions were developed, implemented and evaluated. The main contributions include (1) development and evaluation of a real-time capable motion compensation method for percutaneous abdominal interventions, (2) development and evaluation of a guidance method to allow for fast and precise insertion of a needle-shaped instrument along a predetermined trajectory and (3) development of a respiratory liver motion simulator for evaluating the proposed methods in a realistic setting. Furthermore, a prototypical system for navigated liver punctures was developed and evaluated based on the proposed methods to demonstrate the clinical applicability of the novel navigation approach. According to various *in-silico*, *in-vitro* and *in-vivo* experiments, the method is highly accurate compared to state of the art work and outperforms the conventional CT-guided needle insertion method with respect to accuracy and radiation exposure to the patient.

A major advantage of the navigated needle insertion approach compared to the conventional CT-guided method is that it can be applied when traditional image guidance is not feasible, i.e., when the tumor is too small, in-plane needle insertion is not possible, or patients cannot cooperate with respiratory instructions for breath-hold approaches. Due to the high targeting accuracy, the approach is suitable for targeting small lesions that are located deeply within the tissue. Additional advantages include low radiation exposure to the patient, high flexibility with respect to path planning and low extent of operator training. A limitation of the proposed method could be seen in the fact that it initially increases the invasiveness of an intervention due to the insertion of the fiducial needles. As repeated redirecting and advancing of the instrument is not required, however, the use of needles can be justified. Furthermore, the invasiveness can be minimized by combining fiducial needles with skin markers and by choosing a suitable configuration of fiducials for a given tumor size and location, considering the tradeoff between high accuracy and low invasiveness.

This thesis showed that the proposed navigation approach features major benefits compared to related methods as well as to the conventional needle insertion approach. Future work includes optimization of individual system modules to decrease intervention time, development of algorithms for automatic fiducial configuration and path planning and integration of a robot for needle insertion. To assure that the developed methods will eventually benefit patient care, the new technology must further be effectively integrated with hospital information systems. As the proposed concepts are broadly applicable to various organs and procedures, this work is an important contribution to the field of computer-assisted medical interventions.

BIBLIOGRAPHY

[1] N. Abolhassani, R. Patel, and M. Moallem. Needle insertion into soft tissue: A survey. *Med Eng Phys*, 29:413–431, 2007. (Cited on pages 197 and 205.)

[2] S. A. Ahmad. Limitations of radiofrequency ablation in treating liver metastases: A lesson in geometry. *Ann Surg Oncol*, 11(4):358–359, 2004. (Cited on page 16.)

[3] M. Ahmed and S. N. Goldberg. Thermal ablation therapy for hepatocellular carcinoma. *J Vasc Interv Radiol*, 13(9):231–243, 2002. (Cited on page 16.)

[4] M. L. Apuzzo, P. T. Chandrasoma, D. Cohen, C. S. Zee, and V. Zelman. Computed imaging stereotaxy: Experience and perspective related to 500 procedures applied to brain masses. *Neurosurgery*, 20(6):930–937, Jun 1987. (Cited on page 19.)

[5] J. M. Balter, K. L. Lam, C. J. McGinn, T. S. Lawrence, and R. K. T. Haken. Improvement of CT-based treatment-planning models of abdominal targets using static exhale imaging. *Int J Radiat Oncol*, 41(4):939–943, 1998. (Cited on page 33.)

[6] F. Banovac, J. Tang, S. Xu, D. Lindisch, H. Y. Chung, E. Levy, T. Chang, M. F. McCullough, Z. Yaniv, B. J. Wood, and K. Cleary. Precision targeting of liver lesions using a novel electromagnetic navigation device in physiologic phantom and swine. *Med Phys*, 32(8):2698–2705, 2005. (Cited on pages 22, 31, 172, and 185.)

[7] F. Banovac, E. Wilson, H. Zhang, and K. Cleary. Needle biopsy of anatomically unfavorable liver lesions with an electromagnetic navigation assist device in a computed tomography environment. *J Vasc Interv Radiol*, 17:1671–1675, 2006. (Cited on pages 22 and 193.)

[8] P. Bao, T. K. Sinha, C.-C. R. Chen, J. R. Warmath, R. L. Galloway, and A. J. Herline. A prototype ultrasound-guided laparoscopic radiofrequency ablation system. *Surg Endosc*, 21(1):74–79, Jan 2007. (Cited on pages 25, 33, 35, and 198.)

[9] W. L. Bargar, A. Bauer, and M. Börner. Primary and revision total hip replacement using the ROBODOC system. *Clin Orthop Relat Res*, 1(354):82–91, Sep 1998. (Cited on page 20.)

[10] M. Bauer, M. Schlegel, D. Pustka, N. Navab, and G. Klinker. Predicting and estimating the accuracy of n-occular optical tracking systems. In *Fifth IEEE and ACM International Symposium on Mixed and Augmented Reality (ISMAR) 2006*, pages 43–51, 2006. (Cited on pages 29, 32, and 58.)

[11] M. A. Bauer. *Tracking errors in Augmented Reality*. PhD thesis, Technische Universität München, 2007. (Cited on pages 29, 30, 32, 53, 54, 55, 79, 81, and 82.)

[12] M. Baumhauer, M. Feuerstein, H.-P. Meinzer, and J. Rassweiler. Navigation in endoscopic soft tissue surgery: Perspectives and limitations. *J Endourol*, 22(4):751–766, Apr 2008. (Cited on pages 19, 20, 21, and 36.)

[13] M. Baumhauer, T. Simpfendoerfer, I. Wolf, and H.-P. Meinzer. Soft tissue navigation for laparoscopic prostatectomy: Evaluation of camera pose estimation for enhanced visualization. In *SPIE Medical Imaging 2007: Visualization and Image-Guided Procedures*, volume 6509, page 650911, 2007. (Cited on page 27.)

[14] A. Benninghoff and D. Drenckhahn. *Anatomie. Makroskopische Anatomie, Histologie, Embryologie, Zellbiologie (Band 1)*. Urban & Fischer, 2008. (Cited on page 9.)

[15] W. Birkfellner, F. Watzinger, F. Wanschitz, G. Enislidis, M. Truppe, R. Ewers, and H. Bergmann. Concepts and results in the development of a hybrid tracking system for CAS. In *Medical Image Computing and Computer-Assisted Intervention (MICCAI) 1998 (2)*, LNCS, pages 343–351, 1998. (Cited on page 29.)

[16] J. M. Blackall, G. P. Penney, A. P. King, and D. J. Hawkes. Alignment of sparse freehand 3-D ultrasound with preoperative images of the liver using models of respiratory motion and deformation. *IEEE T Med Imaging*, 24(11):1405–1416, 2005. (Cited on pages 25, 26, 35, and 198.)

[17] F. L. Bookstein. Principal warps: Thin-plate splines and the decomposition of deformations. *IEEE T Pattern Anal*, 11(6):567–585, 1989. (Cited on pages 116 and 117.)

[18] Y. Boykov and V. Kolmogorov. An experimental comparison of min-cut/max-flow algorithms for energy minimization in vision. *IEEE T Pattern Anal*, 26(9):1124–1137, 2004. (Cited on pages 48, 167, 168, and 176.)

[19] I. N. Bronstein, K. A. Semendjajew, and G. Musiol. *Taschenbuch der Mathematik*. Harri Deutsch, 25th edition, 1991. (Cited on page 153.)

[20] M. Bublat, R. Ratering, H. Busse, K. Kansy, and A. Schmittgen. LOCALITE Brain Navigator. Ein bildgestütztes Neuronavigationssystem für die interventionelle Kernspintomographie. In *Bildverarbeitung für die Medizin 2000*, pages 431–435, München, Deutschland, 2000. (Cited on page 38.)

[21] T. J. Carter, M. Sermesant, D. M. Cash, D. C. Barratt, C. Tanner, and D. J. Hawkes. Application of soft tissue modelling to image-guided surgery. *Med Eng Phys*, 27(10):893–909, Dec 2005. (Cited on pages 35 and 36.)

[22] D. M. Cash, M. I. Miga, S. C. Glasgow, B. M. Dawant, L. W. Clements, Z. Cao, R. L. Galloway, and W. C. Chapman. Concepts and preliminary data toward the realization of image-guided liver surgery. *J Gastrointest Surg*, 11(7):844–859, Jul 2007. (Cited on pages 32 and 34.)

[23] D. M. Cash, M. I. Miga, T. K. Sinha, R. L. Galloway, and W. C. Chapman. Compensating for intraoperative soft-tissue deformations using incomplete surface data and finite elements. *IEEE T Med Imaging*, 24(11):1479–1491, Nov 2005. (Cited on page 34.)

[24] D. M. Cash, T. K. Sinha, W. C. Chapman, H. Terawaki, B. M. Dawant, R. L. Galloway, and M. I. Miga. Incorporation of a laser range scanner into image-guided liver surgery: Surface acquisition, registration, and tracking. *Med Phys*, 30:1671–1682, 2003. (Cited on page 34.)

[25] Claron Technology, Inc. *MicronTracker Developer's Manual MTC 2.6*, Aug 2006. (Cited on pages 74, 77, 82, and 93.)

[26] S. Clasen and P. L. Pereira. Magnetic resonance guidance for radiofrequency ablation of liver tumors. *J Magn Reson Imaging*, 27:421–433, 2008. (Cited on pages 14, 17, and 18.)

[27] K. Cleary, F. Banovac, E. Levy, and D. Tanaka. Development of a liver respiratory motion simulator to investigate magnetic tracking for abdominal interventions. In S. K. Mun, editor, *SPIE Medical Imaging 2002: Visualization, Image-Guided Procedures, and Display*, volume 4681, pages 25–29, May 2002. (Cited on page 70.)

[28] M. A. Clifford, F. Banovac, E. Levy, and K. Cleary. Assessment of hepatic motion secondary to respiration for computer assisted interventions. *Comp Aid Surg*, 7(5):291–299, 2002. (Cited on pages 1, 2, 10, 12, 13, 17, 18, 69, 108, 197, 205, and 206.)

[29] L. Crocetti, R. Lencioni, S. DeBeni, T. C. See, C. D. Pina, and C. Bartolozzi. Targeting liver lesions for radiofrequency ablation. *Invest Radiol*, 43(1):33–39, 2008. (Cited on pages 16, 171, and 172.)

[30] M. Das, F. Sauer, U. J. Schoepf, A. Khamene, S. K. Vogt, S. Schaller, R. Kikinis, E. vanSonnenberg, and S. G. Silverman. Augmented reality visualization for CT-guided interventions: System description, feasibility, and initial evaluation in an abdominal phantom. *Radiology*, 240(1):230–235, 2006. (Cited on pages 22, 24, 27, 31, 38, 41, and 171.)

[31] M. H. Davis, A. Khotanzad, D. P. Flamig, and S. E. Harms. A physics-based coordinate transformation for 3-d image matching. *IEEE T Med Imaging*, 16(3):317–328, 1997. (Cited on pages 116 and 117.)

[32] M. Dawood, F. Büther, N. Lang, O. Schober, and K. P. Schäfers. Respiratory gating in positron emission tomography: A quantitative comparison of different gating schemes. *Med Phys*, 34(7):3067, 2007. (Cited on page 33.)

[33] S. L. Delp, S. D. Stulberg, B. Davies, F. Picard, and F. Leitner. Computer assisted knee replacement. *Clin Orthop Relat Res*, 1(354):49–56, Sep 1998. (Cited on page 20.)

[34] S. DiMaio, T. Kapur, K. Cleary, S. Aylward, P. Kazanzides, K. Vosburgh, R. Ellis, J. Duncan, K. Farahani, H. Lemke, T. Peters, W. Lorensen, D. Gobbi, J. Haller, L. Clarke, S. Pizer, R. Taylor, R. Galloway, G. Fichtinger, N. Hata, K. Lawson, C. Tempany, and F. Jolesz. Challenges in image-guided therapy system design. *NeuroImage*, 37:144–151, 2007. (Cited on page 21.)

[35] U. Ecke, B. Luebben, J. Maurer, S. Boor, and W. J. Mann. Comparison of different computer-aided surgery systems in skull base surgery. *Skull Base*, 13(1):43–50, 2003. (Cited on page 20.)

[36] U. Engelmann, A. Schröter, U. Baur, M. Schwab, O. Werner, M. H. Makabe, and H.-P. Meinzer. Openness in (tele-) radiology workstations: The CHILI PlugIn concept. In H. U. Lemke, M. W. Vannier, K. Inamura, and A. Farman, editors, *Computer Assisted Radiology and Surgery (CARS) 1998*, pages 437–442, 1998. (Cited on pages 48 and 49.)

[37] R. Ewers, K. Schicho, G. Undt, F. Wanschitz, M. Truppe, R. Seemann, and A. Wagner. Basic research and 12 years of clinical experience in computer-assisted navigation technology: A review. *Int J Oral Max Surg*, 34(1):1–8, Jan 2005. (Cited on pages 20 and 21.)

[38] A. Faller and M. Schünke. *Der Körper des Menschen - Einführung in Bau und Funktionsweise*. Georg Thieme Verlag, 2004. (Cited on page 10.)

[39] M. Feuerstein, T. Mussack, S. M. Heining, and N. Navab. Intraoperative laparoscope augmentation for port placement and resection planning in minimally invasive liver resection. *IEEE T Med Imaging*, 27(3):355–369, 2008. (Cited on pages 33, 35, and 198.)

[40] G. Fichtinger, A. Deguet, G. Fischer, I. Iordachita, E. Balogh, K. Masamune, R. H. Taylor, L. M. Fayad, M. de Oliveira, and S. J. Zinreich. Image overlay for CT-guided needle insertions. *Comp Aid Surg*, 10(4):241–255, 2005. (Cited on pages 22, 24, 38, 42, 178, and 185.)

[41] J. M. Fitzpatrick and J. B. West. The distribution of target registration error in rigid-body point-based registration. *IEEE T Med Imaging*, 20(9):917–927, 2001. (Cited on pages 32, 45, 48, 81, 82, 96, and 107.)

[42] J. M. Fitzpatrick, J. B. West, and C. R. Maurer. Predicting error in rigid-body point-based registration. *IEEE T Med Imaging*, 17(5):694–702, 1998. (Cited on pages 30, 31, 32, 47, 55, 56, 58, 77, and 82.)

[43] D. D. Frantz, A. D. Wiles, S. E. Leis, and S. R. Kirsch. Accuracy assessment protocols for electromagnetic tracking systems. *Phys Med Biol*, 48:2241–2251, 2003. (Cited on page 79.)

[44] R. L. Galloway. The process and development of image-guided procedures. *Annu Rev Biomed Eng*, 3:83–108, 2001. (Cited on page 27.)

[45] D. Gianfelice, L. Lepanto, P. Perreault, C. Chartrand-Lefebvre, and P. Milette. Value of CT fluoroscopy for percutaneous biopsy procedures. *J Vasc Interv Radiol*, 11(7):879–884, 2000. (Cited on pages 2 and 14.)

[46] P. L. Gildenberg. The birth of stereotactic surgery: A personal retrospective. *Neurosurgery*, 54(1):199–207, Jan 2004. (Cited on page 19.)

[47] P. L. Gildenberg and P. Franklin. Survey of CT-guided stereotactic surgery. *Appl Neurophysiol*, 48(1-6):477–480, 1985. (Cited on page 19.)

[48] S. N. Goldberg and D. E. Dupuy. Image-guided radiofrequency tumor ablation: Challenges and opportunities-part I. *J Vasc Interv Radiol*, 12:1021–1032, 2001. (Cited on page 14.)

[49] S. N. Goldberg, C. J. Grassi, J. F. Cardella, J. W. Charboneau, G. D. Dodd, D. E. Dupuy, D. Gervais, A. R. Gillams, R. A. Kane, F. T. Lee, T. Livraghi, J. McGahan, D. A. Phillips, H. Rhim, and S. G. Silverman. Image-guided tumor ablation: Standardization of terminology and reporting criteria. *J Vasc Interv Radiol*, 16:765–778, 2005. (Cited on pages 14 and 17.)

[50] A. Grant and J. Neuberger. Guidelines on the use of liver biopsy in clinical practice. *Gut*, 45:IV1–IV11, 1999. (Cited on page 13.)

[51] M. Grass, P. Koppe, E. Klotz, R. Proksa, M. H. Kuhn, H. Aerts, J. O. de Beek, and R. Kemkers. Three-dimensional reconstruction of high contrast objects using C-arm image intensifier projection data. *Comput Med Imag Grap*, 23(6):311–321, 1999. (Cited on page 24.)

[52] P. Grunert, K. Darabi, J. Espinosa, and R. Filippi. Computer-aided navigation in neurosurgery. *Neurosurg Rev*, 26(2):73–99, May 2003. (Cited on page 21.)

[53] W. A. Hall. The safety and efficacy of stereotactic biopsy for intracranial lesions. *Cancer*, 82(9):1749–1755, May 1998. (Cited on page 19.)

[54] R. L. Harder and R. N. Desmarais. Interpolation using surface splines. *J Aircraft*, 9(2):189–91, 1972. (Cited on page 116.)

[55] A. J. Herline, J. L. Herring, J. D. Stefansic, W. C. Chapman, R. L. Galloway, and B. M. Dawant. Surface registration for use in interactive, image-guided liver surgery. *Comp Aid Surg*, 5(1):11–17, 2000. (Cited on page 32.)

[56] P. Hildebrand, S. Schlichting, V. Martens, A. Besirevic, M. Kleemann, U. Roblick, L. Mirow, C. Bürk, A. Schweikard, and H.-P. Bruch. Prototype of an intraoperative navigation and documentation system for laparoscopic radiofrequency ablation: First experiences. *Eur J Surg Oncol*, pages 418–421, 2007. (Cited on pages 25, 33, 35, and 198.)

[57] J.-S. Hong, T. Dohi, M. Hasizume, K. Konishi, and N. Hata. A motion adaptable needle placement instrument based on tumor specific ultrasonic image segmentation. In *Medical Image Computing and Computer-Assisted Intervention (MICCAI) 2002 (2)*, pages 122–129, 2002. (Cited on page 34.)

[58] B. Horn. Closed-form solution of absolute orientation using unit quaternions. *J Opt Soc Am A*, 4:629–642, 1987. (Cited on pages 31, 68, 81, 82, 96, 107, 118, 141, and 161.)

[59] V. A. Horsley and R. H. Clarke. The structure and functions of the cerebellum examined by a new method. *Brain*, 31:45–124, 1908. (Cited on page 19.)

[60] A. Hostettler, S. A. Nicolau, C. Forest, L. Soler, and Y. Rémond. Real time simulation of organ motions induced by breathing: First evaluation on patient data. *Medical Image Computing and Computer-Assisted Intervention (MICCAI) 2006 (2)*, 4072:9–18, 2006. (Cited on page 36.)

[61] A. Hostettler, S. A. Nicolau, L. Soler, Y. Rémond, and J. Marescaux. A realtime predictive simulation of abdominal organ positions induced by free breathing. In *Biomedical Simulation*, volume 5104 of *LNCS*, pages 89–97, 2008. (Cited on page 36.)

[62] J. B. Hummel, M. R. Bax, M. L. Figl, Y. Kang, J. C. Maurer, W. W. Birkfellner, H. Bergmann, and R. Shahidi. Design and application of an assessment protocol for electromagnetic tracking systems. *Med Phys*, 32(7):2371–2379, 2005. (Cited on pages 79, 82, and 83.)

[63] L. Ibañez, W. Schroeder, L. Ng, J. Cates, and the Insight Software Consortium. *The ITK Software Guide Second Edition*, 2005. http://www.itk.org. (Cited on pages 49 and 99.)

[64] J. Illingworth and J. Kittler. A survey of the hough transform. *Comput Vision Graph*, 44(1):87 – 116, 1988. (Cited on page 103.)

[65] M. Jabero and D. P. Sarment. Advanced surgical guidance technology: A review. *Implant Dent*, 15(2):135–142, Jun 2006. (Cited on page 20.)

[66] F. A. Jolesz. Future perspectives for intraoperative MRI. *Neurosurg Clin N Am*, 16(1):201–213, Jan 2005. (Cited on page 26.)

[67] A. Kato, T. Yoshimine, T. Hayakawa, Y. Tomita, T. Ikeda, M. Mitomo, K. Harada, and H. Mogami. A frameless, armless navigational system for computer-assisted neurosurgery. Technical note. *J Neurosurg*, 74(5):845–849, May 1991. (Cited on page 20.)

[68] H. G. Kenngott, J. Neuhaus, B. P. Müller-Stich, I. Wolf, M. Vetter, H.-P. Meinzer, J. Köninger, M. W. Büchler, and C. N. Gutt. Development of a navigation system for minimally invasive esophagectomy. *Surg Endosc*, 22(8):1858–1865, 2008. (Cited on page 34.)

[69] R. Khadem, C. C. Yeh, M. Sadeghi-Tehrani, M. R. Bax, J. A. Johnson, J. N. Welch, E. P. Wilkinson, and R. Shahidi. Comparative tracking error analysis of five different optical tracking systems. *Comp Aid Surg*, 5:98–107, 2000. (Cited on pages 20, 79, and 83.)

[70] A. Khamene, S. Vogt, F. Azar, T. Sielhorst, F. Sauer, and H. Niemann. Local 3D reconstruction and augmented reality visualization of free-hand ultrasound for needle biopsy procedures. In *Medical Image Computing and Computer-Assisted Intervention (MICCAI) 2003 (2)*, pages 344–355, 2003. (Cited on page 33.)

[71] A. Khamene, J. K. Warzelhan, S. Vogt, D. Elgort, C. Chefd'Hotel, J. L. Duerk, J. S. Lewin, F. K. Wacker, and F. Sauer. Characterization of internal organ motion using skin marker positions. In C. Barillot, D. R. Haynor, and P. Hellier, editors, *Medical Image Computing and Computer-Assisted Intervention (MICCAI) 2004 (2)*, pages 526–533, Saint-Malo, France, 2004. Springer. (Cited on pages 22, 26, 35, 127, and 198.)

[72] M. F. Khan, S. Dogan, A. Maataoui, S. Wesarg, J. Gurung, H. Ackermann, M. Schiemann, G. Wimmer-Greinecker, and T. J. Vogl. Navigation-based needle puncture of a cadaver using a hybrid tracking navigational system. *Invest Radiol*, 41(10):713–720, 2006. (Cited on pages 22, 24, 29, 31, 34, 178, 185, and 193.)

[73] S. H. Kim, H. K. Lim, W. J. Lee, J. M. Cho, and H.-J. Jang. Needle-tract implantation in hepatocellular carcinoma: Frequency and CT findings after biopsy with a 19.5-gauge automated biopsy gun. *Abdom Imaging*, 25(3):246–250, 2000. (Cited on pages 2 and 14.)

[74] V. V. Kindratenko. A survey of electromagnetic position tracker calibration techniques. *Virtual Reality: Research, Development, and Applications*, 5(3):169–182, 2000. (Cited on page 29.)

[75] M. A. Kliewer, D. H. Sheafor, E. Paulson, R. Helsper, B. Hertzberg, and R. Nelson. Percutaneous liver biopsy: A cost-benefit analysis comparing sonographic and CT guidance. *Am J Roentgenol*, 173:1199–1202, 1999. (Cited on page 13.)

[76] A. F. Kolen, N. R. Miller, E. E. Ahmed, and J. C. Bamber. Characterization of cardiovascular liver motion for the eventual application of elasticity imaging to the liver in vivo. *Phys Med Biol*, 49:4187–4206, 2004. (Cited on pages 2, 12, and 205.)

[77] J. Krücker, S. Xu, N. Glossop, W. F. Pritchard, J. Karanian, A. Chiesa, and B. J. Wood. Evaluation of motion compensation approaches for soft tissue navigation. In *Proceedings of SPIE Medical Imaging 2008: Visualization, Image-Guided Procedures, and Modeling*, volume 6918, page 691814, 2008. (Cited on pages 34 and 139.)

[78] J. Krücker, S. Xu, N. Glossop, A. Viswanathan, J. Borgert, H. Schulz, and B. J. Wood. Electromagnetic tracking for thermal ablation and biopsy guidance: Clinical evaluation of spatial accuracy. *J Vasc Interv Radiol*, 18(9):1141–50, 2007. (Cited on pages 22, 29, 31, 34, 181, and 185.)

[79] Y. S. Kwoh, J. Hou, E. A. Jonckheere, and S. Hayati. A robot with improved absolute positioning accuracy for CT guided stereotactic brain surgery. *IEEE Trans Biomed Eng*, 35(2):153–160, Feb 1988. (Cited on page 20.)

[80] D. Laganà, G. Carrafiello, M. Mangini, D. Lumia, L. Mocciardini, C. Chini, G. Pinotti, S. Cuffari, and C. Fugazzola. Hepatic radiofrequency under CT-fluoroscopy guidance. *Radiol Med (Torino)*, 113(1):87–100, 2008. (Cited on page 17.)

[81] E. Levy, H. Zhang, D. Lindisch, B. J. Wood, and K. Cleary. Electromagnetic tracking-guided percutaneous intrahepatic portosystemic shunt creation in a swine model. *J Vasc Interv Radiol*, 18(2):303–307, 2007. (Cited on pages 34, 37, and 39.)

[82] E. B. Levy, J. Tang, D. Lindisch, N. Glossop, F. Banovac, and K. Cleary. Implementation of an electromagnetic tracking system for accurate intrahepatic puncture needle guidance: Accuracy results in an in vitro model. *Acad Radiol*, 14(3):344–354, Mar 2007. (Cited on pages 24, 34, and 171.)

[83] R. Lin, E. Wilson, J. Tang, D. Stoianovici, and K. Cleary. A computer-controlled pump and realistic anthropomorphic respiratory phantom for validating image-guided systems. In *SPIE Medical Imaging 2007: Visualization and Image-Guided Procedures*, volume 6509, page 65090E (9 pages), San Diego, CA, USA, Mar 2007. (Cited on page 70.)

[84] B. Ma, M. H. Moghari, R. E. Ellis, and P. Abolmaesumi. On fiducial target registration error in the presence of anisotropic noise. In *Medical Image Computing and Computer-Assisted Intervention (MICCAI) 2007 (2)*, pages 628–635, 2007. (Cited on pages 32, 82, and 91.)

[85] R. J. Maciunas. Computer-assisted neurosurgery. *Clin Neurosurg*, 53:267–271, 2006. (Cited on page 21.)

[86] L. Maier-Hein, A. M. Franz, J. Neuhaus, H.-P. Meinzer, and I. Wolf. Comparative assessment of optical tracking systems for soft tissue navigation with fiducial needles. In K. R. Cleary and M. I. Miga, editors, *SPIE Medical Imaging 2008: Visualization, Image-Guided Procedures, and Modeling*, volume 6918, page 69181Z (9 pages), Feb 2008. (Cited on pages 3, 6, 54, and 207.)

[87] L. Maier-Hein, D. Maleike, J. Neuhaus, A. M. Franz, I. Wolf, and H.-P. Meinzer. Soft tissue navigation using needle-shaped markers: Evaluation of navigation aid tracking accuracy and CT registration. In K. R. Cleary and M. I. Miga, editors, *SPIE Medical Imaging 2007: Visualization and Image-Guided Procedures*, volume 6509, page 650926 (12 pages), Feb 2007. (Cited on pages 5, 6, and 207.)

[88] L. Maier-Hein, S. A. Müller, F. Pianka, A. Seitel, B. P. Müller-Stich, C. N. Gutt, U. Rietdorf, G. Richter, H.-P. Meinzer, B. M. Schmied, and I. Wolf. In-vitro evaluation of a novel needle-based soft tissue navigation system with a respiratory liver motion simulator. In K. R. Cleary and M. I. Miga, editors, *SPIE Medical Imaging 2007: Visualization and Image-Guided Procedures*, volume 6509, page 650916 (12 pages), San Diego, CA, USA, Mar 2007. (Cited on pages 5, 6, 123, and 207.)

[89] L. Maier-Hein, S. A. Müller, F. Pianka, S. Wörz, B. P. Müller-Stich, A. Seitel, K. Rohr, H.-P. Meinzer, B. M. Schmied, and I. Wolf. Respiratory motion compensation for CT-guided interventions in the liver. *Comp Aid Surg*, 13(3):125–38, 2008. (Cited on pages 5, 6, 120, 207, and 208.)

[90] L. Maier-Hein, F. Pianka, S. A. Müller, U. Rietdorf, A. Seitel, A. M. Franz, I. Wolf, B. Schmied, and H.-P. Meinzer. Respiratory liver motion simulator for validating image-guided systems ex-vivo. *Int J CARS*, 2(5):287–92, 2008. (Cited on pages 3, 63, and 206.)

[91] L. Maier-Hein, F. Pianka, S. A. Müller, A. Seitel, U. Rietdorf, I. Wolf, B. M. Schmied, and H.-P. Meinzer. Atembewegungssimulator für die in-vitro Evaluation von Weichgewebe-Navigationssystemen in der Leber. In A. Horsch, T. M. Deserno, H. Handels, H.-P. Meinzer, and T. Tolxdorf, editors, *Bildverarbeitung für die Medizin 2007*, pages 379–83. Springer, 2007. (Cited on pages 3 and 206.)

[92] L. Maier-Hein, F. Pianka, A. Seitel, S. A. Müller, A. Tekbas, M. Seitel, I. Wolf, B. M. Schmied, and H.-P. Meinzer. Precision targeting of liver lesions with a needle-based soft tissue navigation system. In N. Ayache, S. Ourselin, and A. Maeder, editors, *Medical Image Computing and Computer-Assisted Intervention (MICCAI) 2007 (2)*, volume 4792, pages 42–49, Brisbane, Australia, Oct 2007. Springer. (Cited on pages 6, 166, 168, and 209.)

[93] L. Maier-Hein, A. Seitel, I. Wolf, and H.-P. Meinzer. A system for computer assisted targeting in soft tissue, Jun 2008. US 61/075,467. (Cited on pages 5 and 208.)

[94] L. Maier-Hein, A. Tekbas, A. M. Franz, R. Tetzlaff, S. A. Müller, F. Pianka, I. Wolf, H.-U. Kauczor, B. M. Schmied, and H.-P. Meinzer. On combining internal and external fiducials for liver motion compensation. *Comp Aid Surg*, 13(16):369–376, 2008. (Cited on pages 5, 127, 132, 133, and 208.)

[95] L. Maier-Hein, A. Tekbas, A. M. Franz, R. Tetzlaff, S. A. Müller, F. Pianka, I. Wolf, H.-U. Kauczor, B. M. Schmied, and H.-P. Meinzer. Reduktion der Invasivität bei nadelbasierter Bewegungskompensation für navigierte Eingriffe im Abdomen. In *Bildverarbeitung für die Medizin 2009*, pages 82–86, 2009. (Cited on page 5.)

[96] L. Maier-Hein, A. Tekbas, A. Seitel, F. Pianka, S. A. Müller, S. Satzl, S. Schawo, B. Radeleff, R. Tetzlaff, A. M. Franz, B. P. Müller-Stich, I. Wolf, H.-U. Kauczor, B. M. Schmied, and H.-P. Meinzer. In vivo accuracy assessment of a needle-based navigation system for CT-guided radiofrequency ablation of the liver. *Med Phys*, 35(12):5385–5396, 2008. (Cited on pages 5, 6, 44, 174, 177, 182, 185, 208, and 209.)

[97] L. Maier-Hein, A. Tekbas, A. Seitel, F. Pianka, S. A. Müller, S. Schawo, B. Radeleff, R. Tetzlaff, A. M. Franz, A.-M. Rau, I. Wolf, H.-U. Kauczor, B. M. Schmied, and H.-P. Meinzer. In-vivo targeting of liver lesions with

a navigation system based on fiducial needles. In *Bildverarbeitung für die Medizin 2008*, pages 227–231, 2008. (Cited on page 6.)

[98] L. Maier-Hein, C. J. Walsh, A. Seitel, N. C. Hanumara, J.-O. Shepard, F. Pianka, S. A. Müller, B. M. Schmied, A. H. Slocum, R. Guptac, and H.-P. Meinzer. Robotic assisted versus computer guided needle insertion in percutaneous liver interventions. In *SPIE Medical Imaging 2009: Visualization, Image-Guided Procedures, and Modeling*, volume 7261, page 72610Y (12 pages), 2009. (Cited on page 203.)

[99] C. R. Maurer, J. M. Fitzpatrick, M. Y. Wang, R. L. Galloway, R. J. Maciunas, and G. S. Allen. Registration of head volume images using implantable fiducial markers. *IEEE T Med Imaging*, 16:447–462, 1997. (Cited on pages 31 and 55.)

[100] C. R. Maurer, J. J. McCrory, and J. M. Fitzpatrick. Estimation of accuracy in localizing externally attached markers in multimodal volume head images. In *SPIE Medical Imaging 1993: Image Processing*, volume 1898, pages 43–54, 1993. (Cited on pages 32 and 58.)

[101] W. Mayoral and J. H. Lewis. Percutaneous liver biopsy: What is the current approach? Results of a questionnaire survey. *Digest Dis Sci*, 46(1):118–127, 2001. (Cited on page 13.)

[102] J. P. McGahan and G. D. Dodd. Radiofrequency ablation of the liver: Current status. *Am J Roentgenol*, 176(1):3–16, 2001. (Cited on pages 1 and 17.)

[103] Medilexicon International Ltd. www.medilexicon.com/medicaldictionary.php (15/12/2008). (Cited on pages 13, 14, and 203.)

[104] P. Merloz, J. Tonetti, A. Eid, C. Faure, S. Lavallee, J. Troccaz, P. Sautot, A. Hamadeh, and P. Cinquin. Computer assisted spine surgery. *Clin Orthop Relat Res*, 1(337):86–96, Apr 1997. (Cited on page 20.)

[105] R. A. Mischkowski, M. J. Zinser, J. Neugebauer, A. C. Kübler, and J. E. Zöller. Comparison of static and dynamic computer-assisted guidance methods in implantology. *Int J Comput Dent*, 9(1):23–35, Jan 2006. (Cited on page 20.)

[106] M. H. Moghari and P. Abolmaesumi. A high-order solution for the distribution of target registration error in rigid-body point-based registration. In *Medical Image Computing and Computer-Assisted Intervention (MICCAI) 2006 (2)*, pages 603–611, 2006. (Cited on page 32.)

[107] M. H. Moghari and P. Abolmaesumi. Maximum likelihood estimation of the distribution of target registration error. In K. R. Cleary and M. I. Miga,

editors, *SPIE Medical Imaging 2008: Visualization, Image-Guided Procedures, and Modeling*, volume 6918, page 69180I, Feb 2008. (Cited on page 32.)

[108] M. H. Moghari, B. Ma, and P. Abolmaesumi. A theoretical comparison of different target registration error estimators. In *Medical Image Computing and Computer-Assisted Intervention (MICCAI) 2008 (2)*, volume 5242, pages 1032–1040, 2008. (Cited on page 32.)

[109] M. Nagel, M. Hoheisel, R. Petzold, W. A. Kalender, and U. H. W. Krause. Needle and catheter navigation using electromagnetic tracking for computer-assisted C-arm CT interventions. In K. R. Cleary and M. I. Miga, editors, *SPIE Medical Imaging 2007: Visualization, Image-Guided Procedures, and Display*, volume 6509, page 65090J (9 pages), San Diego, CA, USA, Feb 2007. (Cited on pages 22 and 29.)

[110] M. Nagel, G. Schmidt, R. Petzold, and W. A. Kalender. A navigation system for minimally invasive CT-guided interventions. In J. S. Duncan and G. Gerig, editors, *Medical Image Computing and Computer-Assisted Intervention (MICCAI) 2005 (2)*, pages 33–40, Palm Springs, Ca, USA, 2005. Springer. (Cited on pages 22, 24, 27, 31, and 34.)

[111] R. D. Nawfel, P. F. Judy, S. G. Silverman, S. Hooton, K. Tuncali, and D. F. Adams. Patient and personnel exposure during CT fluoroscopy-guided interventional procedures. *Radiology*, 216(1):180–184, 2000. (Cited on pages 2, 14, and 17.)

[112] S. A. Nicolau, X. Pennec, L. Soler, and N. Ayache. A complete augmented reality guidance system for liver punctures: First clinical evaluation. In J. Duncan and G. Gerig, editors, *Medical Image Computing and Computer-Assisted Intervention (MICCAI) 2005 (2)*, volume 3749 of *LNCS*, pages 539–547, Palm Springs, CA, USA, October 26-29, 2005. Springer Verlag. (Cited on pages 37 and 40.)

[113] S. A. Nicolau, X. Pennec, L. Soler, and N. Ayache. Clinical evaluation of a respiratory gated guidance system for liver punctures. In N. Ayache and et al., editors, *Medical Image Computing and Computer-Assisted Intervention (MICCAI) 2007 (2)*, volume 4792, pages 77–85, Brisbane, Australia, Oct 2007. Springer. (Cited on pages 22, 27, 34, 178, and 185.)

[114] G. M. Nielson. Scattered data modeling. *IEEE Comput Graph*, 13(1):60–70, 1993. (Cited on page 116.)

[115] L.-P. Nolte, L. Zamorano, H. Visarius, U. Berlemann, F. Langlotz, E. Arm, and O. Schwarzenbach. Clinical evaluation of a system for precision enhancement

in spine surgery. *Clin Biomech (Bristol, Avon)*, 10(6):293–303, Sep 1995. (Cited on page 20.)

[116] B. Olbrich, J. Traub, S. Wiesner, A. Wiechert, H. Feußner, and N. Navab. Respiratory motion analysis: Towards gated augmentation of the liver. In *Computer Assisted Radiology and Surgery (CARS) 2005*, pages 248–253, Berlin, Germany, Jun 2005. (Cited on page 12.)

[117] C. Ozhasoglu, C. B. Saw, H. Chen, S. Burton, K. Komanduri, N. J. Yue, S. M. Huq, and D. E. Heron. Synchrony - Cyberknife respiratory compensation technology. *Med Dosim*, 33(2):117–123, 2008. (Cited on pages 24 and 35.)

[118] N. Pagoulatos, R. N. Rohling, W. S. Edwards, and Y. Kim. A new spatial localizer based on fiber optics with applications in 3D ultrasound imaging. In *SPIE Medical Imaging 2000: Image Display and Visualization*, 2000. (Cited on page 27.)

[119] G. P. Penney, J. M. Blackall, M. S. Hamady, T. Sabharwal, A. Adam, and D. J. Hawkes. Registration of freehand 3D ultrasound and magnetic resonance liver images. *Med Imag Anal*, 8:81–91, 2004. (Cited on page 33.)

[120] P. L. Pereira. Actual role of radiofrequency ablation of liver metastases. *Eur Radiol*, 17(8):2062–2070, 2007. (Cited on pages 1, 10, 16, and 17.)

[121] T. M. Peters. Image-guided surgery: From x-rays to virtual reality. *Comput Methods Biomech Biomed Engin*, 4(1):27–57, 2000. (Cited on page 27.)

[122] T. M. Peters. Image-guidance for surgical procedures. *Phys Med Biol*, 51(14):R505–R540, Jul 2006. (Cited on pages 19, 20, 21, 23, 24, 26, 29, 31, and 33.)

[123] A. Raabe, R. Krishnan, and V. Seifert. Actual aspects of image-guided surgery. *Surg Technol Int*, 11:314–319, 2003. (Cited on page 21.)

[124] H. Rhim, S. N. Goldberg, G. D. Dodd, L. Solbiati, H. K. Lim, M. Tonolini, and O. K. Cho. Essential techniques for successful radio-frequency thermal ablation of malignant hepatic tumors. *Radiographics*, 21:17–35, 2001. (Cited on pages 1, 16, 17, and 18.)

[125] R. A. Robb. Three-dimensional visualization and analysis in prostate cancer. *Drugs Today (Barc)*, 38(3):153–165, Mar 2002. (Cited on page 25.)

[126] T. Rohlfing, C. Maurer, W. O'Dell, and J. Zhong. Modeling liver motion and deformation during the respiratory cycle using intensity-based free-form registration of gated MR images. *Med Phys*, 31:427–432, Mar 2004. (Cited on page 11.)

[127] K. Rohr. Elastic registration of multimodal medical images: a survey. *KI - Künstliche Intelligenz*, 00(3):11–17, 2000. (Cited on page 116.)

[128] K. Rohr, H. S. Stiehl, R. Sprengel, T. M. Buzug, J. Weese, and M. H. Kuhn. Landmark-based elastic registration using approximating thin-plate splines. *IEEE T Med Imaging*, 20(6):526–534, 2001. (Cited on pages 117 and 126.)

[129] B. Rubinsky, C. Y. Lee, J. Bastacky, and G. Onik. The process of freezing and the mechanism of damage during hepatic cryosurgery. *Cryobiology*, 27(1):85–97, 1990. (Cited on page 16.)

[130] W. Saad, C. Ryan, M. Davies, P. Fultz, D. Rubens, N. Patel, L. Sahler, D. Lee, T. Kitanosono, and T. Sasson. Safety and efficacy of fluoroscopic versus ultrasound guidance for core liver biopsies in potential living related liver transplant donors: Preliminary results. *J Vasc Interv Radiol*, 17(8):1307–1312, 2003. (Cited on page 13.)

[131] R. F. Schmidt. *Physiologie des Menschen*. Springer, 2007. (Cited on page 10.)

[132] W. J. Schroeder, K. M. Martin, L. S. Avila, and C. C. Law. *The Visualization Toolkit User's Guide*, Aug 2003. (Cited on page 49.)

[133] A. Schweikard, G. Glosser, M. Bodduluri, M. J. Murphy, and J. R. Adler. Robotic motion compensation for respiratory movement during radiosurgery. *Comp Aid Surg*, 5:263–277, 2000. (Cited on pages 35 and 139.)

[134] A. Seitel. Entwicklung und Evaluation von Visualisierungsmethoden für computer-navigierte Eingriffe in Weichgewebe. Master's thesis, Universität Karlsruhe (TH), Jun 2007. (Cited on pages 5, 153, 155, 157, and 208.)

[135] A. Seitel, L. Maier-Hein, S. Schawo, B. A. Radeleff, S. A. Müller, F. Pianka, B. M. Schmied, I. Wolf, and H.-P. Meinzer. In-vitro evaluation of different visualization approaches for computer assisted targeting in soft tissue. In *Int J CARS 2 (Suppl 1)*, pages 188–190. Springer, Jun 2007. (Cited on pages 5, 6, and 208.)

[136] D. H. Sheafor, E. K. Paulson, C. M. Simmons, D. M. DeLong, and R. C. Nelson. Abdominal percutaneous interventional procedures: comparison of CT and US guidance. *Radiology*, 207:705–710, 1998. (Cited on page 17.)

[137] S. Shimizu, H. Shirato, H. Aoyama, S. Hashimoto, T. Nishioka, A. Yamazaki, K. Kagei, and K. Miyasaka. High-speed magnetic resonance imaging for four-dimensional treatment planning of conformal radiotherapy of moving body tumors. *Int J Radiat Oncol*, 48(2):471–474, 2000. (Cited on page 12.)

[138] T. Sielhorst, M. Bauer, O. Wenisch, G. Klinker, and N. Navab. Online estimation of the target registration error for n-ocular optical tracking systems. In *Medical Image Computing and Computer-Assisted Intervention (MICCAI) 2007 (2)*, pages 652–659, 2007. (Cited on pages 32 and 55.)

[139] S. G. Silverman, K. Tuncali, D. F. Adams, R. D. Nawfel, K. H. Zou, and P. F. Judy. CT fluoroscopy-guided abdominal interventions: Techniques, results, and radiation exposure. *Radiology*, 212:673–681, 1999. (Cited on pages 2, 14, and 17.)

[140] E. H. Smith. Complications of percutaneous abdominal fine-needle biopsy. *Radiology*, 178:253–258, 1991. (Cited on pages 2 and 14.)

[141] S. B. Solomon, C. Magee, D. E. Acker, and A. C. Venbrux. TIPS placement in swine, guided by electromagnetic real-time needle tip localization displayed on previously acquired 3-D CT. *Cardiovasc Inter Radiology*, 22:411–414, 1999. (Cited on page 31.)

[142] E. A. Spiegel, H. T. Wycis, M. Marks, and A. J. Lee. Stereotaxic apparatus for operations on the human brain. *Science*, 106(2754):349–350, 1947. (Cited on page 19.)

[143] N. Sugano. Computer-assisted orthopedic surgery. *J Orthop Sci*, 8(3):442–448, 2003. (Cited on page 21.)

[144] I. Suramo, M. Paivansalo, and V. Myllyla. Cranio-caudal movements of the liver, pancreas and kidneys in respiration. *Acta Radiol Diagn*, 25:129–131, 1984. (Cited on page 12.)

[145] R. Takamori, L. L. Wong, C. Dang, and L. Wong. Needle-tract implantation from hepatocellular cancer: Is needle biopsy of the liver always necessary? *Liver Transplant*, 6(1):67–72, 2000. (Cited on pages 2 and 14.)

[146] J. Tang, S. Dieterich, and K. Cleary. Respiratory motion tracking of skin and liver in swine for Cyberknife motion compensation. In *SPIE Medical Imaging 2004: Visualization, Image-guided Procedures, and Display*, pages 729–734, May 2004. (Cited on pages 32 and 58.)

[147] A. Tekbas, L. Maier-Hein, S. A. Müller, A. Seitel, B. Radeleff, S. Satzl, R. Tetzlaff, A. M. Franz, F. Pianka, I. Wolf, H.-U. Kauczor, H.-P. Meinzer, and B. M. Schmied. In-vivo comparision of the conventional ct-guided liver biopsy method with a novel computer-assisted approach. In *Int J CARS 3 (Suppl 1)*, pages 142–143, 2008. (Cited on page 6.)

[148] M. Tsuchida, Y. Yamato, T. Aoki, T. Watanabe, N. Koizumi, I. Emura, and J. Hayashi. CT-guided agar marking for localization of nonpalpable peripheral pulmonary lesions. *Chest*, 116(1):139–143, 1999. (Cited on page 166.)

[149] V. Venkatraman, M. H. V. Horn, S. Weeks, and E. Bullitt. Liver motion due to needle pressure, cardiac, and respiratory motion during the TIPS procedure. In C. Barillot, D. Haynor, and P. Hellier, editors, *Medical Image Computing and Computer-Assisted Intervention (MICCAI) 2004 (2)*, volume 3217, pages 66–72. Springer, 2004. (Cited on pages 2 and 205.)

[150] C. Villard, C. Baegert, P. Schreck, L. Soler, and A. Gangi. Optimal trajectories computation within regions of interest for hepatic RFA planning. In *Medical Image Computing and Computer-Assisted Intervention (MICCAI) 2005 (2)*, pages 49–56, 2005. (Cited on page 202.)

[151] F. K. Wacker, S. Vogt, A. Khamene, J. A. Jesberger, S. G. Nour, D. R. Elgort, F. Sauer, J. L. Duerk, and J. S. Lewin. An augmented reality system for MR image-guided needle biopsy: Initial results in a swine model. *Radiology*, 238(2):497–504, 2006. (Cited on pages 22, 26, 171, 181, and 185.)

[152] M. J. Wallace, S. Gupta, and M. E. Hicks. Out-of-plane computed-tomography-guided biopsy using a magnetic-field-based navigation system. *Cardiovasc Inter Rad*, 29:108–113, 2006. (Cited on page 22.)

[153] C. J. Walsh, N. C. Hanumara, A. H. Slocum, J. O. Shepard, and R. Gupta. A patient-mounted, telerobotic tool for CT-guided percutaneous interventions. *J Med Devices*, 2(1):011007 (10 pages), Mar 2008. (Cited on page 203.)

[154] Z. Wei, M. Ding, D. Downey, and A. Fenster. 3D TRUS guided robot assisted prostate brachytherapy. *Medical Image Computing and Computer-Assisted Intervention (MICCAI) 2005 (2)*, 8:17–24, 2005. (Cited on page 25.)

[155] Z. Wei, L. Gardi, D. B. Downey, and A. Fenster. Oblique needle segmentation and tracking for 3D TRUS guided prostate brachytherapy. *Med Phys*, 32(9):2928–2941, Sep 2005. (Cited on page 34.)

[156] W. Wein, A. Khamene, D.-A. Clevert, O. Kutter, and N. Navab. Simulation and fully automatic multimodal registration of medical ultrasound. In *Medical Image Computing and Computer-Assisted Intervention (MICCAI) 2007 (2)*, pages 136–143, 2007. (Cited on pages 35 and 198.)

[157] G. Welch and E. Foxlin. Motion tracking: No silver bullet, but a respectable arsenal. *IEEE Comput Graph*, 22(6):24–38, 2002. (Cited on page 27.)

[158] J. B. West and J. C. R. Maurer. Designing optically tracked instruments for image-guided surgery. *IEEE T Med Imaging*, 23(5):533–545, 2004. (Cited on pages 30 and 89.)

[159] W. H. O. (WHO). The world health organization's fight against cancer: Strategies that prevent, cure and care, 2007. ISBN: 978 92 4 159543 8. (Cited on page 1.)

[160] A. D. Wiles, A. Likholyot, D. D. Frantz, and T. M. Peters. A statistical model for point-based target registration error with anisotropic fiducial localizer error. *IEEE T Med Imaging*, 27(3):378–391, 2008. (Cited on page 32.)

[161] A. D. Wiles, D. G. Thompson, and D. D. Frantz. Accuracy assessment and interpretation for optical tracking systems. In *SPIE*, volume 5367, pages 421–432, 2004. (Cited on pages 20, 27, 55, 74, 77, 79, and 82.)

[162] P. W. A. Willems, J. W. B. van der Sprenkel, C. A. F. Tulleken, M. A. Viergever, and M. J. B. Taphoorn. Neuronavigation and surgery of intracerebral tumours. *J Neurol*, 253(9):1123–1136, Sep 2006. (Cited on page 20.)

[163] E. Wilson. Accuracy analysis of electromagnetic tracking within medical environments. Technical report, Georgetown University, Imaging Science and Information Systems Center, Washington, DC, USA, 2006. (Cited on page 79.)

[164] I. Wolf, M. Vetter, I. Wegner, T. Böttger, M. Nolden, M. Schöbinger, M. Hastenteufel, T. Kunert, and H.-P. Meinzer. The Medical Imaging Interaction Toolkit. *Med Image Anal*, 9(6):594–604, 2005. (Cited on page 49.)

[165] K. H. Wong, J. Tang, H. J. Zhang, E. Varghese, and K. Cleary. Prediction of 3D internal organ position from skin surface motion: Results from electromagnetic tracking studies. In *SPIE Medical Imaging 2005: Visualization, Image-guided Procedures, and Display*, volume 5744, pages 879–887, 2005. (Cited on page 12.)

[166] Z. Yaniv and K. Cleary. Image-guided procedures: A review. Technical report, Georgetown University, 2006. (Cited on pages 2, 9, 21, 23, 24, 25, 26, 27, 29, 33, 36, 197, 198, 203, and 205.)

[167] H. Zhang, F. Banovac, and K. Cleary. Increasing registration precision for liver movement with respiration using electromagnetic tracking. In *Computer Assisted Radiology and Surgery (CARS) 2005*, volume 1281, pages 571–576, May 2005. (Cited on page 139.)

[168] H. Zhang, F. Banovac, N. D. Glossop, and K. Cleary. Two-stage registration for real-time deformable compensation using an electromagnetic tracking device. In J. S. Duncan and G. Gerig, editors, *Medical Image Computing and Computer-Assisted Intervention (MICCAI) 2005 (2)*, pages 992–999, Palm Springs, Ca, USA, 2005. Springer. (Cited on page 127.)

[169] H. Zhang, F. Banovac, R. Lin, N. Glossop, B. J. Wood, D. Lindisch, E. Levy, and K. Cleary. Electromagnetic tracking for abdominal interventions in computer aided surgery. *Comp Aid Surg*, 11(3):127–136, 2006. (Cited on pages 29, 171, 178, and 181.)

Die VDM Verlagsservicegesellschaft sucht für wissenschaftliche Verlage abgeschlossene und herausragende

Dissertationen, Habilitationen, Diplomarbeiten, Master Theses, Magisterarbeiten usw.

für die kostenlose Publikation als Fachbuch.

Sie verfügen über eine Arbeit, die hohen inhaltlichen und formalen Ansprüchen genügt, und haben Interesse an einer honorarvergüteten Publikation?

Dann senden Sie bitte erste Informationen über sich und Ihre Arbeit per Email an *info@vdm-vsg.de*.

Sie erhalten kurzfristig unser Feedback!

VDM Verlagsservicegesellschaft mbH
Dudweiler Landstr. 99   Telefon +49 681 3720 174
D - 66123 Saarbrücken   Fax   +49 681 3720 1749
www.vdm-vsg.de

Die VDM Verlagsservicegesellschaft mbH vertritt

Printed by Books on Demand GmbH, Norderstedt / Germany